Reforming the Liturgy

John F. Baldovin, SJ

REFORMING THE LITURGY

A Response to the Critics

A PUEBLO BOOK

Liturgical Press Collegeville, Minnesota

www.litpress.org

A Pueblo Book published by Liturgical Press

Cover design by David Manahan, OSB. Cover photo courtesy of dreamstime.com, © Tkachuk. Taken in Saint Peter's Basilica, Rome.

Library of Congress Cataloging-in-Publication Data

Baldovin, John F. (John Francis), 1947–
    Reforming the liturgy : a response to the critics / John Baldovin.
        p.   cm.
    "A Pueblo book."
    Includes bibliographical references and index.
    ISBN 978-0-8146-6219-9 (pbk.)
        1. Liturgical movement—Catholic Church—History—20th century.
    2. Catholic Church—Liturgy—History—20th century.   I. Title.

BX1975.B35 2008
264'.02001—dc22

                                                          2008028273

To the memory of

Edward J. Kilmartin, SJ (1923–1994)
Aidan J. Kavanagh, OSB (1929–2006)
Thomas Julian Talley (1924–2006)

Contents

Preface

This work originated in a series of articles for various publications. The first was a *Festschrift* for Nathan Mitchell in which I published an article on Catherine Pickstock's treatment of medieval liturgy.[1] The second was an article solicited by Paul Bradshaw, editor of *Studia Liturgica*. That essay dealt with the post–Vatican II liturgical critique of Klaus Gamber.[2] Finally, there was an essay on Joseph Ratzinger in a volume in honor of Paul Bradshaw.[3] After finishing those essays I decided to embark on a project that would survey the various types of criticism that have been aimed at the post–Vatican II reform of Roman Catholic worship. The present book is the result.

Writing a book is a solitary activity, but one never really does it alone. I am grateful to the editors of the volumes and journal in which the original three essays appeared, as well as to R. Kevin Seasoltz, OSB, and Joyce Ann Zimmerman, CPPS, the editors of *Worship* and the *Proceedings of the North American Academy of Liturgy* in which the appendix first appeared. The bulk of this work was done while I was on a sabbatical granted by Weston Jesuit School of Theology (now the Boston College School of Theology and Ministry). I am grateful to then-President Robert Manning, SJ, and Dean Randy Sachs, SJ, for granting me this sabbatical. The writing was done at the Fairfield University Jesuit community, and I am most grateful to its rector, Walter Conlan, SJ, and the president of the university, Jeffrey von Arx, SJ, as well as the most genial Jesuit community for their gracious hospitality. I am also indebted to Martin Jean, director of Yale's Institute of Sacred Music, who facilitated my use of Yale's wonderful libraries. I am also thankful for

---

[1] Clare V. Johnson, ed., *Ars Liturgiae: Worship, Aesthetics and Praxis: Essays in Honor of Nathan D. Mitchell* (Chicago: Liturgy Training Publications, 2003), 55–76.

[2] "Klaus Gamber and the Post–Vatican II Reform of the Roman Liturgy," *Studia Liturgica* 33 (2003): 223–39.

[3] Maxwell Johnson and L. Edward Phillips, eds., *Studia Liturgica Diversa: Essays in Honor of Paul F. Bradshaw* (Portland: Pastoral Press, 2004), 211–28.

the kind invitations of Paul Lakeland (Fairfield University), Walter Conlan, SJ (the Fairfield Jesuit Community), the Catholic Academy of Liturgy, James Hayes, SJ (Jesuit Community at the College of the Holy Cross), and Jerome Maryon (Committee on Contemporary Spiritual and Public Concerns, St. Paul Parish, Cambridge, MA) for their invitations to share the results of my study.

I also owe a debt of gratitude to Gregory Semeniuk, CM, for assembling the bibliography, and to Brian Flanagan who compiled the index, not to mention Linda Maloney, Peter Dwyer, Michelle Verkuilen, and Hans Christoffersen of Liturgical Press.

Several friends and colleagues read all or part of the manuscript. They kept me from making a number of egregious errors, with regard to both style and fact. I am very grateful to my faculty colleagues at Weston Jesuit, as well as to Lawrence Borchardt; Andrew Cameron-Mowat, SJ; Paul Cavendish; John Page; Marc Reeves, SJ; and Joseph Villecco.

This book is dedicated to the memory of three of my significant mentors in liturgical studies.

Abbreviations

CDWDS   Congregation for Divine Worship and the Discipline of the Sacraments

DOL   *Documents on the Liturgy 1963–1979: Conciliar, Papal, and Curial Texts* (Collegeville, MN: Liturgical Press, 1982)

DS   Denzinger/Schönmetzer

EACW   *Environment and Art in Catholic Worship*

GIRM   *General Instruction of the Roman Missal*

ICEL   International Commission on English in the Liturgy

LA   *Liturgiam Authenticam*

SC   *Sacrosanctum Concilium*

SP   *Summorum Pontificum*

TS   *Theological Studies*

Introduction

Since the very beginnings of the implementation of Vatican II's Constitution on the Sacred Liturgy (*Sacrosanctum Concilium*, hereafter SC), the reform and renewal of Roman Catholic worship has been severely criticized. This criticism by scholars and writers on many fronts has taken on new force since the publication of the Congregation for Divine Worship's 2000 instruction, *Liturgiam Authenticam* (*On the Correct Translation of Liturgical Texts*) and even more recently with Pope Benedict XVI's *motu proprio, Summorum Pontificum* (July 2007). The present book arises from the conviction that serious critique of the reform—both in its formulation in the Liturgy Constitution and in the subsequent reformed liturgical books and their implementation—needs to be attended to. It also arises from the conviction that these criticisms need an equally serious assessment and response.

The liturgical reform prompted by SC was the fruit of decades of research and conversation about the state of Catholic worship. Beginning with the adoption of historical method in the retrieval of ancient and medieval texts and continuing with the monastic revival of Dom Prosper Gueranger and others in the mid-nineteenth century, the liturgical movement was initiated in earnest at the beginning of the twentieth century by Dom Lambert Beauduin and a host of other liturgical historians and theologians. That movement has been well documented elsewhere, as has the implementation of the Liturgy Constitution.[1] There is no need to repeat these valuable studies. But one

---

[1] See, for example, Bernard Botte, *From Silence to Participation: An Insider's View of Liturgical Renewal* (Portland, OR: Pastoral Press, 1998); Annibale Bugnini, *The Reform of the Liturgy 1948–1975*, trans. Matthew J. O'Connell (Collegeville, MN: Liturgical Press, 1990); Piero Marini, *A Challenging Reform: Realizing the Vision of the Liturgical Renewal*, Mark Francis, John Page, and Keith Pecklers, eds. (Collegeville,

fact should indeed be emphasized. The post–Vatican II documents, from Paul VI's *motu proprio, Sacram Liturgiam* (25 January 1964) and the Sacred Congregation of Rites' Instruction, *Inter Oecumenici* (26 September 1964) forward are the implementation of the guidelines for reform and renewal provided by the council's Liturgy Constitution.[2] Just as the Council of Trent's decrees could not have reformed the liturgy, but rather laid the groundwork for what has come to be called the Tridentine liturgy, so the general principles given by SC required the difficult and painstaking work of the liturgical commissions created to actually implement it at the end of the council. All too often criticism of the liturgical reform has pretended that the entirety of the reform can be located in the council document itself. What *can* be contested is whether the official implementation was faithful to the Liturgy Constitution.[3] The pastoral implementation of those official reforms can also be debated. Much of what follows hangs on differentiating between the Liturgy Constitution and the subsequent implementation by the Consilium for the implementation of the liturgical reform that Pope Paul VI established under Cardinal Giacomo Lercaro and Vincentian Father Annibale Bugnini in the aftermath of the approval of the constitution. That story has now been ably told by Archbishop Piero Marini, papal master of ceremonies from 1987 to 2007.[4]

I have decided to select a number of serious critiques of the liturgical reform with a view to engaging the opposition to the reform as a whole. The bibliography of these works and authors is very large indeed, and so some discretion is required in dealing with the volume of criticism that has been offered. My selection is inevitably somewhat subjective, but I do think that I have chosen to examine some of the most impor-

---

MN: Liturgical Press, 2007). For the period immediately preceding Vatican II see Carlo Braga, "Per la Storia della Riforma Liturgica: La Commissione di Pio XII e di Giovanni XXIII," *Ephemerides Liturgicae* 117 (2003): 401–04.

[2] The official documents of the reform in English translation can be found in International Commission on English in the Liturgy, *Documents on the Liturgy 1963– 1979: Conciliar, Papal, and Curial Texts* (Collegeville, MN: Liturgical Press, 1982). I will cite the document numbers from this collection—here at 276ff. and 293ff.

[3] For example: "Those who claim to have 'implemented' *Sacrosanctum Concilium* have repudiated the foundations of that document, have conceived a different inspiration, and have led the Roman Church in quite a different direction from that given by the liturgical movement and ratified by the council." Serge Kelleher, "Whatever Happened to the Liturgical Movement? A View from the East," in Stratford Caldecott, ed., *Beyond the Prosaic: Renewing the Liturgical Movement* (Edinburgh: T&T Clark, 1998), 74.

[4] Marini, *A Challenging Reform* (see n. 1 above).

tant and persuasive critics. Needless to say, there have been a number of critics (as well as defenders) of the reform who are less intellectually compelling, but my selection does not imply that every serious critic is accounted for in these pages.[5]

A BRIEF CHRONICLE OF OPPOSITION

As Archbishop Marini's book on the creation of the *Consilium* shows, opposition to the implementation of SC began as soon as the constitution was approved. Paul VI was unwilling to entrust the reform of the liturgy to the Congregation of Rites because its leadership was opposed to the reform in the first place. Therefore he created something new with the awkward name of the *Consilium ad exsequendam Constitutionem de sacra liturgia* (usually shortened to *Consilium*). This office reported directly to the pope and, according to Marini, was the object of a great deal of suspicion in the Roman Curia. The *Consilium*'s work was essentially completed by 1969, when it was absorbed into the newly created Congregation for Divine Worship. In a harbinger of things to come, the Congregation for Divine Worship was dissolved in 1975 and replaced by the current Congregation for Divine Worship and the Discipline of the Sacraments. Bugnini (now an archbishop and secretary of the Congregation) was dismissed (and sent as papal nuncio to Iran). The Vatican's proactive stance toward liturgical reform lasted until 1975. From then on, one document after another drew back on the reforms or at least expressed a good deal of caution with regard to them. In my opinion the year 1994 marked a definitive turning point when the fourth Instruction on the Reform of the Liturgy, *Varietates Legitimae*, on the subject of inculturation, was promulgated.

Marini chronicles the early opposition to the reform, which was associated with the Roman Curia. For example, a book in Italian by Tito Casino that was extremely critical of the work of the *Consilium* appeared in 1967. It was remarkable for the fact that its preface was by a curial cardinal, Antonio Bacci.[6] Bacci also joined with Cardinal Alfredo Ottaviani in 1969 in a letter to the pope that accused the reform

---

[5] I should add that the topic of liturgical reform is much too large to address in this modest book. See the monumental series of books in honor of Angelus Häussling, OSB: Martin Klöckener and Benedikt Kranemann, eds., *Liturgiereformen: Historische Studien zu einem bleibenden Grundzug des christlichen Gottesdienstes.* 2 vols. Liturgiewissenschaftliche Quellen und Forschungen 88–89 (Münster: Aschendorff, 2002). For the post–Vatican II reform and its reception see Vol. II, Part VI.

[6] Ibid., 137.

of serious deviation from Catholic theology and doctrine.[7] Around the same time scholars like Klaus Gamber in Germany were voicing serious discontent with the reform, and an organized opposition under Archbishop Marcel Lefebvre began to call for a return to the traditional (pre–Vatican II) Mass.[8] Paul VI himself exhibited a good deal of caution in his addresses to members of the *Consilium* and the Congregation for Divine Worship.[9] The pope also required changes in the first edition of the *General Instruction of the Roman Missal* because it had been criticized as overly Protestant.[10] Organizations like *Una Voce* as well as Lefebvre's movement had, in fact, begun their work very early. These groups (and their heirs) opposed the reform as a whole. In fact, there have been so many approaches taken to the reform (pro and con) that it is necessary to organize them by categories.

ASSESSING THE REFORM

One of the best templates for assessing the current reform of the liturgy has been provided by M. Francis Mannion in a paper delivered at a congress convened at Oxford in 1996 to discuss the current state of Roman Catholic liturgy.[11] Mannion employs the "models" typology popularized by H. Richard Niebuhr and Avery Dulles to distinguish five discernible agendas at work with regard to contemporary liturgical reform. He admits that these five approaches are not mutually exclusive. Indeed, I can find myself in agreement with four of the five on various points and I am certain that I am not alone. These are the five agendas:

1. Advancing the official reform

2. Restoring the preconciliar

3. Reforming the reform

4. Inculturating the reform

5. Recatholicizing the reform

---

[7] Ibid., 142–43.

[8] Enrico Cattaneo, *Il Culto Cristiano in Occidente: note storiche* (Rome: Centro Liturgico Vincenziano—Edizioni Liturgiche, 1978), 643ff.

[9] Texts quoted in *Il Culto Cristiano*, 645–47.

[10] Ibid., 651, thus causing a confusing double numbering system of the paragraphs, since the addition was made as a preface to the original instruction. This confusion was cleared up by the 2002 edition of the *GIRM*.

[11] M. Francis Mannion, "The Catholicity of the Liturgy: Shaping a New Agenda," in Caldecott, *Beyond the Prosaic* (see n. 3 above), 11–48.

1. *Advancing the official reform*

The basic lines of each agenda are easy enough to describe. The first takes its inspiration from the Liturgy Constitution and the subsequent implementation by the *Consilium for the Implementation of the Sacred Liturgy*, which was subsumed into the Congregation for Divine Worship in 1969. The major architect of the official reform was Archbishop Annibale Bugnini, whose thorough chronicle was referenced above. Even within this particular agenda there are significant differences. Mannion points to a more progressive approach to advancing official documents in the International Commission on English in the Liturgy (ICEL) and a more traditional approach in the Congregation for Divine Worship and the Discipline of the Sacraments. Since this essay was written, the lay of the land has changed considerably and ICEL can no longer be said to represent a progressive approach to advancing official reform.[12] That ground is left to United States groups like *We Believe!* and the Catholic Academy of Liturgy and similar groups in other countries.

2. *Restoring the preconciliar*

As the title suggests, this agenda rejects the conciliar reform of the liturgy completely. In fact, it has grave reservations about most of the council's documents, especially its teachings on episcopal collegiality, ecumenism, and religious liberty. It is important to note that for many of the people supporting this agenda (for example, the followers of the late Archbishop Marcel Lefebvre), liturgical reform is only part of a much larger package that has to do with the contemporary direction of Roman Catholicism as a whole. Aspects of this agenda will be treated in our consideration of Pope Benedict XVI's widening of permission to use the preconciliar rite.

3. *Reforming the reform*

The third of Mannion's agendas is directly relevant to our subject. Many of the authors we shall study in these pages would put themselves in this camp. These are not people who desire a return to the pre–Vatican II liturgy. They recognize that the liturgy needed reform and that the liturgical movement of the twentieth century provided many fruitful avenues for development. If they have a core position, it is founded on paragraph 23 of the Liturgy Constitution:

---

[12] I will deal with the fortunes of ICEL in chapter 5 below.

In order that sound tradition be retained, and yet the way remain open to legitimate progress, a careful investigation—theological, historical, and pastoral—should always be made into each part of the liturgy which is to be revised. Furthermore the general laws governing the structure and meaning of the liturgy must be studied in conjunction with the experience derived from recent liturgical reforms and from the indults granted to various places. Finally, there must be no innovations unless the good of the Church genuinely and certainly requires them, and care must be taken that any new forms adopted should in some way grow organically from forms already existing.[13]

The operative word here is "organically," and we shall deal with it at greater length in a later chapter. The major theme of these writers is that the reform happened too quickly and too radically (although, as we shall see, Catherine Pickstock will argue that it was not radical enough). The variations on this theme will be clarified in later chapters. In the United States the "reform of the reform" is represented by Jesuit Father Joseph Fessio and by an organization he helped to found—Adoremus: Society for the Renewal of the Sacred Liturgy.[14] One of the more outspoken representatives of this agenda in Great Britain is Father Aidan Nichols, OP. [15]

4. *Inculturating the reform*

If "reforming the reform" is most relevant to the subject of this book, this next agenda is probably least relevant. The project of inculturating the reform is based on the premise that the reform of the official books of the Roman Rite is only the first step in the process of a thorough adaptation of Catholic liturgy to the various cultures in which it finds itself celebrated.[16] The charter for this agenda can be found in the famous paragraphs on culture in SC (§§37–40). Mannion points to the North American Academy of Liturgy, an ecumenical/interfaith association of liturgical scholars and experts in allied disci-

---

[13] SC §23. Translation from Austin Flannery, OP, ed., *Vatican Council II. Volume 1: The Conciliar and Postconciliar Documents* (new rev. ed. Northport, NY: Costello, 1996).

[14] This group publishes a newsletter: http://www.adoremus.org.

[15] See Aidan Nichols, *Looking at Liturgy: A Critical View of Its Contemporary Form* (San Francisco: Ignatius Press, 1996).

[16] Mannion, "Catholicity of the Liturgy," 21.

plines (e.g., architecture) as the foremost representative of this agenda.[17]

Of course, there is a sense in which this agenda is also aimed at criticizing the current Roman Catholic liturgical reform, especially given the cautious (if not backtracking) statements of the Congregation for Divine Worship and the Discipline of the Sacraments (CDWDS) on inculturation, beginning with the so-called Fourth Instruction on liturgical inculturation, *Varietates Legitimae*, of 1994.[18] The focus of this study, however, is on critics who mainly consider the Vatican II reform to have gone too far or to have betrayed the tradition of Roman Catholic worship.

5. *Recatholicizing the reform*

As Mannion frankly admits, the fifth agenda is not so much separate from the rest as it is meant to transcend the current debate over the liturgy. As with many typologies or models approaches, Mannion saves his preferred model until last. His basic inspiration is the important work on ecclesiology by Avery Dulles, *The Catholicity of the Church*,[19] with its treatment of catholicity from above, from below, in breadth, and in length. As Mannion puts it, "the recatholicizing agenda is primarily committed to a vital recreation of the ethos that

[17] In the interests of transparency I note that I am a past president of this organization and have been actively involved in it since its inception at Scottsdale, Arizona in 1973. I should probably add—with reference to the first agenda, advancing the official reform—that I have in the past served on ICEL's Advisory Committee and its Subcommittee on Translations and Revisions. I have also served as an advisor to the U.S. Bishops' Committee on the Liturgy. So I have been quite actively involved in two of Mannion's agendas.

[18] See David Lysik, *The Liturgy Documents: Volume Two* (Chicago: Liturgy Training Publications, 2000), 107–36; the theme continues with the "Fifth Instruction" on translation (*Liturgiam Authenticam*), ET published by the United States Conference of Catholic Bishops (Washington, DC: USCCB, 2001). There is also a new chapter on inculturation (chapter 9) in the third edition of the *General Instruction of the Roman Missal* (Washington, DC: USCCB, 2003). Finally, we should mention the instruction of the CDWDS (*Redemptionis Sacramentum*) that followed Pope John Paul II's encyclical on the Eucharist, *Ecclesia de Eucharistia* (2003). This instruction can be found at http://www.vatican.va/roman_curia/congregations/ccdds/documents/rc_con_ccdds_doc_20040423_redemptionis-sacramentum_en.html.

[19] Avery Dulles, *The Catholicity of the Church* (Oxford: Clarendon Press, 1985).

has traditionally imbued Catholic liturgy at its best—an ethos of beauty, majesty, spiritual profundity and solemnity."[20]

This agenda is not concerned with rewriting the liturgical books, either in a progressive or in a traditional direction, but rather with a deepening of the spirit of the liturgy, the inculcation of a liturgical spirituality. Two aspects of the recatholicizing agenda strike me as quite pertinent to the subject of criticizing the reform. The first is the aesthetic dimension of worship. People with academic degrees (like me) find it convenient and comfortable to deal with texts. Scarce though texts may be for some of the earlier centuries of Christian worship, they can be analyzed by various accepted methods. We find it more difficult to deal with the nonverbal or aesthetic aspects of liturgy including art, architecture, music, gesture, and movement. But much of the lived experience of the recent liturgical reform has precisely to do with those aesthetic elements in the liturgy. Thus I agree with Mannion's claim that "there does not exist today an adequate theology of ceremonial in Catholic liturgical life,"[21] and much of the present study will inevitably deal with aesthetic issues.

A second pertinent aspect of the recatholicizing agenda has to do with how contemporary students of the liturgy view history. We shall frequently see the claim that the guild of liturgical historians is biased toward a kind of antiquarianism. That claim, most importantly made by Joseph Ratzinger (now Pope Benedict XVI), does at times have validity and needs to be dealt with in the chapters that follow. How to discern from liturgical tradition what may be normative is no easy matter, but it lies at the center of the debate we are about to survey.[22]

I think it worthwhile to repeat some of the cautions Mannion makes elsewhere—especially since this book is written from the point of view of a North American and has as its main (though by no means exclusive) intended audience North American Roman Catholics. In 1988 he published a very important article in *Worship*, titled "Liturgy and

---

[20] Mannion, "Catholicity of the Liturgy," 27.

[21] Ibid., 29.

[22] I have made a plea for the ongoing relevance of liturgical history in "The Usefulness of Liturgical History," *Proceedings of the North American Academy of Liturgy* (2007): 18–32, also published as "The Uses of Liturgical History," *Worship* 82 (2008): 2–18. It is an appendix to this study.

the Present Crisis of Culture."[23] Mannion argues that, contrary to the perception of many students of the liturgy, one of the greatest problems of the contemporary liturgical renewal has not been the insufficient adaptation of liturgy to culture but rather the fact that the liturgy was too inculturated, that we had surrendered to a number of features of contemporary Western culture that were positively harmful to authentic liturgical celebration. He outlines three, the first of which is "the subjectification of reality" or the radical individualism that has been so characteristic of our world and has been illuminated by authors like Robert Bellah, Christopher Lasch, and Richard Sennett. The impact on liturgy of this cultural feature is not too difficult to assess. If the supreme criterion for judging a liturgy is my own intellectual, emotional, and spiritual satisfaction, the liturgy falls prey to manipulation and technique rather than the mediation of divine presence. Many of the authors we shall deal with are very concerned with this trend. It is also related (as are the following two aspects) to a certain congregationalist drift found in many U.S. Catholic parishes.[24]

A second negative cultural dynamic is "the intimization of society," by which Mannion means that formal or ritual elements in worship are felt to be inauthentic or hypocritical. Ritual etiquette is merely a concession to the scale of worship services. The ideal would be small intimate gatherings of worshipers where everyone would be comfortable with everyone else. Then we could have truly "meaningful" liturgies. Anyone who has read Aidan Kavanagh's *On Liturgical Theology* will recognize that we are lounging here in his suburbia of personal taste in our flight from the *civitas*, the city or civilization where difference is encountered and redeemed.[25]

The third and final feature is named "the politicization of culture." Mannion is quick to point out that he is not referring to the sensitivity to social justice and the "Christian commitment to systemic social reform" that are a significant outcome of the Second Vatican Council.

---

[23] *Worship* 62 (1988): 98–123, reprinted in Eleanor Bernstein, ed., *Liturgy and Spirituality in Context* (Collegeville, MN: Liturgical Press, 1990), 1–26. Much of the following paragraphs can be found in John F. Baldovin, "Lo, the Full Final Sacrifice: On the Seriousness of Christian Liturgy," *Antiphon* 7 (2002): 10–17.

[24] M. Francis Mannion, "Catholic Worship and the Dynamics of Congregationalism," *Chicago Studies* 33 (1994): 57–66.

[25] See also M. Francis Mannion, "The Church and the City," *First Things* 100 (2000): 31–36.

Rather he is concerned with the manipulation of the liturgy for specific and narrow political outcomes. His concern seems to be with left-wing groups, but it seems to me one finds the very same tendency to manipulate on the right. I am reminded of the exasperated plea of Robert Hovda, who wrote: "What do you mean 'we need more peace liturgies.' Peace liturgies are the only kind we have."[26] In other words, the eucharistic liturgy in particular and all Christian worship in general is a celebration of God's vision of a redeemed world, or to use Kavanagh's phrase, "Church Doing World."[27]

THE PLAN OF THIS BOOK

In my attempt to analyze and (more to the point) to respond to the contemporary critics of the post–Vatican II Catholic liturgical reform I shall pursue the following itinerary. A number of approaches and methods have been employed to criticize the reform. Although authors sometimes overlap in the approaches they use—e.g., no one completely avoids historical arguments[28]—it will be instructive to see the variety of angles from which the critique has come. The first part of the book (four chapters) will outline and analyze philosophical, historical, theological, and sociological/anthropological approaches. The second part of the book will focus more precisely on the issues that arise from these approaches: liturgical music, architecture (especially the placement of the altar and the orientation of the presider), liturgical language, and finally the 2007 papal *motu proprio*, *Summorum Pontificum*, and the liberalization of the use of pre–Vatican II liturgy—the so-called Missal of Blessed John XXIII (1962).

We shall begin with the very challenging critiques of the reform made by a philosopher, the British Anglican scholar Catherine Pickstock, and the Oratorian Jonathan Robinson. The next chapter will deal with the historical critique as represented by three figures: Klaus Gamber, a German scholar; Alcuin Reid, at one time a Benedictine at Farnborough Abbey in England; and a French musicologist, Denis Crouan. The third approach examined will be that of theology, and the chosen representative will be the current pope, Benedict XVI, especially in his

---

[26] See John Baldovin, ed., *Robert Hovda: The Amen Corner* (Collegeville, MN: Liturgical Press, 1994), 170–76.

[27] Aidan Kavanagh, *On Liturgical Theology* (Collegeville, MN: Liturgical Press, 1984), 52ff.

[28] See the appendix.

influential writings as Cardinal Joseph Ratzinger. Criticism of the liturgical reform under Paul VI has also involved the work of sociologists and anthropologists as well as of philosophers, historians, and theologians. Therefore a fifth chapter will analyze the critiques launched by Kieran Flanagan and David Torevell, both from Great Britain. Needless to say there have been many more significant authors, e.g., Aidan Nichols, Uwe Lang, Thomas Kocik, and Laszlo Dobszay, who have made important contributions to the critique we are examining. These authors will certainly appear in the pages of this study, but I have chosen for better or worse to focus on several representative figures, especially since much of the critique (as the reader will surely discover) has a somewhat repetitive quality.

The second part of the book begins with chapter 5, which deals not with approaches but with issues: language, space, translation, and the liberal use of the preconciliar liturgy. A final chapter will summarize the conclusions and (much more important) suggest some ways forward in what has become a war over the liturgy.

CONCLUSION

One of the more serious debates in Catholic historiography during the past few years has been over the significance of Vatican II. Various authors have challenged the so-called Alberigo School of interpreting Vatican II. Italian church historian Giuseppe Alberigo and others considered the council a monumental watershed in the history of modern Catholicism.[29] Much of the implementation of the council, significantly represented by Pope John Paul II and his prefect of the Congregation for the Doctrine of the Faith, Joseph Ratzinger, has been undertaken on the premise that the council did not change anything important in the church. Certainly the council documents themselves can yield both interpretations. This has been one of the problems in assessing the significance of the liturgy constitution. My sympathies lie with

---

[29] See Giuseppe Alberigo, *A Short History of Vatican II* (Maryknoll, NY: Orbis, 2006); idem, ed., with Joseph Komonchak, *History of Vatican II*. 5 vols. (Maryknoll, NY: Orbis, 1995–2006). For the anti-Alberigo camp see Rino Fisichella, ed., *Il Concilio Vaticano II: Recezione e attualità alla luce del Giubileo* (Milan: San Paolo, 2000); as well as Pope Benedict XVI's Christmas address to the Roman Curia for 2005, available at http://www.vatican.va/holy_father/benedict_xvi/speeches/2005/december/documents/hf_ben_xvi_spe_20051222_roman-curia_en.html; and an interview given in 2007 by Cardinal Camillo Ruini, former papal vicar of Rome, available at http://www.cathnews.com/news/506/122.php.

two Jesuit colleagues, John O'Malley and Stephen Schloesser, who in recent articles in *Theological Studies* have articulated the understanding that Vatican II represents a change in Roman Catholicism that transcends the documents themselves.[30] That has clearly been true of the reform of the liturgy.

As we move forward let me make it clear that I would not have written this book if I had thought the critics had nothing to offer. My hope is that in a respectful and non-polemical atmosphere the positive contributions made by the critics can be appreciated by a wider audience, including what might be called "the academic liturgical establishment." Why has there been so much contention over the reform? Why the current battles over the liturgy? There are several reasons, I think. First, we are at a crucial point in world history when the fate of Christianity, at least as we know it, seems to be in the balance. Second, one of the clearest signs of change in the Catholic Church in the past century has been the liturgical reform following Vatican II. That reform coincided with a virtual cultural revolution in the West and the various interconnections between culture and the reform of worship are extremely difficult to disentangle. Third, the liturgy lies at the very heart of Catholic identity and practice. Decades of teaching have taught me that very little inflames the passions and commitment of my theological students more than liturgical and sacramental questions. While this can be frustrating at times, I suppose it is as it should be. No matter where we stand, the liturgy is precious to all who bear the name Christian—and so thinking about it, even arguing about it, is an important and necessary endeavor.

[30] John O'Malley, "Vatican II: Did Anything Happen?" *TS* 67 (2006): 3–33; Stephen Schloesser, "Against Forgetting: Memory, History, Vatican II," *TS* 67 (2006): 275–319.

Chapter One

The Philosophical Critique

Some of the most fundamental criticisms of the Vatican II reform of the liturgy stem from the conviction that the entire reform program (in the Liturgy Constitution) and its application (in the subsequent reform) were founded on bad philosophical premises. We shall deal with two representative figures, each with a distinctive understanding of the philosophical errors at the basis of the reform.

CATHERINE PICKSTOCK: *AFTER WRITING*

Catherine Pickstock is a theologian who has dealt with some of the most fundamental philosophical presuppositions of the liturgical reform. A number of the scholars we shall review in the course of this book accept the Constitution on the Liturgy as Vatican II proposed it, but take issue in one way or another with its implementation. This is not the case with Pickstock, who has questioned the very foundations of the reform. For her the reform proceeds from "modern" presuppositions such as the triumph of "mapping" reality after the sixteenth century, the victory of nouns over verbs, the supposed virtues of simplicity and non-repetition, and a preference for writing over orality or speaking. What results is perhaps the most intriguing critique of the reform in recent years, a powerful and difficult book, *After Writing: On the Liturgical Consummation of Philosophy*.[1] Since its publication she has captured the interest of a number of liturgical scholars.[2] This chapter will first situate Pickstock's treatment of liturgy within her overall project and also within the movement known as Radical Orthodoxy.

---

[1] Catherine Pickstock, *After Writing: On the Liturgical Consummation of Philosophy* (Oxford: Blackwell, 1998).

[2] Nathan Mitchell, "The Amen Corner: Worship as Music," *Worship* 73 (1999): 249–59, especially 254–59.

Second, I will offer an analysis of her treatment of the medieval Roman liturgy of the Mass and the theology it represents. Third, I will consider her views on liturgy and society. An assessment of Pickstock's questioning of some of the fundamental basics of the Vatican II reform of the liturgy will conclude this section.

Catherine Pickstock is associated with Radical Orthodoxy, a theological movement begun in Cambridge in the 1990s and spearheaded by John Milbank, Graham Ward, and herself. These three scholars edited *Radical Orthodoxy: A New Theology*, which serves as a kind of summary of the "movement."[3] In their words, Radical Orthodoxy "in the face of the secular demise of truth, seeks to reconfigure theological truth."[4] In other words, these authors are self-consciously responding to the modern and postmodern critiques of power. What makes them self-conscious, and not merely restorationist, is their recognition of the place of language in construing reality. In this sense they understand themselves to be thoroughly postmodern. Language is unavoidable, as the deconstructionists like Derrida and Foucault have well understood. On the other hand, Radical Orthodoxy is a direct response to the cynicism and relativism that come in the wake of the postmodern deconstructionists. In that sense they are not postmodern at all. They seek to revive an Augustinian Neoplatonism as a holistic vision of the world and social order,[5] and consider themselves to be Christian Socialists.[6] After all, it is difficult to call oneself a theologian if one takes a completely agnostic attitude toward understanding truth, which seems to be the position of a good number of postmodern thinkers.

For a critic like Russell Reno, the project of Radical Orthodoxy fails to preserve the specific identity of Jesus Christ in favor of theological abstraction, thus sliding back into "modern" presuppositions. Reno lays this failure at the door of Milbank et al.'s Anglo-Catholicism, which he regards as an invented tradition.[7] Perhaps this is also why

---

[3] John Milbank, Catherine Pickstock, and Graham Ward, eds., *Radical Orthodoxy: A New Theology* (London: Routledge, 1999). See also Milbank's *Theology and Social Theory: Beyond Secular Reason* (Oxford: Blackwell, 1991).

[4] Milbank, Pickstock, and Ward, *Radical Orthodoxy*, 1.

[5] See the perceptive analysis of Russell R. Reno, "The Radical Orthodoxy Project," *First Things* 100 (2000): 37–44.

[6] See Stratford Caldecott, "Radical Orthodoxy," a 2001 interview with Pickstock, at http://www.catholicculture.org/library/view.cfm?recnum=4174.

[7] Reno, "Radical Orthodoxy Project," 40–41. We shall see below whether a similar criticism can be applied to Pickstock's treatment of medieval liturgy.

this movement is criticized by Stratford Caldecott as lacking an ecclesiology.[8]

Of course Milbank, Ward, and Pickstock hardly fall into the category of radical postmodernism, one of whose characteristics is the principle of the indeterminacy of meaning and truth, based on the ever-fluid interpretation of the written word. The contemporary French philosopher Jacques Derrida is well known for this kind of deconstruction of meaning. Derrida's target is the Western metaphysical tradition with the privilege it gives to the spoken word, the *Logos*.[9] One can guess immediately that the defense of the spoken word, so central to both christology and the performance of liturgy, will be a major element in Pickstock's program. For her, many contemporary postmodernist philosophers (and their progenitors) have put dissecting reality over the act of praise (doxology), which is precisely what liturgy ultimately is. For Pickstock, doxology (= liturgy) is not just an event that happens now and then, but rather constitutes a whole way of life.[10]

And so *After Writing* begins with a rereading of Plato's *Phaedrus* in an attempt to show why Jacques Derrida's denigration of orality (as opposed to writing) is an error. It is important to note that Pickstock has a rather particular reading of Plato—one in which reality (Being) is not static but rather dynamic and inevitably incarnated in time and space. This rather opaque passage gives some idea of what she is after:

> In the *Phaedrus*, reliance on the written word is seen as representing an immanentist attempt to *circumvent* temporality and contingency and to spatialize time by gathering up the present moment with a view to offering it to an anonymous posterity, not for the sake of interpersonal benefit through time, but as a means to ensure lasting reputation, a

reflexive "gift" which does not freely inhabit time, but seeks to reclaim identically the anterior moment of donation, thus transposing time into a spatial domain.[11]

In fact, Derrida (and those who think like him) create "the polity of death" by isolating snapshots on the written page. Pickstock eventually refers to this process as "spatialization"[12] and it will have an impact on contemporary understanding of the liturgy. Spatialization refers to the tendency in writers from Petrus Ramus (sixteenth century) onward to privilege static analysis and mapping (*mathesis*) over the dynamism given by temporality. The deconstructionists therefore represent the dead end of a project of mapping and dissecting reality begun by Petrus Ramus and solidified for Western philosophy by René Descartes in the seventeenth century.[13] The result is the loss of the narrative connections that hold reality together, and the technical name for this process in terms of language is "asyndeton, syntax characterized by the absence of coordinating and subordinating conjunctions."[14] Hence we have another symptom of the frenzy to map and categorize everything by lists. Verbs lose out to nouns in the process.[15] The passion for nouns leads to what Pickstock calls "necrophilia." I will let her speak for herself:

> modernity seeks less to banish death, than to prise death and life apart in order to preserve life immune from death in pure sterility. For in seeking *only* life, in the form of pseudo-eternal permanence, the "modern" gesture is secretly doomed to necrophilia, love of what has to die, can only die. In seeking only life, modernity gives life over to death. . . .[16]

In other words, since modernity (as Pickstock conceives it) cannot allow for the truly transcendent and thus for having to take some account of death, it is ironically left only with death itself. And so it is essential that the continuum that could be called "the great chain of

---

[11] Ibid., 9.

[12] Ibid., 47ff.

[13] Ibid., 49–61.

[14] Ibid., 95. See also her "Liturgy and Modernity," *Telos* 113 (1998): 26.

[15] Pickstock perceives a good example of this process in the contemporary English translation of the Creed: "Asyndeton: Syntax and Insanity. A Study in the Revision of the Nicene Creed," *Modern Theology* 10 (1994): 321–40.

[16] Pickstock, *After Writing*, 104.

being" is maintained. Along with other members of the Radical Orthodoxy "school" she thus argues for a return to an Augustinian Neoplatonism, which we shall see below is vital to her interpretation of St. Thomas on transubstantiation.

One final step in Pickstock's program must be described before I deal directly with her treatment of medieval liturgy and the question of liturgy and culture. She lays the modern problematic not at the doorstep of Petrus Ramus in the sixteenth century but rather at that of the fourteenth-century Franciscan theologian John Duns Scotus, whose denial of the Thomistic analogy of being (*analogia entis*) made the concept of being univocal. In other words, if the idea of being must be predicated in exactly the same way for everything that exists, then ultimately God is constrained to behave like every being. This idea is not so much an attempt to control God as it is to make the universe intelligible. But this denial of what is called the ontological difference (between God and the created order) ultimately leads to an arbitrary God (the *potentia absoluta Dei*) since the effort to make God unique must also (in Scotus' system) make him somewhat despotically irrational.[17] By the same token, dispensing with the analogy of being leads to what is called "occasionalism" in sacraments—crudely put, the sacraments are not effective because of a certain fittingness in their constitution and operation but simply because God has decided that it shall be so. In other words, instead of being able to construe a logic to the activity of God in a sacrament, we must posit God's activity on the basis of the divine will.[18] Thus Pickstock blames ("blames" is not too strong a word here) Scotus for the turn to the priority of epistemology over metaphysics—a turn she finds disastrous for modern theology.[19] Because he denies the analogous nature of being, Scotus cannot maintain the real distinction between essence and existence, which for Pickstock allows for a being's "always arriving, always coming." She puts it this way:

> The real distinction between existence and essence is therefore the inner kernel of both *analogia entis* and participation because it permits essence to be realized as essence only through the Being from which it always remains distinct: essence forever simply participates in that

[17] Ibid., 122–23.
[18] Ibid., 132.
[19] Ibid., 127.

which alone realizes and fully determines it. Thus, ontological difference invites the possibility of likeness and proximity, whereas univocity of Being produces unmediable difference and distance.[20]

And so Scotus is forced into a postulation of the divine will with regard to transubstantiation. Moreover, this means transubstantiation can only be understood as a locative presence—i.e., presence as of an object in a place. St. Thomas had argued against such a flat-footed, unnuanced understanding of presence in his treatment of transubstantiation.[21] For Thomas, Christ is not in the sacrament as an object is in a place. But the result for Scotus, at least according to Pickstock,[22] is that Christ's soul is only partially present in the eucharistic elements and ". . . His Body is here effectively presented in the manner of a corpse. Here, therefore, in the very heart of piety, the cult of necrophilia is begun."[23] There is, after all, something breathtaking about such a sweeping claim!

I have tried in the above paragraphs to make an exceedingly long story short. And the reader may be thinking that we have lost our way in the thickets of a very complex critique of Western philosophy. But I cannot agree with reviewers who advise skipping over the first part of Pickstock's *After Writing*, since the more "liturgical" part of her work very much rests on the case she builds in the more philosophical part. It is also important to have some sense of her philosophical position to be able to judge her assessment of the ("modernist") foundations of the liturgical reform. The first part of the book, which we have just reviewed, is indeed very difficult—not only because of the complexity of the subject and of her logic, but also because she insists on being obscure and opaque (playfully like the postmodernists she opposes) when she could be much clearer.

At the end of the next section I shall argue that Pickstock has a rather abstract notion of liturgy, but we need to postpone that until we consider what she has to say about Christian worship. At this point it is important to understand that Pickstock is after rather large game in claiming that liturgy (or better, doxological language) is the true con-

[20] Ibid., 129.

[21] Thomas Aquinas, *Summa Theologiae* IIIa, 76, a 5.

[22] I must disclaim direct knowledge of Scotus. See the critical remarks on Pickstock's reading of Scotus in Bryan Spinks, "Review of *After Writing*," *Scottish Journal of Theology* 51 (1998): 510; also the review by Regis Duffy, a Franciscan, in *TS* 60 (1999): 175.

[23] Pickstock, *After Writing*, 134.

summation of philosophy. All thought, all language has praise as its true goal. One is reminded of Alexander Schmemann's understanding of the human being as fundamentally *homo adorans*—the creature whose main goal is to adore[24]—or even the First Principle and Foundation of the *Spiritual Exercises* of St. Ignatius of Loyola: "Human beings are created to praise, reverence and serve God our Lord, and by means of doing this, to save their souls."[25] Pickstock has a dynamic understanding of being that is rooted in her reading of Plato. Not everyone will agree with that reading. For example, the contemporary French Roman Catholic sacramental theologian Louis-Marie Chauvet interprets Plato (in the *Timaeus*) as the beginning of a tradition that favors Being over Becoming.[26]

In any case, Pickstock has provided a philosophical construct that places liturgy at the center of life and thought. The second part of her book, titled "The Sacred Polis," is a good indication of the role she expects liturgy to play in society. It is to that role of liturgy—and specifically medieval liturgy—that we turn.

Medieval Liturgy as Model

One of the aspects of her work that has made Pickstock well known and, in fact, something of a hero to those who question the wisdom of modern liturgical reform is her critique that appears as a commentary on "the impossibility of liturgy" in the second part of the book.[27] For Pickstock the post–Vatican II reform of the liturgy was fundamentally flawed because it did not adequately contextualize the liturgy in contemporary culture. As she puts it:

---

[24] *For the Life of the World: Sacraments and Orthodoxy* (Crestwood, NY: St. Vladimir's Seminary Press, 1973), 15.

[25] George E. Ganss, *The Spiritual Exercises of Saint Ignatius: A Translation and Commentary* (St. Louis: Institute of Jesuit Sources, 1992), 32.

[26] See Louis-Marie Chauvet, *Symbol and Sacrament: A Sacramental Rereading of Christian Existence* (Collegeville, MN: Liturgical Press, 1995), 26–33.

[27] Classifying Pickstock as a conservative is much too simple. As becomes clear in her interview with Caldecott (see n. 6 above), she is enthusiastically in favor of women's ordination as well as a very active role for the laity in liturgical celebration. In addition to *After Writing*, her critique of the reform has appeared in a number of places. Catherine Pickstock, "A Sermon for St. Cecilia," *Theology* 100 (1997): 411–18; eadem, "Medieval Liturgy and Modern Reform," *Antiphon* 6 (2001): 19–25; eadem, "A Short Essay on the Reform of the Liturgy," in Paul Bradshaw and Bryan Spinks, eds., *Liturgy in Dialogue* (London: SPCK, 1993).

. . . because the Vatican II reforms of the mediaeval Roman Rite failed to take into account the cultural assumptions which lay implicit within the text [of the pre–Vatican II Roman Rite], their reforms were themselves to a certain extent imbued with an entirely more sinister conservatism. For they failed to challenge those structures of the modern secular world which are wholly inimical to liturgical purpose: those structures, indeed, which perpetuate a separation of everyday life from liturgical enactment.[28]

Here we meet a claim that will appear fairly frequently among the critics: twentieth-century liturgical historians have a bent toward antiquarianism. They have idealized the late Patristic period (4th–6th centuries) and refuse to appreciate the healthy aspects of development in the Middle Ages. The main villains of the piece are the usual suspects: Theodor Klauser and Josef Jungmann, the German and Austrian liturgical historians on whom the liturgical reformers relied so heavily.[29] Summing up several centuries of liturgical scholarship and nearly a century of advocacy for liturgical reform, these scholars both revealed how very accidental much of the development of the liturgy actually was. These efforts have been matched for the Christian East by scholars like Juan Mateos and Robert Taft, both of Rome's Pontifical Oriental Institute.[30] On the basis of the research of these great historians, Vatican II's Constitution on the Liturgy made the following well-known prescription with regard to the reform of the liturgy:

> The rites should be marked by a noble simplicity; they should be short, clear and unencumbered by useless repetitions; they should be within the people's powers of comprehension and as a rule not require much explanation.[31]

---

[28] Pickstock, "Short Essay on the Reform of the Liturgy," 56.

[29] Theodor Klauser, *A Short History of the Western Liturgy*, trans. John Halliburton (2nd ed. New York: Oxford University Press, 1979); Josef Jungmann, *Missarum Sollemnia: The Mass of the Roman Rite*, trans. Francis Brunner. 2 vols. (New York: Benziger Bros., 1950).

[30] Juan Mateos, *La célébration de la parole dans la liturgie byzantine* (Rome: Pontifical Oriental Institute Press, 1971); Robert Taft, *A History of the Liturgy of St. John Chrysostom*. 6 vols. (Rome: Pontifical Oriental Institute Press, 1975). See especially Taft's apologia for the method of comparative liturgy in "Anton Baumstark's Comparative Liturgy Revisited," in Robert Taft and Gabriele Winkler, *Comparative Liturgy Fifty Years After Anton Baumstark (1872–1948)* (Rome: Pontifical Oriental Institute Press, 2001), 191–232.

[31] Vatican II, Constitution on the Sacred Liturgy, §34.

Much of the postconciliar reform of the Eucharist and other liturgical rites took its inspiration from this call for simplification. This is precisely what Pickstock wants to call into question. As I noted earlier, this means that Pickstock is critical not only of the reform but of its roots in the Liturgy Constitution. Far from the rationalized logic of the contemporary Mass of Paul VI, Pickstock finds the deepest meaning of the traditional Roman Rite (the so-called Tridentine Mass) in its very stops and starts, its hesitancies and "impossible logic." Moreover, she finds that the theological basis of the reform would have been more profound had it paid more attention to certain theologians: ". . . the reform of the liturgy instigated by Vatican II was itself not adequate to its theology, for example, the work of de Lubac, Hans Urs von Balthasar, Yves Congar, and the influence of the restored Thomism of Etienne Gilson."[32]

This is certainly an astute observation, and we shall have to return to it in the last chapter. Was adequate theological reflection incorporated in the reform of the liturgy in addition to the results of historical-critical analysis? Clearly Pickstock thinks it was not.

What, then, are the main lines of Pickstock's appreciation of the Mass in the Middle Ages? First she analyzes the opening rites of the Mass as a series of recommencements and repetitions starting with the use of "impersonation" (assuming another's name) at the very outset: "In the name of the Father and of the Son and of the Holy Spirit." There is ambiguity here, for "in the name" could be understood both as "within" and "taking the name." This ambiguity is essential because it reveals the very impossibility of liturgy—the fact that it must be experienced both as gift and sacrifice and thereby overcome the dead ends of modern philosophy.[33] In other words, we are actors in the liturgy, but we can only be actors because we impersonate the one who gives us the ability to worship in the first place.

"I will go to the altar of God," the psalm (43) recited at the foot of the altar is another example of this impossibility. Since the altar is by

---

[32] Pickstock, "Short Essay on the Reform of the Liturgy," 63.

[33] Pickstock, *After Writing*, 169–70; see also 208; the question of the possibility of true gift was raised by Derrida. Pickstock's Radical Orthodoxy partner, John Milbank, has responded in *On Being Reconciled: Ontology and Pardon* (London: Routledge, 2003). For another view of the question see Jean-Luc Marion, *Being Given: Toward a Phenomenology of Givenness* (Stanford: Stanford University Press, 2002), and John Caputo, *God, the Gift and Postmodernism* (Bloomington: Indiana University Press, 1999).

definition the place of alteration (her word, not my pun), it is always "receding," not within human grasp:

> The altar is therefore a [sic] supplementary, and, in worldly terms, destination which is also a beginning, the place towards which we must travel in order to be able to offer our sacrifice of praise. It follows that the liturgy of our text is always about to begin, not in a "hollowed out" sense, but as a necessarily deferred anticipation of the heavenly worship towards which we strive. Our liturgy in time can only be the liturgy we render in order to be able to render liturgy. . . . And one can only ever have begun; there is no other way to be than to be on the way.[34]

In this way Pickstock argues for the eschatological nature of the liturgy so strongly emphasized by a number of contemporary theologians.[35] In her reading of the medieval Roman Mass the approach to the altar represents yet another beginning—the request for purification in the *Confiteor* to the incensation, and the *Kyrie eleison* chant that follows. At this point the liturgy impersonates the angelic voices in the singing of the hymn *Gloria in excelsis Deo*. Yet another request for purification comes with the priest's prayer, *Munda cor meum* (Cleanse my heart), in preparation for the Gospel.[36] Here she perceives a play on the word *munda*—both "cleanse" (the meaning of the verb) and "worlded" from the Latin noun for the world, *mundum*, as in "mundane." By the end of her treatment of what we now refer to as the Liturgy of the Word, Pickstock writes:

> The same dialectic of exaltation and subsidence or self-abasement occurs throughout the Rite . . . the passage of the worshipper's advance is not construed as unicursally progressive, nor as undertaken

---

[34] Pickstock, *After Writing*, 183, 185. (Thus Pickstock proves herself a worthy sparring opponent for the likes of Derrida and Foucault. The number of times my word processing program has suggested spell check in the composition of this chapter is another pointed example!)

[35] E.g., Geoffrey Wainwright, *Eucharist and Eschatology* (New York: Oxford University Press, 1981), and especially in the work of Joseph Ratzinger, *The Spirit of the Liturgy* (San Francisco: Ignatius Press, 2000), which we shall see in a later chapter. The notion of eschatology will be particularly relevant in the argument about the position of the presider at the altar.

[36] Pickstock, *After Writing*, 189.

by one worshipping voice alone, but as stuttering, constantly retracing its syllables, and calling for aid by means of many voices.[37]

By the same token she finds that the contemporary liturgical criticism of the offertory prayers and repetition of offering in the Roman Canon is misdirected, for it fails to appreciate how we are constituted as liturgical subjects by the constant reentering into God and in the dialectic of giving and receiving.

Another important feature Pickstock finds in the language of the liturgy is "apostrophe": "a rhetorical figure used to signify vocative address to an absent, dead, or wholly other person, idea or object."[38] In this case, of course, we are speaking to one who is "wholly other." For Pickstock, such apostrophizing language dispossesses the subject so that the worshiper receives himself or herself from God. The triumph of nouns over verbs so characteristic of the modern mania for mapping and categorizing is countered by this kind of praying. An example is provided in the address made to the incense in the initial incensation of the altar: *Ab illo benedicaris in cuius honorem cremaberis* ("May you be blessed by him in whose honor you will be burned"). The incense only becomes its true self when it goes up in smoke. Moreover, the absence of the one to whom prayers are addressed requires that the Mass be "rehearsed" again and again "in the hope that there might be worship."[39]

One final comment on Pickstock's treatment of the medieval Mass: The fact that a multiplicity of genres is employed in the Mass is crucial to her argument that the liturgy is no simple linear or rational progression. Rather, the Roman Rite is "polyphonal." It uses "narrative, dialogue, antiphon, monologue, apostrophe, doxology, oration, invocation, citation, supplementation, and entreaty."[40] In other words, it always keeps us on our toes and prevents us from becoming self-satisfied.

These are the main lines of Pickstock's assessment of the medieval Mass of the Roman Rite. What to make of this analysis whose aim is to

---

[37] Ibid., 189–90.

[38] Ibid., 193.

[39] Ibid., 200; see also the interpretation of *haec quotiescumque feceritis* ("as often as you do this") from the words of institution as an example of the repetition inherent in the liturgy, 223.

[40] Ibid., 213.

demonstrate that the contemporary Roman Rite (and its cousins in the Anglican communion, for example) is inadequate to the task of worship that can stand up to secular society? In the first place we need to note that the phrase "medieval liturgy," while handy, is not terribly useful. One can begin treatment of the medieval Roman Rite in fifth-century Rome and follow it through an immense number of permutations and variations both temporally and geographically up to the end of the sixteenth century—perhaps even to the last third of the twentieth. As Bryan Spinks points out, the Sarum Rite did not begin the Mass with the Prayers at the Foot of the Altar that Pickstock cites as so significant.[41] A cursory glance at a synoptic chart of offertory prayers in the various medieval usages would demonstrate a good deal of variety, a point even Pickstock must concede.[42]

Second, Pickstock makes a plea for understanding the medieval liturgy in its context, but apparently that does not include taking a hard look at the development of the text or its surroundings—the church building, for example. There is some irony in the fact that while in the first part of the book she champions the spoken over the written, her argument in the second part of the book is tied to a text—the Ordinary of the Mass.

Third, although the Eucharist is clearly the high point of medieval worship, it is also part of an enormously complex system of services including the Divine Office, processions, and other sacramental rites. It will not do to isolate the Eucharist from other liturgical rites. This isolation has also been characteristic of many (though not all) of the contemporary critics of the reform.

In the fourth place, many of Pickstock's textual analyses are playful, much in the same way that some postmodern theorists play with language. Take, for example, the priest's prayer before the Gospel, *Munda cor meum*, cited above. In the context of this formula there is only one meaning that can be sustained by the word *munda*, and that is the verb "cleanse." Pickstock's notion that the use of the word could imply a "request to be *worlded*" is utterly fanciful, even if claiming that the Gospel makes us more citizens of the world is a wonderful idea. Many of Pickstock's interpretations are a template imposed upon the rite, much like the medieval allegorical interpretations of Amalar of Metz

[41] "Review of *After Writing*," (see n. 22 above): 510.
[42] See Craig Wright, *Music and Ceremony at Notre Dame of Paris 500–1500* (Cambridge: Cambridge University Press, 1989), 118; Pickstock, *After Writing*, 179.

(ninth century) or William Durandus (thirteenth century). They make for excellent material for meditation but do not really do justice to the rite or provide an adequate critique for its reform.

Fifth, Pickstock is fond of taking the plural "we" of the Roman Rite seriously. For example, she writes of the entrance rite: "But as soon as we arrive at this state of purity, sufficient to bless one another in this way (the dialogue 'The Lord be with you . . .') we must again repeat our request for purification."[43] This is fine until one asks the question: just who exactly is this "we" she is speaking of? Being in touch with the text of the liturgy as a corporate exercise ended as soon as Latin was no longer the common language of the people. Many of the prayers of the Roman Rite that Pickstock finds so meaningful entered the liturgy after the people no longer understood, and in any case were recited *sotto voce*. The priest did indeed speak for the congregation, but the percentage of people who understood this (at least in terms of language) must have been very small.[44]

Sixth, Pickstock acknowledges the need for reforming a liturgy in which receiving holy communion had become infrequent, devotional practices individualistic, and the liturgy itself a kind of spectacle.[45] The latter two features did indeed arise rather late in the Middle Ages and flourished in the period of the Baroque right through the early twentieth century. But the decline in the reception of holy communion, which one can argue is the most important, is a problem that begins in the sixth century at the latest. All this is to say that Pickstock's medieval Mass is a construct that seems to have little to do with the actual performance of the rite.[46] Just as the Middle Ages were romanticized in the novels of Sir Walter Scott, the Gothic Revival of architecture in the early nineteenth century, and Cambridge Ritualists like John Mason Neale and Benjamin Webb, so too we have here a view of

[43] Pickstock, "Medieval Liturgy and Modern Reform," 22.

[44] Chapter 4 below, on the sociological and anthropological critique, deals with the arguments of Eamon Duffy, John Bossy, and others that the liturgy was indeed understood by the people as a corporate activity.

[45] Pickstock, "Medieval Liturgy and Modern Reform," 21. In fact, she is quite strong on the notion of participation in her interview with Caldecott. I repeat that it would be incorrect to think that she aims at restoring medieval liturgy; see n. 27 above.

[46] For further critique by liturgical historians see the excellent reviews by Kenneth Stevenson, *Journal of Theological Studies*, n.s. 50 (1999): 452–54, and Bryan Spinks, cited above in n. 22.

medieval liturgy that is alluring but not quite the case.[47] There is a kind of sanitized medievalism at work here—a very romanticized notion that the Middle Ages represent an ideal of Christian society. One must ask if that kind of romanticism is really helpful in understanding how to reform and renew Catholic worship.

Liturgy, Theology, and Society

All this is not to say that Pickstock is completely off the point. On the contrary, much of what she has to say is insightful, even brilliant. And there is no rule saying that the historical-critical interpretation of the liturgy is the only one allowed.[48] Just like the Scriptures, the liturgy is open to the historical triad of spiritual (allegorical), moral (tropological), and eschatological (anagogical) analysis. This does not mean, however, that each of these forms of analysis provides an adequate basis for reforming the liturgy.

Pickstock is also clearly on the right track in suggesting that a certain linear rationality has informed the contemporary liturgy of the Roman Rite Eucharist—a point made by sociologists and anthropologists, as we shall see in a later chapter. The model used by the post–Vatican II reformers in order to reconstruct the eucharistic liturgy was pretty clearly the late-seventh-century Roman Mass described in the *Ordo Romanus Primus*. Yet only the bare structure of the rite was taken, not the no-longer-relevant court etiquette that is so meticulously laid out.[49] Perhaps since she is not a liturgical scholar (nor does she claim to be), Pickstock can be forgiven for ignoring the wise observations of Anscar Chupungco and others that what we have in the books of the reformed Roman Rite is the basic script for the liturgy, not the liturgy

---

[47] Russell Reno, "Radical Orthodoxy Project," 41, may be correct in seeing the root of this romanticism in the writer's Anglo-Catholicism: "But monuments are not living institutions, and Gothic buildings are no substitute for enduring practices. Radical Orthodoxy cannot invent the flesh and blood of a Christian culture, and so must be satisfied with describing its theoretical *gestalt*, gesturing in postmodern fashion, toward that which was and might be."

[48] I have, nevertheless, tried to argue elsewhere that a rigorous historical-critical investigation of the liturgy is essential for liturgical theology and liturgical studies in general. See the appendix.

[49] See the superb 2007 Harvard dissertation by John Romano, *Ritual and Society in Early Medieval Rome*, an extremely thorough and convincing analysis of the text and context of *Ordo Romanus Primus*.

itself as it must be adapted in various cultures.[50] At the same time, Pickstock's notion of the liturgical stutter and stammer read off the medieval rite is an important reminder that putting the liturgy into understandable language does not make God understandable. Liturgical language still needs to point to the transcendent. Divine grace makes the impossible possible in our worship. One of the persistent problems with the liturgical reform (*any* liturgical reform) is going to be a kind of Pelagian attitude that we have constructed the liturgy, because reform is always and inevitably self-conscious.[51]

In this vein what Pickstock has to say about "asyndeton" is also useful. In an article contrasting the translation of the Nicene Creed in the 1980 *Alternative Service Book* (*ASB*) of the Church of England (the common ecumenical text developed by the International Consultation on English Texts [ICET] in the 1970s) with the previous translation in the *Book of Common Prayer* of 1549 she attempts to show how contemporary translators have bought into the modern use of asyndeton, the literary practice that tends to multiply and shorten sentences and especially to eliminate subordinate and relative clauses. Thus "it converts six sentences to become thirteen, twenty coordinating conjunctions into nine, and five subordinating conjunctions into one."[52] Her point, although worked out in twenty pages of extremely dense prose, is relatively straightforward. The Nicene Creed is not a list of true doctrinal statements about God but rather a doxological hymn that *enacts* or *performs* the Holy Trinity by its intricate conjunctions and references that leap over one another and entwine with one another. The modern translation smoothes these complications out—but it does so at the cost of losing the performativity of the Creed itself. It also (unwittingly) surrenders to a capitalist notion of desire as lack

[50] Anscar Chupungco, *Liturgies of the Future: The Process and Methods of Inculturation* (New York: Paulist Press, 1989), 7.

[51] We shall return to this subject in the final chapter. For Chupungco on text and reform, see ibid.

[52] Pickstock, "Asyndeton" (see n. 15 above), 325. The *ASB* translation is in fact the ecumenical translation of the International Consultation on Common Texts (ICET) and is used as well in most contemporary English versions of the liturgy, including the Roman Catholic. With very few alterations the same version appears in the text of the Roman Catholic Eucharist employed in the United States. Pickstock's analysis corresponds to the connections and clauses not only in the *BCP* 1549 but also in the Greek and Latin versions of the Creed. See Heinrich Denziger, *Enchiridion Symbolorum* §§54, 86.

rather than the Christian/Augustinian notion of desire as excess. In other words, desire is ultimately more about what God wants to give us than it is about what we do not have. This is a very fruitful trajectory for liturgical theology.

Pickstock is correct: the Nicene Creed employed at the Sunday Eucharist is not a "loyalty oath" or a series of doctrinal statements that ought to be recited instead of sung—if it is to be recited at all. To be sure, the Creed's native home is the baptismal liturgy. The Nicene Creed[53] entered into the Eucharist in the Orthodox East as a reaction against its polemical use by the Monophysites (or better "Non-Chalcedonians"), who claimed the Creed as their own, refusing to accept the doctrinal conclusions about the two natures of Christ affirmed by the Council of Chalcedon. Be that as it may, the Sunday Eucharist is fundamentally the weekly renewal of Christian initiation begun at baptism. Moreover, the Creed has more to do with praise or doxology than information or a series of doctrines. Pickstock is right on the money—the value of the Creed is in the enacting of the Trinity as relation. The ICET translation does blur that enactment by its tendency to make the flow of doctrine seem more logical and rational. Moreover, her point that short sentences mimic the disorientation of modern society is an idea worth pondering, though I cannot go more deeply into it here.[54] As she puts it:

> Since meaning resides in the connections between things, readers of asyndetic texts have much more work to do in supplying what is absent. The several elements of salvation history are related as isolated units, devoid of syntactic lexical indication of their purpose, or connection with the text as a whole. . . . This would-be 'accelerated' narrative is not one that is continuous, but one that starts and stops with every clause. It effects a reification of singular verbal units, a list of semelfactive actions, the arbitrary disjunctive components of a catalogue.[55]

In *After Writing* Pickstock goes on to analyze the asyndetic nature of the Institution Narrative of the Eucharist—coming to the opposite

---

[53] Technically the Creed affirmed by Nicea (325 CE) and supplemented by Constantinople I (381 CE).

[54] I am not as sure that I would agree with her argument about the replacement of the traditional Latin form of the Creed: "I believe" (Credo) with "We believe." The latter reflects the Greek of the Creed handed down from Nicea and Constantinople I. See Pickstock, "Asyndeton," 333. We shall deal further with questions of language in a later chapter.

[55] Ibid., 331–32.

conclusion, namely that it is useful in throwing the hearers off balance in their inability to control the words of Christ.[56]

Mention of the Institution Narrative leads us to a second aspect of Pickstock's interpretation of medieval liturgy and the theology that accompanies it. Here her interpretation of St. Thomas Aquinas is extraordinarily insightful. She understands the difficulty that arises in a Counter-Reformation understanding of the Eucharist that "fetishizes" the elements—i.e., turns them into objects subject to the gaze of human beings. On the contrary, following Jean-Luc Marion and Henri de Lubac, she insists that Christ's body and blood are present in the passing of time as a gift as opposed to being objects under the gaze of human beings; thus she argues that transubstantiation is a certain kind of presence.[57] To stay with de Lubac for a moment, she also recognizes that the gift of the sacramental Body and Blood of Christ is at the same time the gift of the church to itself—an Augustinian notion that actually begins to fade from the picture in High Scholasticism.[58] Once again to make an extremely ingenious and complex argument short, the key to her interpretation is the idea of desire—desire for the Body and Blood of Christ, which are given and yet (eschatologically) reserved at the same time, so that there is no possibility (short of heaven) of a perfect Eucharist, one that need not be repeated.[59] Technically, she finds the rationale behind her interpretation in a Neoplatonic participationist understanding of the role of the accidents of bread and wine. In other words, St. Thomas cannot be tagged with the label "poor Aristotelian" because he argues something that Aristotle could not: that accidents exist without their own substance but only in virtue of the substance that is the Body and Blood of Christ. Thomas knows his Aristotle, but he uses Augustinian categories to recognize that the accidents after the consecration are miraculous because they can nourish without being substantive. Thus, says Pickstock, "the operation of matter in a *normal* fashion has been rendered miraculous."[60] Since they

---

[56] Pickstock, *After Writing*, 223–28.

[57] Pickstock, "Thomas Aquinas and the Quest for the Eucharist," *Modern Theology* 15 (1999): 159–80, at 164. This essay parallels her treatment of transubstantiation in the last chapter of *After Writing*, 253–66.

[58] Pickstock, "Thomas Aquinas and the Quest for the Eucharist," 178; also 171.

[59] As was the case with her analysis of the Mass, Pickstock follows St. Thomas here in his rather eisegetical treatment of the unfolding of the rite, ibid., 169–71; Thomas Aquinas, *Summa Theologiae* III:79, 81, 83.

[60] Pickstock, "Thomas Aquinas and the Quest for the Eucharist," 174. For the purposes of the present chapter we can leave aside the question of the relation

manifest the pure (and absurd) gift of Christ himself, these material elements become *more* of what they were before. In other words, transubstantiation represents the *telos* of all things. She puts it this way: "Rather, to exceed the contrast between substance and accident is to attain to createdness as pure transparency, as pure mediation of the divine."[61] She goes on to quote St. Thomas to the effect that it is not so much that this food is incorporated into us as that we are incorporated into this food.[62] In the end result, for Pickstock, the Eucharist becomes the ultimately trustworthy sign, one that confounds or "outwits" the conundrum of presence and absence and thereby transcends postmodernist skepticism. Finally, for her, the Eucharist *is* desire and transubstantiation represents the vocation of all reality. This, I believe, is excellent eucharistic theology since it contextualizes the transformation of bread and wine within the ultimate rationale of the Eucharist: the transformation of human beings, indeed of the whole world.

Finally I would like, by way of coming full circle, to discuss Pickstock's understanding of the relation between liturgy, art, and politics. After all, her project is not so much aimed directly at liturgical renewal or sacramental theology as it is an attempt to argue the necessarily doxological element in society. In several other essays she attempts to show how liturgy holds the worlds of art and politics together. She understands liturgy to fuse "the most realistic with the most ideal."[63] Liturgy stands as the foundation of society because "it relativises the everyday without denying its value." It can critique society from within and at the same time refer it to a transcendent dimension. It

---

between the Institution Narrative and consecration. The recent decision by the Vatican allowing for the validity of the ancient eucharistic prayer of Addai and Mari (Anaphora of the Apostles) of the Assyrian Church raises the question whether one can point to a moment of consecration in the way that St. Thomas and the whole Western tradition after the twelfth century presumed. The Anaphora of Addai and Mari contains no institution narrative. In any case, liturgical scholars and sacramental theologians have been questioning the notion of a "moment of consecration" for some time. See Robert Taft, "Mass Without the Consecration? The Historic Agreement on the Eucharist between the Catholic Church and the Assyrian Church of the East Promulgated 26 October 2001," *Worship* 77 (2003): 482–509.

[61] Pickstock, "Thomas Aquinas and the Quest for the Eucharist," 175.

[62] Citing Thomas Aquinas, *Summa Theologiae* III:73. a. 3. ad 2.

[63] Catherine Pickstock, "Liturgy, Art and Politics," *Modern Theology* 16 (2000): 159–80, at 160; eadem, "Liturgy and Modernity," *Telos* 113 (1998): 19–41; eadem, "A Poetics of the Eucharist," *Telos* 131 (2005): 83–91.

enables the person to be himself or herself without ever resting complacently in that identity. It enables art and real life to be held together, which is something the modern cannot do.[64] A person becomes self-realized only by entering into his or her liturgical role, and so becoming a liturgical or doxological person has implications for the individual as well as communal dimension of human being. Finally, liturgy has direct consequences for economics, since the liturgical act is meant to deal with surplus wealth in public festival. No doubt she has the traditional cultural phenomenon of "potlatch" in mind.[65] She also points to a modern pseudo-liturgy that uses spectacle to induce order. One is reminded of Leni Riefenstahl's horrifying portrayal of the Nazi Nuremberg rallies of the 1930s in her film, *Triumph of the Will*.[66]

In my opinion Pickstock's work is of little use to those who want to know how to reform the liturgy. She offers no specific prescriptions, only critique. It is doubtful that we could simply return to a translated form of the medieval Roman Rite, and I do not think she can be read as simply advocating such a return. In fact, Pickstock is far more radical, since her critique goes to the very roots of capitalist economics, and the conservatives for whom she has become a hero might well want to rethink their position, just as they would have to do if they took the economic writings of Pope John Paul II seriously.

At the outset of this chapter I referred to Pickstock's critique of the liturgy as intriguing. It is indeed intriguing as well as difficult. Although one should not accept her analysis of medieval liturgy without caution, she does raise some very important and fundamental philosophical questions about the nature of the post–Vatican II reform as well as its charter in *Sacrosanctum Concilium*.

---

[64] Pickstock, "Liturgy, Art and Politics," 162. This is reminiscent of the categories "dramatic" and "political" that R. Taylor Scott pointed out in "The Likelihood of Liturgy: Reflections Upon Prayer Book Revision and Its Liturgical Implications," *Anglican Theological Review* 62 (1980): 103–20. See also the tripod of Christian existence (sacrament-doctrine-ethics) analyzed by Louis-Marie Chauvet, *Symbol and Sacrament* (n. 26 above).

[65] Pickstock, "Liturgy, Art and Politics," 166. For a similar approach to the relation between ritual and economics at the root of culture and society see Ernest Becker, *Escape from Evil* (New York: Free Press, 1974).

[66] See the excellent essay by James Alison, "Worship in a Violent World," *Studia Liturgica* 34 (2004): 133–46.

1. Do the Constitution and the subsequent reform too easily accept "modern" preconceptions about society?

2. Does the reform of the liturgy rationalize the Mass in a way that evades its "impossibility"?

3. Have the strategies of translation (in the 1970s) adequately captured the genius of the genres to which they were applied?

and perhaps most important:

4. Was there adequate dialogue among liturgical historians, pastoral specialists, and theologians in the construction of the reform?

THE MASS AND MODERNITY: JONATHAN ROBINSON

Another major philosophical critique has been proposed by Jonathan Robinson, an Oratorian with an excellent background in modern philosophy. For Robinson it is not only the liturgy that is problematic but also the way contemporary Catholicism understands the truth of revelation and how it is communicated. The liturgy is a prime example of the crisis of contemporary Catholicism and serves as the focus of his work. The liturgical movement of the twentieth century relied on a number of (unspoken) presuppositions that stem from the Enlightenment, the philosophical reaction of Georg W. F. Hegel, the scientism of Auguste Comte, the romantic movement, and postmodern cynicism.[67] The end result is a liturgy in which the church no longer worships God, but rather itself. Liturgy is replaced by autocelebrations, the community turned in upon itself.[68] Of course, he is far too sophisticated to reject the legitimate gains wrought by the Enlightenment, like human rights and religious liberty,[69] but he does see the dark side in the threefold movement from rejection of revelation (Latitudinarianism) to dismissal of the church and the sacraments (Deism) to ultimate rejection of God altogether (Atheism).[70]

[67] Jonathan Robinson, *The Mass and Modernity: Walking to Heaven Backwards* (San Francisco: Ignatius Press, 2005), 19.

[68] Ibid., 34. Robinson is referring to an article by Bishop Tena Garriga, "La sacra liturgia fonte e culmine della vita ecclesiale," in Rino Fisichella, *Il concilio Vatican II: Recezione e attualità alla luce del Giubileo* (Milan: San Paolo, 2000), 52.

[69] Robinson, *The Mass and Modernity*, 41.

[70] Ibid., 62.

Each of these Enlightenment moves has a(n indirect) result in the reform of the liturgy. For example, with regard to the loss of belief that revelation actually has any content: "This sapping away of belief in revelation has created a climate of opinion in which liturgy as the celebration of the central mysteries of revelation is becoming less and less meaningful to most people."[71] Therefore Robinson rejects what he considers a one-sided reading of the axiom *lex orandi lex credendi* (the law of prayer is the law of belief), insisting that the correct reading of the original form of the axiom: *legem credendi lex statuat supplicandi* should read "Let the rule of prayer *support* the rule of belief" instead of the more frequent translation ". . . *determine* the rule of belief."[72]

The dismissal of sacramental religion by Immanuel Kant in favor of a rational moral system has resulted in the weakening of Catholicism itself: "If we take the sacraments seriously, then we have to take the importance of the visible Church seriously. The Church is more than a society for the promotion of an ethics of duty; she is Christ's Mystical Body here on earth where the mercy of God is found in the sacraments."[73] I do not think that Robinson is so much dismissing the idea that ethics and liturgy have much to do with one another as he is commenting on the not infrequent case of Catholic churches in which ethical engagement seems to have swallowed the sacramental life completely—or where the sacraments are a convenient venue for the presentation of moral values.

The third Enlightenment challenge is Atheism. Here Robinson finds an outcome in the way Catholic funeral liturgy has replaced concern for the fate of the deceased with concern for mourners. I will quote him at some length:

> Even though Hume's dismissal of the Resurrection of Christ and of eternal life have not often been taken up explicitly by Catholics, the atmosphere his work engendered has had a profound influence on Catholic worship, and this can be seen from the way the funeral Mass is often celebrated today.

---

[71] Ibid., 75.

[72] See ibid., 233. To be fair, Robinson will allow a stronger translation of *statuere*, such as "buttress" or "firm up," but he would clearly not adhere to the use of the axiom by a contemporary liturgical theologian like Aidan Kavanagh. See the latter's *On Liturgical Theology* (Collegeville, MN: Liturgical Press, 1992).

[73] Robinson, *The Mass and Modernity*, 94.

What goes on at funerals shows what is really believed about the passage from this life. If the rite of Christian burial does not clearly show that funerals are in the first place intimately connected with the state of the person who has died, then it fails to be Catholic. What I am objecting to is the all too common conviction that funerals are a sort of instant canonization of the dead person in the interests of the community left behind; or, as the stronger version of this goes, "funerals have nothing to do with the dead person." . . . It seems to me obvious in the light of what I have written that wearing white vestments for funerals ought to be the exception, not the norm. Funerals are about, and for, the person who has died.[74]

Besides the threefold challenge represented by the Enlightenment, Robinson also finds that the philosophy of Georg W. F. Hegel has done significant damage to the church and to the liturgy. To make a rather long and complex story short, he argues that Hegel ultimately has the community swallow God or, as the chapter is subtitled: "God becomes the community."[75] Understanding Hegel is somewhat tricky since he uses the traditional vocabulary of Christian theology, but for his own purposes. In the end there is no transcendent object of Christian worship and there is "little room for adoration and contemplation."[76] One can see the same dynamic at work in Francis Mannion's critique of "the intimization of society," where the feelings of the assembly and individuals within it take precedence over the worship of a transcendent God.

Robinson discerns a third source of the destruction of modern Catholic liturgy in the program of Auguste Comte, the idiosyncratic nineteenth-century French inventor of sociology. For Robinson, Comte's empiricism and confidence in the rule of experts is mirrored in the triumph of the liturgical experts in the post–Vatican II reform.[77] This seems to me something of a stretch, but the disparagement of liturgical experts is certainly a theme that will recur.

[74] Ibid., 110, 115.

[75] Ibid., 116.

[76] Ibid., 142. As with Pickstock on Scotus, I must acknowledge that I am far from being an expert on Hegel's philosophy. There are clearly many approaches to his usefulness for Christian theology; see, e.g., Charles Taylor, *Hegel* (Cambridge: Cambridge University Press, 1975).

[77] Robinson, *The Mass and Modernity*, 159–63.

A final philosophical blow to Catholic liturgy (for Robinson) can be found in postmodernism's (cynical) objection to metanarratives, all encompassing grand schemes like religious belief systems: "everything is in flux, and this includes the person who experiences a world in which there are no stable centers or fixed meanings."[78] The result of accepting postmodernism, at least in its more radical guise, is clearly the evacuation of the Creed and of Christian liturgy of all meaning.[79] Robinson summarizes this way:

> Religion has also been taught to deliver the same ambiguous and hidden message [of the indeterminacy of meaning]. Only the very naïve, we are assured, would imagine that statements in the Creed, for example, have anything to do with stating the way things are. What religious language shows us is a complicated structure of hidden meanings that are not open to ordinary believers. The hidden meanings are not, however, buried in total obscurity, because they are open to the inspection of experts who are trained to describe what lies behind the worship and religious language in general.[80]

To the extent that this is an accurate description of the current state of affairs it represents a devastating critique of the theological enterprise in general and the work of liturgical scholars in particular. I think it is fair to say that theologians and liturgists of all stripes do sometimes sound like experts who employ esoteric knowledge and methods to impose their will on others. This is why they never have the last word—the church's authority does.

Before we can begin to answer the questions raised by Robinson and Pickstock we need to consider other angles from which the contemporary Roman Rite has been criticized. Since liturgical history was such an important factor in understanding the need for reform, and since liturgical historians were so influential in its implementation, it is to their critique that we now turn.

---

[78] Ibid., 171 (see also 175, 234). There seems to be no end to the various meanings and analyses of postmodernism/postmodernity. Two good places to begin are: Paul Lakeland, *Postmodernity* (Minneapolis: Fortress Press, 1997); Paul Borgmann, *Crossing the Postmodern Divide* (Chicago: University of Chicago Press, 1993).

[79] For an argument in favor of "meeting" rather than "meaning," see Nathan Mitchell's recent *Meeting Mystery: Liturgy, Worship, Sacraments* (Maryknoll, NY: Orbis, 2007).

[80] Robinson, *The Mass and Modernity*, 208.

Chapter Two

The Historical Basis of the Reform

Religious faith and practice are by nature traditional. Even as they might adapt to new times and situations, they appeal to history for their warrant. And so in any contest over the nature of liturgical reform it is inevitable that history—and especially understanding what continuity in history might mean—will have a major place. This chapter will deal with some important criticisms of the contemporary liturgical reform that have been made by several significant historians.

KLAUS GAMBER

One of the most vocal critics of the post–Vatican II liturgical reform was the Regensburg scholar, Monsignor Klaus Gamber (1919–1989). Gamber cofounded and served as director of the Institute of Liturgical Science, where he published a number of distinguished series including *Studia Patristica et Liturgica* and *Textus Patristici et Liturgici*. He compiled the extraordinarily useful *Codices Liturgici Latini Antiquiores*, a description of the important medieval Latin liturgical manuscripts.[1] Gamber also authored a number of monographs on topics such as early church architecture and the early theology of the Mass as sacrifice.[2] In

---

[1] Klaus Gamber, *Codices Liturgici Latini Antiquiores*. Spicilegii Fribourgensis Subsidia 1. (2nd ed. Fribourg: Universitätsverlag, 1968; supplement 1988). A full list of Gamber's publications can be found in idem, *Fragen in der Zeit: Kirche und Liturgie nach dem Vatikanum II* (Regensburg: Pustet, 1989), 204–32. It includes 361 items.

[2] See, e.g., Klaus Gamber, *Domus Ecclesiae: Die ältesten Kirchenbauten Aquilejas sowie in Alpen- et Donaugebiet bis zum Beginn des 5. Jh. liturgiegeschichtlich untersucht.* Studia Patristica et Liturgica 2 (Regensburg: Pustet, 1968); *Liturgie und Kirchenbau: Studien zur Geschichte der Meßfeier und des Gotteshauses in der Frühzeit.* Studia Patristica et Liturgica 6 (Regensburg: Pustet, 1976); *Sacramentorum: Weitere Aufsätze zur Geschichte der Meßritus und der frühen Liturgie.* Studia Patristica et Liturgica 13 (Regensburg: Pustet, 1984).

addition, his works include a valuable edition and commentary on the Gallican eucharistic liturgy.[3] Our main concern here will be with his sharp criticism of the reform of the Roman Rite.

A number of subjects interested Gamber and inspired him to write on the liturgical reform. The first we shall deal with here is the question of whether the *Missal of Paul VI* (and the other rites of the reform) represent a development of the Roman Rite or rather a *new* rite. Second, we shall deal with questions related to the *Ordo Missae*, the use of the vernacular, concelebration, the theology of eucharistic sacrifice, and the priesthood. In a separate chapter we shall review the issue Gamber found even more important than the reform of the liturgical books: the position of the priest at the altar.

A New Rite?

Gamber began his attack on the liturgical reform almost as soon as the *Missal of Paul VI* was published. His *The Modern Rite: Collected Essays on the Reform of the Liturgy*[4] appeared in 1972, only three years after the *Missal* itself. His last publication before his death in 1989 was a larger collection of material about the reform of the liturgy that incorporated some of the earlier essays from *The Modern Rite.*[5] The book that caused the biggest stir, however, was *The Reform of the Roman Liturgy: Its Problems and Background.*[6] One reason for its notoriety was the laudatory introduction to the French edition by Cardinal Joseph Ratzinger, Prefect of the Vatican Congregation of the Doctrine of the Faith—and now, of course, Pope Benedict XVI. Ratzinger is cited in a preface to the English edition as describing Gamber as "the one

---

[3] Klaus Gamber, *Ordo Antiquus Gallicanus: Der gallikanische Meßritus des 6, Jh.* Textus Patristici et Liturgici 3 (Regensburg: Pustet, 1965); idem, *Die Meßfeier nach altgallikanischem Ritus anhand der erhaltenen Dokumente dargestellt.* Studia Patristica et Liturgica 14 (Regensburg: Pustet, 1984); idem, *Der altgallikanische Meßritus als Abbild himmlischer Liturgie.* Beiheft zu den Studia Patristica et Liturgica (Regensburg: Pustet, 1984).

[4] Klaus Gamber, *Ritus Modernus: Gesammelte Aufsätze zur Liturgiereform.* Studia Patristica et Liturgica 4 (Regensburg: Pustet, 1972), trans. Henry Taylor, *The Modern Rite: Collected Essays on the Reform of the Liturgy* (Farnborough: St. Michael's Abbey Press, 2002). Some of the articles collected there were published as early as 1969.

[5] Klaus Gamber, *Fragen in der Zeit: Kirche und Liturgie nach dem Vatikanum II* (Regensburg: Pustet, 1989).

[6] Klaus Gamber, *The Reform of the Roman Liturgy: Its Problems and Background*, trans. Klaus D. Grimm (Harrison, NY: Foundation for Catholic Reform, 1993).

scholar who, among the army of pseudo-liturgists, truly represents the thinking of the center of the Church."[7]

From the very start Gamber claimed that the post–Vatican II reform of the liturgy was not so much a reform of the Roman Rite as it was a completely new creation done by "experts" and having little to do with the pastoral and spiritual needs of the people.[8] As we shall see, he was far from alone in finding himself appalled by the liturgical abuses that followed the council. He refers to the situation of the early 1970s as "complete liturgical anarchy."[9] He also heaps scorn on those who would make the liturgy relevant. For example:

> It is certainly foolish to think that, by goading the participants into activity and by constantly dragging into worship the forms current in the world, one can make these services more attractive, especially amongst younger people, in the way that people are attempting in many places, especially by rock-Masses. . . . Young people who like rock music don't look for it in church, but in pubs and clubs. The fact is that it is much "better" there. In the long term, young people come to church only on account of religious beliefs.[10]

On the one hand, Gamber is certainly correct in stating that merely pandering to people's tastes does not make for good liturgy. On the other hand, his approach begs the question of which cultural forms *are* appropriate for worship. Do not religious beliefs need to be expressed in media that can be appreciated by people of a certain place and time, even if this surely does not exclude the treasures of the past? To be fair, he admits that cultural forms have changed in the course of liturgical history. He cites, for example, the use of full orchestras at Baroque Masses. This still leaves us with the question of precisely how cultural forms change and the appropriate response of the church's liturgy to those changes.

Gamber's criticism of the liturgical reform goes deeper than his dissatisfaction with liturgical abuses, faddishness, or bad taste. For him liturgy develops organically and the post–Vatican II rite is anything but organic. It is "manufactured." He actually begins here not

---

[7] Ibid., xiii. The preface is by Msgr. Wilhelm Nyssen.

[8] See, e.g., Gamber, *Fragen in der Zeit*, 71.

[9] Gamber, *Modern Rite*, 7.

[10] Ibid., 74.

with the post–Vatican II reform but with the reform of the rites of Holy Week under Pope Pius XII in the early 1950s:

> The only standard of judgement is the personal opinion of a group of "Liturgy manufacturers," who create news forms on the basis of their own, often narrow, view of things. One has the impression that they don't take the trouble to study the history of worship in any detail, so as to discover why the previous forms of the cult developed as they did.[11]

Gamber finds the liturgy of the 1951/52 Paschal Vigil lacking in comparison with the Byzantine Rite's exuberantly joyful and endlessly repeated *troparion*: "Christ is Risen from the dead, trampling down death by death, and on those in the tombs bestowing life" at their Paschal Matins. He also questions the pride of place that baptism has taken in the post–Vatican II Easter Vigil rite, noting that it might be useful in mission countries.[12] Anyone who has seen the *Rite of Christian Initiation of Adults* in practice would be loath to call the renewed Easter Vigil "a matter of artificially resurrecting an Early Christian custom," or to use it as an example of creating "a new rite from the foundations up."[13] Admittedly, despite the common opinion that the Vigil was always the home of adult Christian initiation, baptism did have a significant effect on how the Vigil was celebrated, and today it has become an important part of the celebration of the Vigil.

Gamber finds another opportunity to question the new "manufactured liturgy" in a caustic review of Archbishop Annibale Bugnini's *The Reform of the Liturgy*, a long memoir of the postconciliar reform.[14] He infers that Bugnini and the other postconciliar reformers must have been working secretly and with knowledge of other curial

---

[11] Ibid., 79–80.

[12] For a historical criticism of the often facile argument about Easter baptism see Paul Bradshaw, "*Diem baptismo sollemniorem*: Initiation and Easter in Christian Antiquity," in Maxwell Johnson, ed., *Living Water, Sealing Spirit: Essays on Christian Initiation* (Collegeville, MN: Liturgical Press, 1995), 137–47; idem, *The Search for the Origins of Christian Worship* (2nd ed. Oxford: Oxford University Press, 2002), 223.

[13] Gamber, *Modern Rite*, 82.

[14] Annibale Bugnini, *The Reform of the Liturgy 1948–1975* (Collegeville, MN: Liturgical Press, 1990). Bugnini himself seems to be the object of much "conspiracy theory" around the reform: see Didier Bonneterre, *The Liturgical Movement from Dom Gueranger to Annibale Bugnini: or The Trojan Horse in the City of God* (Kansas City: Angelus Press, 2002; original 1980).

officials. The reason he gives is that Cardinal Amleto Cicognani, the Vatican Secretary of State, wrote a laudatory preface to the German "Schott Meßbuch (Missal)" in 1969 (shortly before the appearance of the *Missal of Paul VI*), saying that it represented the fulfillment of Vatican II's liturgical reform. This missal had the text of the Mass as it had been altered just after the council in 1965/1967.[15] Of course, Cicognani's preface might just as well have been an attempt at an end run. Gamber does not seem to reckon with the fact that Cicognani and others in the Roman Curia (famously Cardinal Alfredo Ottaviani of the Holy Office) were opposed to Paul VI's reforms. Moreover, Bugnini amply documents the fact that Paul VI himself was intimately involved in the details of the reform, including the decision to add three new eucharistic prayers instead of the proposed rewriting of the Roman Canon.[16]

In his book *The Reform of the Roman Liturgy* Gamber repeats many of the criticisms he had launched in *The Modern Rite*. Like many of the reform's critics, he appeals to a very close reading of *Sacrosanctum Concilium*, the council's Constitution on the Liturgy, especially when it says "there must be no innovations unless the good of the Church genuinely and certainly requires them."[17] We shall see that he wavers in his defense of the Liturgy Constitution. But his judgment of the reforms that were subsequently carried out is that they were clearly a failure because they were too radical for some and too tame for others.[18] One could also interpret this dissatisfaction as a sign of the reform's success. The fact that the reform was unsatisfactory to both extremes in the church is not necessarily a strike against it, since we will always have to reckon with progressive and conservative elements in the church claiming that they hold the true center and thus are authentically in continuity with tradition.

At times it is hard to find a consistent Gamber. On the one hand, he disparaged the Constitution on the Sacred Liturgy, with its call for active participation, and found that even the scholarly work of Jungmann (his "tentative conclusions") was an insufficient basis for

---

[15] Gamber, *Fragen in der Zeit*, 70; see also *Reform of the Roman Liturgy*, 33–34.

[16] See Piero Marini, *A Challenging Reform: Realizing the Vision of the Liturgical Renewal*, Mark Francis, John Page, and Keith Pecklers, eds. (Collegeville, MN: Liturgical Press, 2007), 140–41.

[17] Constitution on the Sacred Liturgy, §23.

[18] Gamber, *Reform of the Roman Liturgy*, 3; see n. 9.

carrying out a reform of the Mass.[19] At the same time he claimed that Bugnini and the other architects of the reform deliberately moved away from the council's intent.[20] So not only was the reform itself flawed but also the principles in the Liturgy Constitution that were its basis. One of his greatest problems with the reform itself was its movement in the direction of Protestantism instead of the Oriental Rites.[21] It is true that many of the issues of the sixteenth-century Reformation were addressed in the post–Vatican II liturgical reforms, e.g., the cup for the laity, the use of Scripture, and the vernacular. There are profound theological questions operative here and we shall return to them in the conclusion, but suffice it to say that accommodation to some of the Protestant concerns with worship in the sixteenth century is not necessarily a mistake. One can at least argue that reforms like the giving of the cup and the use of the vernacular might have been implemented by the Roman Church in the sixteenth century, were it not for the polemical atmosphere that surrounded the Council of Trent.

Gamber finds six root causes (most of them the result of history) for what he calls "the debacle of modern liturgy."[22]

1. The Frankish co-optation of what had been the rite of the city of Rome; i.e., the adoption and eventual transformation of the rite of the city of Rome in eighth- and ninth-century Gaul. This assimilation, he claims, never quite "took."

2. The medieval alienation of the West from Eastern Christianity, thus losing the East's cosmic and dramatic dimensions of worship.

3. The introduction and triumph of individualist piety in the Gothic period—the thirteenth century onward.

4. The success of vernacular music—especially with Luther and the German reformation.

5. The paralysis of the Roman Rite with the Missal of Pius V, which made normal organic development impossible.

6. Most of all, the age of the Enlightenment with its rationalistic reaction to Baroque imbalance and enthusiasm.

[19] Ibid., 5; see also Gamber, *Modern Rite*, 51–57.
[20] E.g., Gamber, *Reform of the Roman Liturgy*, 38–39, 61.
[21] Ibid., 9.
[22] See ibid., 11–20.

One way to explain Gamber's attitude to modern liturgical reform is to say that he considered the entire development of Western culture a disaster. This lament seems to be common to many of the liturgical reform's critics—for example Gamber's compatriot, Joseph Ratzinger. One must ask of these and other critics whether it is so much the post–Vatican II liturgical renewal that disturbs them, or rather the development of Western culture in general. Allowing the liturgy to find its place in *both* forming culture (and criticizing contemporary culture when it is wrongheaded and sinful) and being appropriately formed by culture is indeed one of the most significant challenges facing the church in any age. Neither a wholesale rejection nor an uncritical acceptance of contemporary culture is helpful in this endeavor.

For Gamber the result of the Catholic Church's accommodation to contemporary culture, what was popularly called *aggiornamento* at the time of the council, was a new liturgy, disconnected from the past. Thus he challenges the position of the German liturgical scholar Heinrich Rennings, who claimed that the *Missal of Paul VI* was in basic continuity with the Roman Rite throughout the centuries.[23] Gamber neglects to add that this is very strongly asserted by the *General Instruction of the Roman Missal* itself, a claim made necessary precisely because of the criticisms of Gamber and those who agree with him.[24]

One should note that Gamber perceives a certain sleight of hand in the common use of the term "Tridentine Mass" to refer to the *Missal of Pius V*. Although the calendar was reorganized and the *Missal of the Roman Curia* made standard for the entire Roman Church (except for those local churches, like Toledo with its Mozarabic Rite that could claim usages over two hundred years old), Pius V did not really introduce a new Mass at all. With the fifteenth-century introduction of printing, Trent was able to codify the medieval Mass in a way that would have hitherto been impossible. Gamber criticizes Rennings for confusing the elimination and addition of proper prayers for the Mass (i.e., on a given feast day) in the *Missal of Pius V* with the transforma-

[23] Gamber, *Reform of the Roman Liturgy*, 23. Unfortunately Gamber does not cite the review in which Rennings' article appeared.

[24] The first edition of the *General Instruction* did not contain the current "preamble" of fifteen paragraphs. The preamble was quickly added after sharp criticism that the instruction did not witness to the sacrificial nature of the Mass. It was not until the 2002 edition of the *General Instruction* that the paragraphs were renumbered so that the first chapter now begins with paragraph 16.

tion of the "Ordinary" (invariable text) of the Mass itself. So Gamber refuses to call the *Missal of Paul VI* the Roman Rite, but rather insists on calling it the "Modern Rite," no doubt a term meant in derision. His point is that the *Missal of Pius V* represents continuity with the "organic" development of the Roman Rite whereas the *Missal of Paul VI* represents a radical and unwarranted departure from that tradition.

He goes further than this and questions whether popes have the authority to change the rites at all. His basic principle is stated thus: "Since the liturgical rite has developed over time, further development continues to be possible. But such continuing development has to respect the timeless character of all rites; and its development has to be organic in nature."[25]

This last statement has become something of a slogan for the critics of the liturgical reform—as we shall see in great detail when we deal with the work of Alcuin Reid. The reform was faulty because it was radical and therefore nonorganic. One certainly cannot deny the radical nature of a reform that swept away the use of a common language and simplified the liturgy to the extent that the *Missal of Paul VI* did. But to assess whether or not the reform had solid roots in the liturgical tradition of the Western church is an issue with which the rest of this chapter will wrestle. Gamber tends to take an "all or nothing—take no prisoners" approach, as is evident in this statement of principle: "Every liturgical rite constitutes an organically developed, homogeneous unit. To change any of its essential elements is synonymous with the destruction of the rite in its entirety."[26]

This statement seems to ignore the fact that all Christian rites borrowed from Jewish liturgical forms (and vocabulary like "Amen," "Hosanna," "Alleluia") and that the Roman Rite itself borrowed elements from the Christian East such as the *Kyrie eleison* and *Agnus Dei* chants. The history of the liturgy has always been constituted by cross-fertilization. Therefore to argue that there is such a thing as a pristine rite is problematic.

In addition, there is a kind of "idolatry" in Gamber's approach to the nature of a rite. Now and again we need to ask ourselves the question: what needs to take priority for the church today—worshiping the liturgical rite or the God whom the liturgy addresses? At times

[25] Gamber, *Reform of the Roman Liturgy*, 29.
[26] Ibid., 30–31.

it seems that some of the critics are more interested in the former than the latter. Of course, one cannot even ask this question if one takes a completely uncritical attitude toward the development of the Roman Rite.

We shall have to leave the question of the particular reforms of the eucharistic liturgy to the next section, but note that we also have before us a question of what would constitute a change in an *essential* element of the rite. On the basis of his reading of church history Gamber concludes that no pope before Paul VI ever attempted as sweeping a reform and that therefore he had no authority to do so.[27] While it is certainly clear that there are limitations to papal authority (the pope may not contradict Scripture or commonly held Catholic doctrine), it is not at all clear that he may not make even radical changes to the church's worship. Of course it is fair enough to ask questions about the speed of the reform or the nature of its implementation and thus to question this or that pope's judgment. Ironically enough, Gamber's position leads him to claim that "it is not the function of the Holy See to introduce Church reforms."[28] In any case, he is certain that the council's understanding of the reform of the liturgy had been misconstrued (to put the best interpretation on it) by the postconciliar reformers.

Gamber's solution to the disastrous state of liturgy as he saw it was to propose that two forms of the liturgy be allowed to coexist side by side.[29] The Roman Rite, with certain changes like the translation of the Scripture readings into the vernacular, would remain basically intact. On the other hand, the "Modern Rite," or what is sometimes called the *Novus Ordo*, would be allowed to remain, but with the proviso that the position of the priest at the altar should be returned to the traditional eastward-facing posture.[30] He seems to have been confident that, given parity between the two, the traditional rite would eventually win out.

---

[27] We shall see a variation of this argument in the work of Alcuin Reid.

[28] Gamber, *Reform of the Roman Liturgy*, 38.

[29] This is the situation we find ourselves in today with Pope Benedict XVI's insistence that an ordinary (*Missal of Paul VI*) and extraordinary (1962 *Missal of John XXIII*) form of the Roman Rite exist side by side.

[30] Gamber, *Reform of the Roman Liturgy*, 91–95.

The Revised Order of Mass and Other Questions

As we saw above, Gamber was convinced that the changes introduced in the 1969 *Missal of Paul VI* were so radical as to constitute an entirely new rite, and one that was inimical to Roman Catholicism at that. We shall turn, then, to the specifics of his critique of the reform of the Mass as well as several other important issues including concelebration, the priesthood, the theology of eucharistic sacrifice (three obviously interrelated issues), and the use of the vernacular.

We have already noted that one of the main targets of Gamber's critique of the post–Vatican II reform of the liturgy is its accommodation to Protestantism. For Gamber, Martin Luther was the first radical liturgical reformer[31]—but a clever one since he did not go out of his way to offend popular piety. For example, Luther "purposely did not dispense with the elevation of the Host and Chalice, at least not initially, because the people would have noticed that change."[32] This is indeed a very poor reading of Luther's intentions, as the citation in Gamber's own footnote demonstrates. Luther retained the elevation of the host (he was actually an innovator with regard to elevating the chalice) not because he wanted to pull the wool over the people's eyes, but because according to his theological understanding the Institution Narrative communicated the Gospel message of the forgiveness of sins—as opposed to the works-righteousness that he found rife in the Roman Canon. For the same reason he argued that the Institution Narrative should be sung in the *gospel tone*—since it was a privileged proclamation of the Gospel itself.

For Gamber the reform of the Mass brought about after Vatican II was even more radical than that of Luther and the other sixteenth-century reformers. He finds fault with the freedom given to the presider[33] (celebrant) of the liturgy: "The many 'may' instructions provided for in the Introductory Rite, a feature particular to the Missal's German-language edition, literally invite the celebrating priest

---

[31] Ibid., 41–42. Technically he is incorrect. Much of what Luther did as a liturgical reformer was in response to Andreas Carlstadt and others he considered "fanatics" who had a very iconoclastic approach to Christian worship. See Frank Senn, *Christian Liturgy: Catholic and Evangelical* (Minneapolis: Fortress Press, 1997).

[32] Gamber, *Reform of the Roman Liturgy*, 42.

[33] I have adopted the usage "presider," which is common among many North American Roman Catholics. It should be noted that the official books use the term "celebrant," and that there is controversy over this terminology.

to come up with his own fanciful ideas of what to do. What twaddle the faithful must listen to in so many of our churches at the beginning of Mass!"[34] He further objects to giving the option of either the Nicene or the Apostles' Creed on Sundays and other solemnities.[35] The placement of a communal penitential rite at the beginning of Mass is another innovation unwarranted by the traditional Roman Rite, in which such prayers were privately recited by the priest and ministers as a means of preparation for worthy celebration. If there were to be a common penitential rite, he would prefer to see it placed with the intercessions after the homily.[36]

Gamber does not reject every aspect of the reform. For example, he considers it a good idea to use the vernacular for the Liturgy of the Word and applauds the addition of readings from the Old Testament. He also welcomes the restoration of the general intercessions. On the other hand, he has grave reservations about the rearrangement of the lectionary, which he views as a preference for modern exegesis over the traditional liturgical hermeneutic of Scripture in the Roman Rite. The result is an emphasis on edification (Protestant) rather than epiphany (Catholic).[37] This objection is raised by a number of critics and we shall return to it when dealing with the liturgical chants in a later chapter. The single cycle of Sunday readings accompanied by musical elements in the proper of the Mass did have a venerable antiquity in the Roman Rite, mainly from the early Middle Ages. For Gamber and others this arrangement of readings substantially constitutes what we call the Roman Rite. Gamber also objects to the *ad lib* nature of the general intercessions and the fact that the priest directs them from the chair rather than from the altar, a "novelty which stands completely in isolation against liturgical tradition."[38] Gamber

---

[34] Gamber, *Reform of the Roman Liturgy*, 49. The German translations are not alone in the liberty they give to presiders.

[35] Ibid., 59. That option has been retained in the third edition of the *Missal of Paul VI*.

[36] This is in fact the practice of Rite II in the American Episcopal *Book of Common Prayer 1979*. Others have also found fault with placing a communal penitential rite at the beginning of the celebration: see John F. Baldovin, "Kyrie Eleison and the Entrance Rite of the Roman Eucharist," *Worship* 60 (1986): 334–47.

[37] Gamber, *Reform of the Roman Liturgy*, 69–75. On the difference between Catholic and Protestant approaches to the lectionary see Fritz West, *Scripture and Memory: The Ecumenical Hermeneutic of the Three-Year Lectionary* (Collegeville, MN: Liturgical Press, 1997).

[38] Gamber, *Reform of the Roman Liturgy*, 53.

seems to be referring to the Solemn Prayers of the Good Friday celebration of the Lord's Passion. On the other hand, we have no idea of
the physical disposition of the presider and other ministers at this
point in the liturgy before the disappearance of intercessory prayers at
this point in the Mass in the sixth century.[39]

Gamber agrees with the elimination of the offertory formulas that
had been added to the Roman Rite Mass in the course of the Middle
Ages, but objects to the German translation of the Latin "Blessed are
You, Lord God of all creation" formulas that have been put in their
place, since they use the German translation "bringen" (to bring) for
the Latin *offerimus*. There is, to be sure, a good deal of ambiguity in the
rite of "Preparation of the Altar and Gifts," as it is now called. While
the rite itself is no longer called an "offertory," the term "offertory
chant" (*offertorium*) is used in the rubrics. Many contemporary liturgical theologians argue that any notion of offering or sacrifice prior to
the eucharistic prayer is misplaced and even hints at a Pelagian notion
that we have something to offer apart from Christ's self-offering,
which we receive in the eucharistic prayer itself. There is some irony
in the desire to retain formulas that use offertory terminology, since so
many of the critics object to the Pelagianizing tendencies of the ICEL
translations.[40]

Gamber has the most difficulty with the eucharistic prayer itself.
His criticisms can be summarized in four points:[41]

1. The traditional Roman Rite had variable prefaces combined with
a stable Canon (= Eucharistic Prayer I). There is no warrant for
the addition of prayers based on models from other traditions:
Gallican (EP III) and Antiochene (EP II and IV).

2. A corollary: Insisting on the combination of preface with the
remainder of the eucharistic prayer, as in EP IV (as well as the
prayers for use with children and the prayers for reconciliation)
is contrary to the Roman tradition. This feature is found only in
Eastern Christian eucharistic prayers.

3. The traditional Institution Narrative in the Roman Canon included
the words "mystery of faith" (*mysterium fidei*) in the formula over

---

[39] The last notice we have of the ordinary use of the general intercessions is
during the pontificate of Gelasius I (492–496); see Jungmann, *Missarum Sollemnia*
1:58, 336.

[40] This topic will be treated in the chapter on liturgical language.

[41] Gamber, *Reform of the Roman Liturgy*, 54–56.

the cup. In the Mass of Paul VI this formula has been turned into an invitation to the assembly's acclamation. Gamber also objects to the change of address in the prayer at this point from God the Father to Christ, e.g., "Dying, you destroyed our death. . . ."[42]

4. Finally—most significant and repeated by many of the critics—there is the translation of the words *pro multis* in several modern languages (English, German, Italian) by "for all" instead of "for many." The translation "for all" was prompted by modern Scripture scholarship, which understood the Semitic usage behind the Greek of the New Testament inclusively rather than exclusively. The Greek πολλῶν then would mean "many" not in the sense of "some" but rather in the sense of "the vast majority or all." Gamber refers to John Chrysostom's exegesis of Hebrews 9:28, in which the great bishop argued that Christ's death is applied to many but not all, since all do not have faith. To be fair to Gamber (and others who make this or a similar argument), he does not want to deny God's desire to save all in Christ, but rather to safeguard an element he considers to be integral to the Roman Rite.[43]

This last issue is worthy of further reflection since it raises a significant hermeneutical question—and one that will have many consequences. To what extent should contemporary scriptural exegesis as well as accepted methods of historical criticism govern and even correct elements of the tradition? To illustrate, let us take an example from classic Christian anthropology. Much of the theology with regard to original sin rested on a translation of a phrase in Romans 5:12: "Therefore, just as sin came into the world through one man, and death came through sin, and so death spread to all because *all have sinned*" (NRSV). Here Paul is contrasting the work of Christ with that of Adam. The Vulgate translated the ἐφ᾽ ᾧ (because all have sinned) incorrectly by "in whom (Adam) all have sinned." St. Augustine, and with him the rest of the Western Christian tradition, was strongly

---

[42] The acclamation "Christ has died, Christ is Risen . . ." is not in the Latin (typical) edition of the Missal but was an addition in the ICEL translation of 1973. The United States Conference of Catholic Bishops has petitioned for its retention in the forthcoming translation of the Mass.

[43] The Congregation for Divine Worship and the Discipline of the Sacraments issued a clarification of this issue in favor of "for many" on 17 October, 2006: http://www.usccb.org/liturgy/innews/November2006.pdf.

influenced by this (mis)translation, which has led us today to reinterpret what we mean by the transmission of original sin. Similarly, one can argue that *multis* is a mistranslation of *pollon* and therefore needs to be corrected.

Gamber's critique of the Mass of Paul VI does not end with the eucharistic prayer. The traditional Roman Rite reserved the recitation of the Lord's Prayer to the priest alone, as a kind of summary of the eucharistic prayer. For him, having the assembly recite or chant this prayer is a major and unwarranted change to the tradition. He also suggests that the addition of the doxology ("for the kingdom, the power . . .") to the embolism after the Lord's Prayer is an unwarranted concession to Protestant usage. One might well ask: "Is an ecumenically conciliatory gesture necessarily a bad thing?" With regard to this issue, as with so many questions raised by the critics, one's answer will depend on the weight one gives to maintaining the tradition of the Roman Rite versus the need to adapt the liturgy to contemporary circumstances. By the same token he objects to the elimination of the traditional "The Lord be with you" before the three presidential[44] prayers of the Mass. This raises another important issue. Following paragraphs 34 and 50 of *Sacrosanctum Concilium*,[45] the reformed Mass eliminated a number of historical inconsistencies, e.g., the repetition of a greeting that had already been made. There is, to be sure, a certain rationalization and streamlining at work here.[46] There is also the recognition that there are three main transition (or action) points in the eucharistic rite: the entrance procession, the procession of the gifts, and the procession for holy communion. Robert Taft has shown that,

[44] Opening Prayer, Prayer over the Gifts, and Prayer after Communion.

[45] SC 34: "The rites should be distinguished by a noble simplicity; they should be short, clear, and unencumbered by useless repetitions; they should be within the people's powers of comprehension, and normally should not require much explanation." SC 50: "The rite of the Mass is to be revised in such a way that the intrinsic nature and purpose of its several parts, as also the connection between them, may be more clearly manifested, and that devout and active participation by the faithful may be more easily achieved. For this purpose the rites are to be simplified, due care being taken to preserve their substance; elements which, with the passage of time, came to be duplicated, or were added with but little advantage, are now to be discarded; other elements which have suffered injury through accidents of history are now to be restored to the vigor which they had in the days of the holy Fathers, as may seem useful or necessary."

[46] See the similar objection made by Catherine Pickstock, chapter 1 above.

just as for the Roman Mass, so also for the Byzantine Liturgy of St. John Chrysostom the same basic structure can be discerned: a procession, covered by a chant and concluded by a prayer.[47] There is a tendency, discernible in the historical evolution of these rites, to add elements to this basic structure: e.g., the prayers at the foot of the altar in the *Missal of Pius V*. The post–Vatican II reform has arguably uncovered the original shape of the rite.

One final example of Gamber's quarrel with the structure of the reformed Mass is the placement of the final blessing. The *Missal of Pius V* has the final blessing come after the dismissal. This historical anomaly is the result of the displacement of the blessing from its original place before holy communion. A blessing before communion had been given in the Gallican liturgies so that those who were not communicating could take something away with them. Eventually this blessing "migrated" to the end of the liturgy—presumably in an effort to get non-communicants to stay through the whole Mass. It was eminently sensible for the reformers to redress this anomaly by shifting the dismissal after the blessing. Gamber's objection shows the depth of his disagreement with the reform.

Eucharistic Sacrifice

Gamber raises some important objections to the sacramental theology that undergirds the post–Vatican II reform. As in the matters already discussed, he is representative of other critics. The major problem is that the reform of the Mass replaced the notion of eucharistic sacrifice with that of the celebrative meal, especially in the first edition of the *General Instruction of the Roman Missal*.[48] Although the second edition, with its new preamble asserting the continuity of the *Missal of Paul VI* with that of Pius V, was a move in the right direction, some terminological problems remain. For example, the eucharistic prayer is now called *Prex Eucharistica*,[49] but the previous title, *Prex Oblationis*, brought out the sacrificial dimension more clearly. Gamber realizes, of course,

---

[47] Robert Taft, "The Structural Analysis of Liturgical Units: An Essay in Methodology," in idem, *Beyond East and West: Problems in Liturgical Understanding* (2nd rev. ed. Rome: Pontifical Oriental Institute Press, 2001), 201–202. See also Josef Jungmann, *Missarum Sollemnia: The Mass of the Roman Rite* (New York: Benziger, 1951) 1:261–71.

[48] See n. 24 above.

[49] See Gamber, *Modern Rite*, 15–24, where he also rehearses the history of sacrificial terminology with regard to the Eucharist.

that we are not dealing with a question of either sacrifice or meal. But for him the understanding of the Eucharist has shifted unhealthily in favor of the meal dimension. The issue of eucharistic sacrifice is one of the most delicate in sacramental/liturgical theology. Today, it seems to me, one must take into account the questions that have been raised with regard to an unnuanced theology of sacrifice, either with regard to the Cross or to the Eucharist.[50]

A related issue is the identity and function of the ordained minister/priest, especially with regard to the practice of concelebration. Gamber laments the contemporary change in the image of the priest from "father of believers" to that of "pastoral social-worker," or "psychotherapist" rather than "pastor of souls," or "manager of the sacred" as opposed to "liturgist."[51] He disagrees with the decision to allow many priests to receive a stipend for the celebration of one concelebrated Mass, since there is only one offering of the Eucharist at any particular celebration. I would have to agree that the decision to allow a number of priests to accept stipends for a single celebration has never gotten a convincing rationale from the magisterium.[52] In any case, Gamber opposes large concelebrations and argues that the number of concelebrants should not exceed that of the Apostles at the Last Supper. Under no condition, on the other hand, should a priest assist at the Eucharist after the manner of a layperson.[53] In considering the theology of the ministerial priesthood in conjunction with the liturgical reform, Gamber has put his finger on an extremely important and neuralgic subject. As we shall see in the last chapter, a good deal of one's attitude toward the reform of the liturgy is shaped by one's theology of the priesthood—and vice versa.

THE QUESTION OF ORGANIC DEVELOPMENT: ALCUIN REID

No treatment of the critique of the reform from the side of historians would be complete without dealing with the question of whether the

---

[50] The literature on this subject is vast and growing. See, e.g., Robert Daly, "Sacrifice Unveiled or Sacrifice Revisited: Trinitarian and Liturgical Perspectives," *TS* 64 (2003): 24–42; S. Mark Heim, *Saved from Sacrifice: A Theology of the Cross* (Grand Rapids: Eerdmans, 2006).

[51] Gamber, *Fragen in der Zeit*, 163–67.

[52] See, e.g., John Baldovin, "Concelebration: A Problem of Symbolic Roles in the Church," *Worship* 59 (1985): 32–47.

[53] Gamber, *Fragen in der Zeit*, 138–43. Priests might, however, receive communion instead of concelebrating, especially at meetings and retreats.

post–Vatican II liturgy represents an organic development from the previous Roman Rite or a radical and uncalled-for departure. Alcuin Reid has been in the forefront of this discussion. His recent *The Organic Development of the Liturgy*[54] is a historical survey of the principles and practice of liturgical reform in the Western church up to the eve of Vatican II. Reid leaves no doubt that he considers the post–Vatican II liturgical reform a radical departure from what he calls the objective liturgical tradition. Reid's work is significant since it acts as a kind of prolegomenon to many of the criticisms brought against the reform. If one accepts his reading of the nature of the liturgical tradition and the nature of genuine reform, then many of the post–Vatican II reforms can be judged to have been executed badly.

Briefly, the book's argument is as follows: Authentic change and reform in the liturgy have always been gradual and careful. Even the popes did not feel free to make radical changes in the liturgy or, when they did, found that the changes needed to be undone. On this basis one can fault Pope Paul III's acceptance of Cardinal Quinognez's reform of the breviary in 1536, the breviary reform of Pope Urban VIII in the early seventeenth century, Pope Pius X's subsequent breviary reform in 1911, and even the transformation of the Easter Vigil and Holy Week rites under Pius XII from 1952 to 1956. There is no room for Ultramontanism in the reform of the liturgy, since even popes do not have the authority to change the essentials of the church's faith. Therefore, one of the principal arguments of the book is that the changes made by the authority of Paul VI were unwarranted and unwise.[55]

Besides the improper arrogation of papal authority, two major problems characterize the misguided or nonorganic approach to reform. The most widespread is antiquarianism, the idea that a better liturgy can be found by archaeological means—unearthing the treasures of past eras when the liturgy was celebrated more authentically. Antiquarianism was criticized by Pope Pius XII in his 1947 encyclical on

---

[54] Alcuin Reid, *The Organic Development of the Liturgy: The Principles of Liturgical Reform and Their Relation to the Twentieth-century Liturgical Movement Prior to the Second Vatican Council* (Farnborough: St. Michael's Abbey Press, 2004).

[55] Joseph Ratzinger makes a similar observation with regard to the wisdom of ecclesiastical authority imposing a radical reform of the liturgy; see his *Milestones: Memoirs 1927–1977*, trans. Erasmo Leiva-Merikakis (San Francisco: Ignatius Press, 1998), 148.

the liturgy, *Mediator Dei*.[56] One example the pope gives is the reforms attempted by the 1786 regional Synod of Pistoia which legislated, for example:

- that there should be only one altar in any church,

- that the priest should not recite readings and chants that were also being done by other ministers, and

- that the entire Roman Canon be prayed aloud.[57]

The archaeological approach was also characteristic of the work of probably the best-known twentieth-century liturgical historian, the Jesuit Josef Andreas Jungmann. Reid devotes an entire section to the work of Jungmann, mainly to argue that his premises about uncovering pristine and cleaner liturgical forms from the past were faulty.[58] Time and again the so-called experts (= liturgical historians) are blamed for the failures and errors of the reform.[59]

The other villain of the piece is Annibale Bugnini, CM, who acted as secretary to the pre–Vatican II commission on liturgical reform under Pius XII as well as the conciliar and postconciliar liturgy commissions. It is commonly agreed that Bugnini, who became Archbishop-secretary to the Congregation for Divine Worship, was the major architect of the liturgical reform.[60] For Reid, Bugnini's major error was his espousal of a liturgical reform that would accommodate the liturgy to the mentality and culture of modern men and women.[61] This approach destroys the objective nature of the liturgy as a gift. Reid refers to this latter approach as "pastoral expediency."

Reid's study begins with a historical overview of liturgical reform in Western Christianity supporting the conviction that the liturgy has

---

[56] *Mediator Dei*, §§61–64.

[57] Reid, *Organic Development*, 41.

[58] Ibid., 151–59.

[59] Ibid., 250, 260.

[60] See Bugnini's own memoir (cited in n. 14 above) as well as the rather intemperate book of Bonneterre cited in the same note. A more balanced critique of Bugnini and his work can be found in Laszlo Dobszay, *The Bugnini-Liturgy and the Reform of the Reform* (Front Royal, VA: Publications of the Catholic Church Music Associates, 2003).

[61] Reid, *Organic Development*, 200–04, 222–23. Bugnini is also criticized for upholding an antiquarian approach to reform.

always been a living reality—an organism—and this organism has represented an objective tradition.[62] After an extremely brief summary of the first six centuries, he arrives at the Carolingian period (late eighth to early ninth century) during which a number of the Roman books[63] were adopted north of the Alps from the rite celebrated in the city of Rome itself. For Reid the adaptation of the Roman books to conditions in the Carolingian realm serves as an exemplar of organic liturgical development.[64] The book in question is the Gregorian Sacramentary (Hadrianum) sent to Charlemagne. This book contained the papal (stational) liturgies for the city of Rome. It was lacking a number of Sunday formulae, e.g., Sundays after Epiphany and after Pentecost. The sacramentary was therefore supplemented by a Carolingian editor, most probably Benedict of Aniane, who filled in the missing material from other traditional sources. Reid discerns the following principles in the finished product:

1. a necessity for the development (the sacramentary supplied was inadequate; further texts were required);

2. a profound respect for liturgical tradition (insofar as possible the compilation of required texts using elements already belonging to the tradition, in this case Roman);

3. little pure innovation (the editor collects rather than composes);

4. the tentative positing of newer liturgical forms alongside the old (his preface accepts that they may be considered a "superfluity");

5. the integration of newer forms following their acceptance over time.[65]

This is a key point in Reid's argument and therefore needs to be analyzed carefully. His "test case" for organic development is somewhat loaded. In the first place, we are not dealing here with a centralized and systematic reform of the liturgy or one that followed centuries of relative liturgical fixity. In addition, the supplement to the *Hadrianum* had far more to do with formulae for the liturgical year (collects, prayers over the gifts, prefaces, prayers after communion)

---

[62] Ibid., 12–13. Reid consistently capitalizes "Liturgy" and "Tradition."
[63] See Cyril Vogel, *Medieval Liturgy: An Introduction to the Sources* (Washington, DC: Pastoral Press, 1986), 61ff.
[64] I am grateful to my licentiate student, Joseph Villecco, for pointing this out.
[65] Reid, *Organic Development*, 17.

than with what is usually called the "Ordinary of the Mass." His example is not comparable to the change from the *Missal of Pius V* (1570) to the *Missal of Paul VI* (1969). A better analogy would be the shift from the second edition of the *Missal of Paul VI* (1975) to the third under Pope John Paul II in which adjustments were made to the prefatory material (the *General Instruction of the Roman Missal*), and prayers for newer feasts and memorials were added.

This analysis of Reid's principles does beg the question of whether such a radical reform of the Roman Rite was necessary in the 1960s. As was the case with Pickstock and with Gamber, it seems that there is a certain romanticism at work with regard to the pre–Vatican II liturgy. It is one thing to laud the beauty and the glories of the traditional Roman Rite. Appreciating how the rite was actually celebrated is something altogether different. Consider Dom Bernard Botte's description of daily Mass at the beginning of the twentieth century in his memoir of the liturgical reform:

> Every morning at eight o'clock there was a Mass in the students' chapel. . . . Up front there was only one altar in a little apse located between two sacristies. Mass was said by an old, more or less voiceless, priest—even in the first row the only thing you'd hear was a murmur. The group rose for the gospel, but nobody dreamed of telling us what gospel it was. . . . You could lose yourself in any prayerbook at all, but we were pulled out of our drowsiness from time to time by the recitation of a few decades of the rosary, or by the singing of either a Latin motet or a French hymn. . . . Receiving communion at this Mass was out of the question. For that matter, no one at the time seemed to notice a relationship between the Mass and communion. . . . When one of my sisters asked the advice of the dean of the upper end of Charleroi, Monsignor Lalieu (a doctor of theology and an author of a book on the Mass), about the best time to receive communion, he recommended she receive before Mass and then offer Mass in thanksgiving for communion. This sounds strange to us, but we ought to keep in mind the ideas then current. Mass was no longer the prayer of the Christian community. The clergy prayed entirely in place of and in the name of the community. As a result, the faithful were only remotely involved and paid attention to their own personal devotion. Communion appeared to be a private devotion without any special link to the Mass.[66]

---

[66] Bernard Botte, *From Silence to Participation: An Insider's View of Liturgical Renewal* (Washington, DC: Pastoral Press, 1988), 2–3. Botte was a Belgian Benedictine liturgical historian and one of the major consultants in the reform.

Admittedly one can take legitimate exception to some of the details of the contemporary liturgical reform, but descriptions like that of Botte, which could be multiplied hundreds of times, leave no doubt of the need for a radical reform. What then of the famous paragraph 23 of *Sacrosanctum Concilium*?

> In order that sound tradition may be retained, and yet the way remain open to legitimate progress, a careful investigation—theological, historical, and pastoral—should always be made into each part of the liturgy which is to be revised. Furthermore the general laws governing the structure and meaning of the liturgy must be studied in conjunction with the experience derived from recent liturgical reforms and from the indults granted to various places.
>
> Finally, there must be no innovations unless the good of the Church genuinely and certainly requires them, *and care must be taken that any new forms adopted should in some way grow organically from forms already existing.*[67]

The word "organically" needs some interpretation. The adjective "organic" is essentially a biological term referring to a living organism. So from the start we are clearly in the realm of metaphor, as Reid admits.[68] Understanding liturgy by way of biological metaphors clearly has limits. The liturgy is not an organism in the same way that a plant or animal is. The question really comes down to the nature of tradition. Is it possible to see a misguided trajectory in certain of the developments, e.g., the silent recitation of the Canon of the Mass, infrequency of reception of holy communion, the retention of Latin? To capitalize on the biological metaphor, is it not possible or necessary that broken limbs must be reset to become useful again to the whole organism? And is tradition to be understood in all of the details of what has been passed on to us, or rather in taking into account the very process of its transmission? As Jaroslav Pelikan wisely commented in the introduction to his magisterial history of Christian doctrine: "Tradition is the living faith of the dead; traditionalism is the dead faith of the living."[69] To insist that the pre–Vatican II liturgy of the

[67] SC §23. Emphasis supplied.

[68] Reid, *Organic Development*, 289. In my opinion this admission should have come in the introduction to the book rather than the conclusion.

[69] Jaroslav Pelikan, *The Christian Tradition: A History of the Development of Doctrine.* Vol. 1: *The Emergence of the Catholic Tradition (100–600)* (Chicago: University of Chicago Press, 1971), 9.

Catholic Church represented an objective tradition that should not have been radically reformed is traditionalism.

At the same time, if one were to understand the council's language to refer to the pace and extent of the reform, one could certainly take issue with the finished product. I am not trying to argue here that the reform was perfect, nor is it fair to contend that Reid and others who agree with him reject any and every attempt at liturgical reform. His assessment of the need for reform is balanced: "Now, a wise reform of the Liturgy must balance the two tendencies: that is, conserve good and healthy conditions, verified on historico-critical bases, and take account of new elements, already opportunely introduced and needing to be introduced."[70]

What is at issue here is both how one understands the role of critical historical study with regard to the tradition and how one judges the new elements that are proposed. Moreover, the twentieth-century discipline of comparative liturgy has indeed relativized our understanding of the tradition as a whole.[71] It is no longer appropriate to attempt a history of a single rite in isolation from others.[72] Even the notion of "rite" needs to be handled gingerly. As Nathan Mitchell has put it:

> The myth [of the substantial unity of the Roman Rite, SC 38] arises from an uncritical assumption that the Roman liturgy has had, from time immemorial, an unbroken history of invariable rites and rubrics, texts and gestures, that everyone recognizes as *Roman* in origin, content and structure. But even the slightest acquaintance with Western liturgical history would expose this myth as little more than wishful thinking or euphoric recall. In one sense, there *is* no "Roman Rite" and never has been.[73]

---

[70] Reid, *Organic Development*, 142.

[71] See Robert F. Taft and Gabriele Winkler, eds., *Comparative Liturgy Fifty Years After Anton Baumstark (1872–1948): Acts of the International Congress, Rome, 25–29 September 1998*. Orientalia Christiana Analecta 265 (Rome: Pontifical Oriental Institute, 2001).

[72] For my own attempt to address some of these questions from the point of view of comparative liturgy and the nature of the liturgical historian's task see the appendix.

[73] Nathan Mitchell, "The Amen Corner: Back to the Future?" *Worship* 73 (1999): 63. In the same vein see idem, "The Amen Corner: Life Begins at Forty?" *Worship* 77 (2003): 65.

Another way of putting this is to say that the notion of "rite" is a convenient way of talking about the style of a tradition of liturgical prayer. In this sense one *can* talk about a "Roman Rite" or a "Byzantine Rite," but one also needs to be careful about isolating and exalting rites in such a way that they themselves become the object of devotion. As we noted above in dealing with the work of Klaus Gamber, there has been a tendency to emphasize devotion to a liturgical tradition over the needs of the contemporary worshiping community within that tradition. For Reid such an approach leads to a subjectivism that destroys the notion of a liturgical tradition altogether.[74]

The Organic Development of the Liturgy ends with the beginning of Vatican II and so does not deal directly with *Sacrosanctum Concilium* or with the postconciliar application of its principles. The author's attitude toward the conciliar constitution and subsequent reform of the liturgy can fairly easily be culled from his work. His objections can be summarized as follows:

1. A major reform of the liturgy has never been successfully undertaken by centralized authority in the church. For the papacy to mount a wholesale reform lies outside the ambit of papal authority, since the pope may not alter tradition. This reform was much too quick and too radical.[75]

2. Although it may make sense to translate the readings of the liturgy into the vernacular, there was no good reason to vernacularize the entire liturgy.[76]

3. The replacement of the traditional Sunday readings by a three-year cycle did "unprecedented violence to the objective traditional Liturgy."[77]

---

[74] Reid, *Organic Development*, 280. In reviewing a 1961 article by Frederick McManus, Reid states: ". . . asserting that 'each generation' should evaluate the liturgical books is tantamount to advocating the subjectifying of objective liturgical Tradition and the relativising of its content."

[75] I cannot agree, however, with Nathan Mitchell, who argues that "the liturgical reforms prompted by the Council of Trent were far more unprecedented and untraditional than those which followed Vatican II" ("The Amen Corner: Rereading Reform," *Worship* 80 [2006]: 465). Trent standardized the liturgy in the West in a way that was unprecedented because it could: Printing had been invented in the previous century. It did not, however, radically change the basic text or Ordinary of the Mass.

[76] Reid, *Organic Development*, 288.

[77] Ibid., 177.

4. The same can be said for the addition of new eucharistic prayers to the Missal.

5. The reforms are founded on the erroneous assumption that Catholic worship needs to be accommodated to historical times and cultures. This is a mistaken understanding of the meaning of "Pastoral Liturgy."[78]

6. The historical-critical findings of scholars must be assessed very carefully since there is a tendency among many liturgical historians to advocate for a forgotten "Golden Age" of the liturgy to the detriment of the organic, living tradition of the Roman Rite and thus to submit the objective tradition to ideological currents.

7. Catholic liturgy is "essentially incarnational";[79] i.e., its external forms cannot be changed without changing the meaning of the liturgy.

One can agree that the reformed rite significantly changed how Catholics understood their worship. The reform was no mere minor adjustment of some of the externals of Catholic piety but a thorough reshaping of the Catholic imagination with regard to liturgy. This is why, as we shall see in the next chapter, the theological element in the reform is extremely important. One can also agree that reforming the liturgy cannot simply be left to the conclusions of liturgical historians. It never has been. The decisions about the reform have always been in the hands of the magisterium and then implemented on the local level. Although his quotation is often used rather maliciously, Aidan Nichols is of course right when he states that "liturgy is too important to be left to the liturgists."[80] I know of no serious liturgist who would disagree. Liturgy is God's gift entrusted to the church, but the church (i.e., ecclesiastical authority) has the obligation to use all of the resources at its disposal to celebrate that gift. And that includes liturgical historians, theologians, and other experts.

Let us take a closer look at one of the issues raised by Reid—the change in the Sunday lectionary. The gospel readings for the Sundays in Lent can serve as a good example of the nature and extent of the change brought about with the *Missal of Paul VI*.

---

[78] Ibid., 138.

[79] Ibid., 203.

[80] Aidan Nichols, *Looking at Liturgy: A Critical View of Its Contemporary Form* (San Francisco: Ignatius Press, 1996), 9.

	Missal of 1570	Missal of 1969 A	Missal of 1969 B	Missal of 1969 C
Lent 1	Matt 4:1-11 Temptation in the Desert	Matt 4:1-11 Temptation in the Desert	Mark 1:12-15 Temptation in the Desert	Luke 4:1-13 Temptation in the Desert
Lent 2	Matt 17:1-9 Transfiguration	Matt 17:1-9 Transfiguration	Mark 9:2-10 Transfiguration	Luke 9:28b-36 Transfiguration
Lent 3	Luke 11:14-28 Jesus exorcizes a demon	John 4:5-42 Woman at the well	John 2:13-25 Purification of the Temple	Luke 13:1-9 Parable of the fig tree
Lent 4	John 6:1-15 Feeding of the multitude	John 9:1-41 Healing of the blind man	John 3:14-21 Jesus and Nicodemus	Luke 15:1-3, 11-32 Prodigal Son
Lent 5	John 8:46-59 Debate with the Jews	John 11:1-45 Raising of Lazarus	John 12:20-33 Unless a grain of wheat falls . . .	John 8:1-11 Woman caught in adultery
Passion/ Palm Sunday	Passion according to Matthew	Passion according to Matthew	Passion according to Mark	Passion according to Luke

The first two Sundays remain the same, at least with regard to their themes: the Temptation in the Desert and the Transfiguration. The new lectionary follows the general pattern of using the parallel gospels in Mark and Luke in the B and C cycles. The same pattern holds for the reading of the Passion. In the older missal the Passions according to Mark and Luke had been read on Tuesday and Wednesday of Holy Week. In the *Missal of Paul VI* each of the Synoptic accounts of the Passion is read in the ABC cycle. The biggest change is evident in the A cycle's reading of three major Johannine gospels (John 4, 9, and 11) on the third, fourth, and fifth Sundays. This change is one of the clearest results of twentieth-century historical-critical study. With the demise of adult initiation (at least by and large) in the early Middle Ages, the gospels that had formerly been read at the scrutinies (exorcisms) on Sundays in preparation for Easter baptism were transferred to weekdays, as was the formal entrance into the catechumenate on Wednesday of the fourth week, a ceremony that took place, fittingly enough, at the Roman basilica of St. Paul Outside the Walls. The desire to reemphasize paschal baptism, which was a feature even of the 1952 reform of the Easter Vigil, led to Vatican II's mandate that the initiatory aspect of Lent be recovered (SC 109). Restoring the initiatory character of Lent and Easter is one of the greatest gains in the reforms of the past forty years—and it is due to patient historical research.[81]

Reid goes somewhat further in several subsequent articles. Taking a different tack, he argues that the reform produced by the post–Vatican II *Consilium* was not faithful to the Liturgy Constitution's directives and particularly to *Sacrosanctum Concilium*'s stipulation that there be no liturgical innovations except as required by the good of the church (§23).[82]

THE HISTORICAL CRITIQUE

To this point we have surveyed two important and representative critics of the historical dimensions of the liturgical reform. Now we shall turn to one more critic, Denis Crouan. Crouan, a historian and specialist in Gregorian chant, is much more sympathetic to the reforms inspired by Vatican II's Liturgy Constitution. In fact, his basic position is that the reforms as instituted by the church in the aftermath of the council are laudable. The problem is that they have not been put into practice.[83] Obviously this stance puts him at odds with the historians we have just examined: Klaus Gamber and Alcuin Reid.

More than most of the critics, Crouan is convinced that the pre–Vatican II Roman liturgy was in serious need of repair. In particular he takes issue with the traditionalists who maintain the persistence of the "Rite of Pius V." There is no "Rite of Pius," he asserts. There is only the Roman Rite, which is enshrined in the current reformed books.[84] How this squares with Pope Benedict XVI's decision in *Summorum*

[81] E.g., in the work of Antoine Chavasse, "La structure du carême et les lectures des messes quadragésimales dans la liturgie romaine," *La Maison-Dieu* 31 (1952): 76–120.

[82] Alcuin Reid, "*Sacrosanctum Concilium* and the Reform of the *Ordo Missae*," *Antiphon* 10 (2006): 277–95. See also idem, "The Fathers of Vatican II and the Revised Mass: The Results of a Survey," *Antiphon* 10 (2006): 170–90.

[83] Denis Crouan, *The Liturgy Betrayed* (San Francisco: Ignatius Press, 2000), 15; idem, *The History and the Future of the Roman Liturgy* (San Francisco: Ignatius Press, 2005), 190–205.

[84] Crouan, *Liturgy Betrayed*, 35; idem, *The Liturgy after Vatican II: Collapsing or Resurgent?* (San Francisco: Ignatius Press, 2001), 31–34.

Pontificum that we have one Roman Rite with two usages is a subject we shall defer to a later chapter. Moreover, Crouan accuses the traditionalists of a certain duplicity when it comes to their argument that the Liturgy Constitution never meant for the pre–Vatican II Mass to be abrogated. The traditionalists' argument rests on their reading of *Sacrosanctum Concilium* 4: "Lastly, in faithful obedience to tradition, the council declares that the Church holds all lawfully acknowledged rites to be of equal right and dignity and wishes to preserve them in the future and to foster them in every way."

No, argues, Crouan. Paragraph 4 is referring to the Byzantine, Armenian, Coptic Rites and the like:

> Both in the East and in the West the different rites recognized by the Church are autonomous rites that were born in socio-historical contexts that are distinct from one another and that developed in uninterrupted traditions all related to a common liturgical source. Thus, these rites, all accepted by the Magisterium, did not stem from the rejection or acceptance of an older ritual form as would be the case with regard to the Roman Rite if one wanted to uphold the arguments made by traditionalist groups.[85]

These conclusions are in line with Crouan's support for and approval of the Roman Missal of 1970. As we saw above, his major complaint is not with the reform itself but rather with what he considers its haphazard implementation. The reform was necessary because a number of romantic and sentimental elements had crept into the liturgy. Unlike most of the critics we have examined, Crouan does not consider the Tridentine liturgical reform an unmixed blessing. One of its most significant difficulties was that in its context it took for granted the ritual development of the Middle Ages and especially the strong spiritual movements of individual piety of the late Middle Ages. The result was a Mass that took the Low Mass rather than the corporate sung Mass as its model:

> The reform of Saint Pius V owed much to the climate of controversy in which it was carried out, and it was enclosed within a social context in which the *sensus Ecclesiae* was lost and an individualism was emerging that was rooted in the *devotio moderna*. This reform, despite the unquestionable progress that it brought about, remained in certain

[85] Crouan, *Liturgy after Vatican II*, 35–39, at 37.

respects distant from the intended return "to the norms of the Church Fathers."

Thus, on giving priority to the "Low Mass," the Tridentine reform would progressively develop a practice of making the Eucharistic celebration an act of private devotion of the priest, whereas the faithful were simply invited to attend the Mass and to unite their prayers with it as sincerely as possible.[86]

One of the major problems of many of the critics of the reform is that they do not understand the criticisms Crouan makes here—or how far the Tridentine liturgy and the priestly spirituality that accompanied it had departed from the spirit of the early liturgy. The Baroque, with its fondness for theatricality, would further distance the liturgy from being a true exercise of the Body of Christ. Another unfortunate consequence of the combination of post-Tridentine polemical theology and Baroque style was the placement of grand tabernacles atop altar retables, which "transformed sanctuaries into religious dioramas."[87] The overall result was an appeal to sentiment and emotion ill-suited to the experience of the liturgy as an act of objective worship. In addition, the invention of printing, which made regularization of the liturgy possible (for the first time really) also turned the book itself with its rules and rubrics into a kind of object of worship: "instead of tradition guaranteeing the missal, the missal becomes the guarantee for tradition."[88] Add the Pietism of the eighteenth century and the Romanticism of the nineteenth and one has prime conditions for the liturgical movement. For Crouan, then, the reform of the liturgy that followed Vatican II was well warranted. His assessment of the Mass produced by the *Consilium* is very positive:

- The connection between the congregation and the celebrant is affirmed more clearly.

- The essential rites have been trimmed of late additions that had grown cumbersome—and esoteric—over time.

- The roles of the individual participants in the liturgy are better defined and do not encroach upon one another.

[86] Crouan, *History*, 92.
[87] Ibid., 94.
[88] Ibid., 100.

- Duplicated prayers have been eliminated.

- The form of the liturgy that has been determined in this way—when it is properly observed—is astonishingly close to that of the first known Roman Rite.[89]

Why, then, would one class this historian among the critics of the post–Vatican II liturgy? The answer lies in the pregnant phrase "when it is properly done." Crouan sees no reason for most celebrations to take place *versus populum*. He also thinks that the abandonment of chant and of Latin is a great mistake. Ironically, the practice of the post–Vatican II liturgy is just as theatrical and subjective as the liturgy it reformed. The main problem lies not with the architects of the reform but with the diocesan and local committees that have put it into practice and with the bishops who have not exercised due diligence.[90] In the Mannion typology surveyed in the introduction, Crouan would most fittingly be classified among those who wish to "recatholicize" the reform.

CONCLUSION

This chapter has reviewed an extremely important approach to the critique of the reform. Since liturgy relies so heavily on tradition, appeals will always be made one way or another to history and to the process of historical development. We have examined three historians who have criticized the reform from the point of view of liturgical history. Two of them, Gamber and Reid, were severely critical of the reform itself. In the course of the chapter we have also considered one of the most consistent complaints about the reform—that it was not an organic development from previously existing forms.

Now it is time to turn to the heart of the matter—theology—and to one of the major representatives of the theological critique of the liturgical reform: Joseph Ratzinger, now Pope Benedict XVI.

[89] Ibid., 188–89.
[90] Crouan, *Liturgy Betrayed*, 77–92.

Chapter Three

A Theological Critique

The bottom line of any critique of the liturgy will necessarily be theological: serious reflection on the nature and content of Christian faith. Perhaps no single figure besides Pope John Paul II has dominated the ecclesiastical and theological consciousness over the past twenty years as much as Cardinal Joseph Ratzinger, Prefect of the Congregation for the Doctrine of the Faith since 1981 and now, of course, Pope Benedict XVI. Ratzinger began his career as a systematic theologian. He taught at Bonn (1959–1963), Münster (1963–1966), and Tübingen (1966–1969) before moving to help found the new Bavarian University of Regensburg in 1969. In 1977 he was made archbishop of Munich-Freising in Bavaria. Ratzinger has been and is a theologian of great talent and accomplishment. For thirty years his theology has served as a touchstone for critics of the reform. Therefore his writings will be the focus of this chapter.

Ratzinger's early theology was received well by progressive theologians in the Roman Catholic Church. In particular his *Introduction to Christian Faith* is a masterful and inspiring treatise on the notion of faith as well as the major aspects of the Apostles' Creed. His theology took a turn after the student riots in the spring of 1968. From that time he distanced himself from the theology represented by Karl Rahner and the theologians who supported the journal *Concilium* and allied himself more closely with Hans Urs von Balthasar, Henri de Lubac, and the journal *Communio*. He apparently had the reputation of being an excellent and very popular teacher who was able to explain technical theology in an accessible way.[1] Reading his written work, one can

---

[1] John Allen, *Cardinal Ratzinger: The Vatican's Enforcer of the Faith* (New York: Continuum, 2000), 103.

easily accept this judgment. Ratzinger's writings are characterized by great clarity combined with a lively imagination and obvious love for God and divine revelation.

My purpose in this chapter is to examine the theological aspect of the critique of the post–Vatican II liturgical reform in light of Ratzinger's theology. This exercise is all the more relevant since he became pope. I will begin by reviewing some of the basic characteristics and direction of Ratzinger's sacramental/liturgical theology. Then the focus will turn to his theology of the Eucharist—especially his emphasis on eucharistic sacrifice and eucharistic adoration. A third section will analyze aspects of his call for liturgical reform in the areas of the liturgy of the Mass, church architecture, and music. Finally, I shall ask how these themes play out in the major document on the liturgy he has written since becoming pope, the 2006 Post-Synodal Apostolic Exhortation *Sacramentum Caritatis*. We shall deal with his *motu proprio, Summorum Pontificum*, in chapter 5.

BASIC THEMES

One of the most striking aspects of Joseph Ratzinger's theology is the facility and frequency with which he turns to biblical exegesis as the foundation of his exposition of aspects of the Christian faith. For example, Ratzinger treats Christ as the Way, the Truth, and the Life in an attempt to get at basic questions for christology. In dealing with Christ as the Way, he turns to the Lukan account of the transfiguration of Jesus and especially Luke's unique use of the word *exodus* for Jesus' passage to Jerusalem.[2] For Ratzinger, Elijah is the key to the story since he prophesies to a people who live in the Promised Land already but in a real sense do not live in it since they have abandoned the covenant. There is no true "way" in this world, in other words, without keeping the covenant. He further explicates the New Testament on the basis of the Old by showing that Jesus' face is transfigured just as Moses' had been by his encounter with the God of the covenant. Finally, he demonstrates that Christ is the fulfillment of the Jewish feasts by showing that the Markan and Matthean accounts of the transfiguration place this event six days after Peter's confession of faith in Jesus—the same period of time separating *Yom Kippur* (the Day of Atonement) from

---

[2] Joseph Ratzinger, *A New Song for the Lord: Faith in Christ and Liturgy Today*, trans. Martha M. Matesich (New York: Crossroad, 1996), 15–20.

Sukkoth (the Feast of Booths), which celebrated the enthronement of Yʜwʜ in his temple.[3]

This example of Ratzinger's use of biblical theology arises in the context of a major theme of his theological work—a lament for the passing of religious values in the contemporary West. At times he sounds very similar to Alexander Solzhenitsyn in decrying the bankruptcy of Western secular values—or the complete lack of them. For him the proof can be found in "the satanic trinity of sex, drugs and collective violence" that characterizes the contemporary world.[4]

For Ratzinger the Enlightenment and post-Enlightenment dismissal of metaphysics is a disaster for Christian faith and theology.[5] He demonstrates great appreciation but even more so a love for the Fathers of the Church, whom he quotes widely. It is no exaggeration to say that he has been deeply affected by the widespread loss of religious consciousness in Northern Europe in particular. In common with many of the critics of the liturgical reform of the past forty years he perceives the liberal or progressive attitude toward liturgy as an unwarranted accommodation to the spirit of the age—going in their door and failing to come out our own. It seems that the once moderately progressive Ratzinger turned very conservative and extremely disillusioned after the student unrest of the spring of 1968, which was particularly virulent in Tübingen.[6]

So one can understand Ratzinger's distress when it seems that the subject of the liturgy has become "neither God nor Christ, but the 'we' of the ones celebrating."[7] This is a constant theme in his thinking and writing about the liturgy. One of the main problems is the triumph of concepts like "celebration," "freedom," and "creativity." The liturgy is valued for its entertainment factor.[8] In fact, I think we can say that the greatest strength of his analysis of liturgy and sacrament today is his insistence on keeping God at the center of the liturgical celebration. Too

---

[3] Note that Ratzinger relies heavily on biblical exegetes for his interpretations, in the case of the transfiguration passage on Hartmut Gese, Jean-Marie Van Cangh, and Michel-Jean van Esbroeck.

[4] Ratzinger, *New Song*, 27; see also his *The Feast of Faith: Approaches to a Theology of the Liturgy*, trans. Graham Harrison (San Francisco: Ignatius Press, 1986), 19.

[5] See the reflections of Jonathan Robinson on the same subject in chapter 1.

[6] See Allen, *Cardinal Ratzinger*, 82–84, 113–18. The decline of faith in Western Europe has of course been a major theme of his papacy.

[7] Ratzinger, *New Song*, 32.

[8] Ratzinger, *Feast of Faith*, 61–62; idem, *New Song*, 112–15.

often one hears or reads a superficial etymology of the word "liturgy" as "the work of the people." But the word is actually more complex than that since in its origins it referred not to work done *by the people* but rather a public work in the sense that we would speak of the "Department of Public Works"—in other words, a benefaction or work done *for the people*.[9] The German term for worship—*Gottesdienst*—captures this double nature of the liturgy well. It can mean both the service (*Dienst*) God does for us and the service we owe to God. I think Cardinal Ratzinger makes a telling point when he underlines the centrality of Christ and thus divine activity in the liturgy. How often does one participate in a Eucharist in a progressive American parish only to find that *all* of the music chosen emphasizes what *we* do in the celebration—"we are church." No doubt this is an extremely valuable insight—but like all good ideas it goes awry when overused. It needs to be balanced by lyrics that emphasize God's activity in our worship. But we will have more to say about this in our chapter on music.

What, then, can one make of Vatican II's Constitution on the Liturgy when it speaks of the importance of active participation (*actuosa participatio*) in the liturgy? In a recent and incisive critique of Ratzinger's *The Spirit of the Liturgy*, Pierre-Marie Gy has pointed out that the author considers this a "dangerous phrase."[10] To be fair, Cardinal Ratzinger has responded vigorously and unequivocally that he does not consider this concept an entreé to "autocelebration"—the church celebrating itself.[11] In fact, in his *A New Song for the Lord* he claims that "the polemical alternative 'priest or congregation as celebrant of the liturgy' is absurd."[12]

Ratzinger's theological vision is both broad and profound. It centers on a cosmic vision of God's going (*exitus*) and drawing all back to himself (*reditus*).[13] As such it is both cosmic and covenant-centered.

---

[9] See ibid., 133, for the same point.

[10] Pierre-Marie Gy, "Is Cardinal Ratzinger's *L'Esprit de la Liturgie* Faithful to the Council?" *Doctrine and Life* 52 (2002): 426–32, at 426 (English translation of an article that originally appeared in *La Maison-Dieu* 229 [2002]).

[11] Joseph Ratzinger, "The Spirit of the Liturgy or Fidelity to the Council: A Reply to Pierre-Marie Gy, O.P.," *Doctrine and Life* 52 (2002): 494–500, at 494 (English translation of an article that originally appeared in German in *Gottesdienst* 36 [2002]: 13).

[12] Ratzinger, *New Song*, 132; see the comments of Eamon Duffy, "Pope Benedict XVI and the Liturgy," *Inside the Vatican* (November 2006): 38.

[13] Once again a theme elaborated by Jonathan Robinson, *The Mass and Modernity: Walking to Heaven Backwards* (San Francisco: Ignatius Press, 2005), 340.

History is creation returning to its source. In this vein he employs the evolutionary thought of Teilhard de Chardin, who saw transubstantiation as "the anticipation of the transformation and divinization of matter in the christological 'fullness.'"[14] God and human beings are involved in a love story that fulfills the purpose of creation. The point of liturgy is "to communicate this vision and to give it life in such a way that glory is given to God."[15] Again employing biblical theology, Ratzinger insists that the goal of the Exodus was not only the Promised Land but the worship of God at Sinai that is a necessary part of that journey. And so for Ratzinger creation has a thoroughly positive value despite human sinfulness. He is careful to avoid any hint of dualism, as though non-divine being were "something negative in itself."[16] Israel's conflicted history of sacrifice finds its fulfillment in the sacrifice of the word—*logikē thusia*—which of course is ultimately the Word-made-flesh, Jesus Christ. The resurrection of Jesus is the end of the old Temple and its worship and the inauguration of a new authentic form of worship.[17] But the resurrection only takes place because of the cross, which Ratzinger describes with great beauty: "In the pierced heart of the Crucified, God's own heart is opened up—here we see who God is and what he is like."[18]

EUCHARISTIC THEOLOGY

The consideration of the resurrection as revelation of God's vindication of Christ's self-sacrifice leads us to examine Ratzinger's eucharistic theology. This aspect of his theology is most thoroughly treated in a book that has recently been translated as *God Is Near Us*.[19] This compilation of articles he wrote and talks he delivered in the late 1970s as archbishop of Munich begins with a meditation on the Nicene Creed's article on the Incarnation: "By the power of the Holy Spirit he was born of the Virgin Mary, and became man."[20] This starting point is

[14] Joseph Ratzinger, *The Spirit of the Liturgy* (San Francisco: Ignatius Press, 2000), 28–29. As we have also seen in chapter 1, this is a theme Catherine Pickstock takes up.

[15] Ibid., 18.

[16] Ibid., 32.

[17] Ibid., 44.

[18] Ibid., 48.

[19] Joseph Ratzinger, *God Is Near Us: The Eucharist at the Heart of Life* (San Francisco: Ignatius Press, 2003).

[20] Ibid., 11–26.

important in itself, since Ratzinger chooses not to begin with the Last
Supper or with Jesus' cross and resurrection—despite the emphasis on
sacrifice, which we shall turn to shortly. Interestingly, a preference for
being over doing has been noted in Ratzinger's theology.[21] Here he
demonstrates a somewhat arbitrary approach to etymology in speaking
of the *skenē* (Greek "tent") of Christ's dwelling with us (John 1:14) as
resonating with the Hebrew word for the divine presence—*shekinah*.[22]

From meditating on "Emmanuel"—God with us—Ratzinger turns
to the origin of the Eucharist in the paschal mystery. In rather traditional fashion he understands Jesus' words at the Last Supper: "This is
my body, which is given for you" and "This is my blood of the covenant" as anticipation and acceptance of Jesus' saving, self-sacrificial
death. Only his death makes sense of these words, and only these
words make sense of his death.[23] Ratzinger also considers the scene of
the washing of the feet in John 13 as a similar effort to reveal the
meaning of Jesus' sacrificial death, which constitutes "the great liturgy
of humanity."[24] At the same time he is intent on distancing himself
from the complaint of some traditionalists that the church has betrayed the Roman liturgy by translating the biblical *peri/hyper hymōn*
and the Roman Canon's *pro multis* (literally "for the many") as "for
you and for all." He can find no justification for limiting God's will for
universal salvation, but at the same time he emphasizes the necessity
of human freedom in accepting that salvation.[25]

In a very moving play on images from John's gospel, Ratzinger
focuses on the wounded and open side of Christ on the cross (John
19:30-37). Like the Church Fathers, he interprets Christ's open side as
the fount of the church and the sacraments. Thus Christ is the new
Adam and from his side springs the new Eve. But Christ's words at
the Last Supper and his death on the cross need a third element for

---

[21] See Allen, *Cardinal Ratzinger*, 35–36, 101–102.

[22] Ratzinger, *God Is Near Us*, 22: "But in the Greek word for tent—*skenē*—we hear
overtones of the Hebrew word *shekina*, that is to say, the term used in early Judaism
to refer to the sacred cloud. . . ."

[23] Ibid., 32–33.

[24] Ibid, 30.

[25] Ibid., 34–38. The Congregation for Divine Worship has recently insisted that
future translations of the eucharistic prayers substitute "for . . . many" in place
of the present "for . . . all." See http://www.usccb.org/liturgy/innews/
November2006.pdf. Apparently there is some disagreement between the pope
(at least writing as Joseph Ratzinger) and the Congregation.

completion: his resurrection. In the unity of these three Ratzinger finds an "intuition" of the Triune God.[26]

In all of this Ratzinger finds ample room to develop a theology of eucharistic sacrifice. He first notes that "God gives himself so that we might give."[27] There is a kind of marvelous exchange (*admirabile commercium*) in all of this. We can give only because God has given first. So he cites the memorable phrase from the Roman Canon that we offer "from the gifts that you have given us" (*de tuis donis ac datis*). This offering is real and not fictitious. It takes place in the "now" of liturgical time, as Jesus has inserted his own words into the memorial *haggadah* (narrative) of the Jewish Passover meal, which in turn becomes the true unbloody sacrifice of prayer.[28] This treatment of eucharistic sacrifice is very attractive—especially since he moves from the question of eucharistic sacrifice to that of eucharistic (real) presence rather than vice versa. In a 2001 address to a conference that focused on his liturgical critique, the Prefect of the Congregation for the Doctrine of the Faith asked the following: "Who still talks today about the divine sacrifice of the Eucharist?"[29] The answer to this question is, actually, that a good number of theologians have taken up this issue in recent years, and Ratzinger acknowledges this. Probably chief among the current writers is Robert Daly, who has employed the work of the late Edward Kilmartin to reconstruct a theology of eucharistic sacrifice and in addition incorporated the very helpful (at least in my opinion) thinking of René Girard.[30] The key to a viable contemporary eucharistic theology is an understanding of sacrifice that makes theological

---

[26] Ratzinger, *God Is Near Us*, 35.

[27] Ibid., 45.

[28] Ibid., 51.

[29] Joseph Ratzinger, "The Theology of the Liturgy,"in Alcuin Reid, ed., *Looking Again at the Question of the Liturgy with Cardinal Ratzinger: Proceedings of the July 2001 Fontgombault Liturgical Conference* (Farnborough: St. Michael's Abbey Press, 2003), 19.

[30] Among his numerous articles see Robert Daly, "Robert Bellarmine and Post-Tridentine Eucharistic Theology," *TS* 61 (2000): 239–60; "Sacrifice Unveiled or Sacrifice Revisited: Trinitarian and Liturgical Perspectives," *TS* 64 (2003): 24–42; "Images of God and the Imitation of God: Problems with Atonement," *TS* 68 (2007): 36–51. Michon Matthiesen, a Ph.D. candidate at Boston College, has currently completed a dissertation rehabilitating Maurice de la Taille's important early-twentieth-century theology of eucharistic sacrifice under my direction.

and liturgical sense.[31] A good deal of what is written about eucharistic sacrifice will depend on the outcome of conversations about the meaning of Christ's atonement and sacrifice on the cross. Much of the complaint about the lack of attention to eucharistic sacrifice in the contemporary reform of the liturgy seems to rely on crude readings of an Anselmian satisfaction theology of the atonement, one in which somehow an injured God is being done justice. Contemporary atonement theology, much of which relies heavily on the work of René Girard and his reading of the cross as ultimately the rejection of human violence, will go a long way toward reviving an intelligible and persuasive theology of eucharistic sacrifice.[32] Ratzinger goes on to state: "A sizeable party of Catholic liturgists seems to have practically arrived at the conclusion that Luther, rather than Trent, was substantially right in the sixteenth century debate; one can detect much the same position in the post-Conciliar discussion on the Eucharist."[33] He has in mind theologians like David Power and Theodore Schnitker, and he goes on to complain that one contemporary problem is that such theology passes easily and quickly from theory to practice. This much is certainly verifiable in the case of the practice of a good number of priests, but Ratzinger's next conclusion seems unwarranted—namely that such a theology of eucharistic sacrifice has led the community to consider itself the subject of the liturgy. Although it is undeniably the case that some liturgical assemblies celebrate as if the community were the sole purpose and object of the celebration, this anomaly cannot be laid at the door of contemporary theologians who are trying to retrieve a viable theology of the cross and eucharistic sacrifice. The heart of the question, as Ratzinger rightly recognizes, is a hermeneutical issue. How does the theologian deal with Scripture and the magisterium? What is the correct balance between parroting the language of Scripture, magisterium, and tradition, and treating it in cavalier fashion? He describes the issue powerfully, but somewhat one-sidedly:

[31] See my attempt to deal with this question in "Lo, the Full Final Sacrifice: On the Seriousness of Christian Liturgy," *Antiphon* 7 (2002): 51–56.

[32] I attempt such a retrieval in the article cited in the previous note as well as in the chapter on eucharistic theology in my *Bread of Life, Cup of Salvation: Understanding the Mass* (Lanham, MD: Rowman and Littlefield, 2003), 151–82. On the atonement see, e.g., S. Mark Heim, *Saved from Sacrifice: A Theology of the Cross* (Grand Rapids: Eerdmans, 2006).

[33] Ratzinger, "Theology of the Liturgy," 20. He does not give references to the works of Power or Schnitker.

For the believing theologian, it is clear that it is Scripture itself which must teach him the essential definition of sacrifice, and that will come from a "canonical" reading of the Bible, in which Scripture is read in its unity and its dynamic movement, the different stages of which receive their final meaning from Christ, to Whom this whole movement leads. By this same standard the hermeneutic here proposed is a hermeneutic of faith, founded on faith's internal logic. Ought not the fact be obvious? Without faith, Scripture itself is not Scripture, but rather an ill-assorted ensemble of bits of literature which cannot claim any normative significance today.[34]

Of course, Ratzinger is right: a reading of Scripture not founded on faith and attentive to the church's reading of the Bible through the ages can end up misleading people—and ultimately (at least in time) that will most likely lead to deficient liturgical celebrations. On the other hand, it is precisely the understanding of Christ that is at issue and needs profound theological reflection based *both* on historical-critical methods and on respect for the church's magisterium.[35] Ratzinger then demonstrates his considerable ability as a theologian, employing St. Augustine (arguably his favorite commentator on the tradition) in relating sacrifice to love, which is at its heart. He concludes by citing *The City of God*:

The initiative of God has a name: Jesus Christ, the God who himself became man and gives Himself to us. That is why Augustine could synthesize all that by saying: "Such is the sacrifice of Christians: the multitude is one single body in Christ. The Church celebrates this mystery by the sacrifice of the Altar, well known to believers, because in it, it is shown to her that in the things which she offers, it is she herself who is offered." Anyone who has understood this will no longer be of the opinion that to speak of the sacrifice of the Mass is at least highly ambiguous, and even an appalling horror. On the contrary, if we do not remember this, we lose sight of the grandeur of that which God gives us in the Eucharist.[36]

---

[34] Ibid., 22.

[35] The importance of this methodological question could well explain the close scrutiny christology has received from the Congregation for the Doctrine of the Faith in recent years, e.g., in the cases of Jacques Dupuis, Roger Haight, Jon Sobrino, and Peter Phan.

[36] Ratzinger, "Theology of the Liturgy," 26–27; the reference to Augustine is *City of God* X:5.

Ratzinger does not take up the relation between the role of the ordained minister and the eucharistic sacrifice in the context of his paper to the Fontgombault Conference, but he does deal with it at some length in *God Is Near Us*. There he insists that the role of the priest in the sacrifice of the Eucharist is the role of one who does not represent himself but rather is chosen to represent Christ on behalf of the entire church. Thus he stresses the gift character of the Eucharist, whose reality is not owed to the organizing capability of the church. No doubt he has the question of the ordination of women in mind here. One can speculate that one of the reasons why Ratzinger opposes ordaining women, in fact thinks it utterly impossible, is that it would make it seem as if the church can take ordination into its own hands—at will. Intercommunion is similarly an issue that must be understood within the category of divine gift: intercommunion can only be the result of the gift of union, a reality that has not yet been given to the church.[37]

Of course, in addition to dealing with eucharistic sacrifice Ratzinger must also deal with Catholic faith in the real presence of Christ in the Eucharist. He begins his consideration of real presence by reflecting on John 6—Jesus' "bread of life" discourse. He connects this reflection with St. Thomas Aquinas' homily on the Feast of Corpus Christi, a homily that makes reference to a classic text: Deuteronomy 4:7 ("For what other great nation has a god so near to it as the LORD our God is whenever we call upon him?" NRSV). Ratzinger's insight into the grumbling of the crowds at Jesus' saying that his flesh is food indeed focuses on the fact that in many ways we prefer a God who is distant to one who is near.[38] His treatment of this passage is illustrative, I think, of a problem with his use of Scripture. Almost offhandedly he remarks that Jesus did not respond to the grumbling of the people by saying "I was talking symbolically. I wasn't really trying to say that my flesh is actually food."[39] The device does work rhetorically and makes a certain point, but at the same time one wonders if he is willing to consider only a rather matter-of-fact reading of the biblical narrative. There is nothing here about how the evangelist constructs a Johannine discourse like "The Bread of Life." It is as if Ratzinger, in accepting the canonical Scriptures, wants to say something like "the church has

[37] Ratzinger, *God Is Near Us*, 51–52.
[38] Ibid., 75.
[39] Ibid., 77.

accepted this as revealed truth; all that historical-critical or literary-critical business is beside the point, if not positively harmful."

He proceeds to pose and respond to three key modern questions with regard to real presence:

1. Does the Bible really speak of it?

2. How can the same body communicate itself in so many different times and places?

3. Does modern science make it impossible to believe the church's doctrine on substance?

He answers the first question with the direct (and somewhat literalistic) biblical exegesis we have just noted. In Augustinian fashion he insists that Christ invites us to be transformed into himself.[40] With regard to the question of a body being in many places at the same time, Ratzinger makes it clear that the problem is mainly with our imagination and our failure to appreciate that this is a risen body. Besides, the realism with which Catholic faith is concerned is not the self-giving of a body but of the entire person. He puts it this way: "That which is given us here is not a piece of a body, not a thing, but him, the Resurrected One himself, the person who shares himself with us in his love which runs right through the cross. This means that receiving communion is always a personal act."[41]

Ratzinger thinks that the recovery of the corporate and communal (one could say horizontal) dimension of holy communion over the past decades has been important, but that it has also involved running the risk of forgetting the dimension of personal and individual encounter with the Lord, an encounter that requires a certain reverential silence.[42] Although he does not follow this line of thought, it seems to me that such a desire for reverential preparation for holy communion might be a good argument for placing the greeting and exchange of peace between the prayer of the faithful and the presentation of the gifts.[43]

---

[40] Ibid., 78.

[41] Ibid., 81. My translation. See Ratzinger, *Spirit of the Liturgy*, 88.

[42] Ratzinger, *God Is Near Us*, 83.

[43] As we shall see, he picks up this line of thought in the post-synodal exhortation, *Sacramentum Caritatis*.

So Cardinal Ratzinger finds that the realism with which the Catholic tradition has approached the presence of Christ in the Eucharist is well founded scripturally. Similarly, he finds no real problem with the church's thinking about substance. Ratzinger skillfully presents the Catholic teaching on transubstantiation as a middle path between a kind of crude realism on the one hand and a symbolism that cannot accept the reality of Christ's presence on the other. "Substance" in the technical language of theology refers not to a *thing* but to the *underlying reality*—in this case, of personal self-donation. Ratzinger here insists on three aspects of traditional Catholic teaching: the transformation is a real one, it is objective, and it is a permanent gift of the Lord—that is to say, the presence is not for communion at the present Mass alone, but remains.[44]

This leads us to a last aspect of Joseph Ratzinger's thought on the Eucharist that has proved timely: eucharistic adoration. First we need to note that he rejects what could be called the "genetic fallacy" that only what is original is best. He freely admits that there were no tabernacles in the church of the first millennium.[45] He is close to Gamber and others we have studied in his constant criticism of the antiquarianism of the liturgical establishment—the notion that it was all downhill in the second millennium. On the contrary, he has a principle of development that insists that Christian teaching can grow more profound on the basis of experience, reflection, and conflict. In another context he claims: "The greatness and beauty of the Church consists in the fact that it grows, it matures, it enters more profoundly into the mystery."[46]

Ratzinger is willing to admit that the eschatological dynamism and a certain corporate understanding of the Body of Christ—in line with the history outlined by Henri de Lubac in his *Corpus Mysticum*—were lost in the course of the Middle Ages, but he also insists that the gains in terms of appreciating the Eucharist were greater than the losses.[47] He rejects any serious conflict between eating the eucharistic species and contemplating them. Because the Catholic tradition has always

[44] Ibid., 86–90.

[45] Ratzinger, *Spirit of the Liturgy*, 85–86; see also his "Assessments and Future Prospects," the concluding reflection given at the end of the Fontgombault Conference in Alcuin Reid, ed., *Looking Again*, 147.

[46] Ratzinger, *God Is Near Us*, 70.

[47] Ratzinger, *Spirit of the Liturgy*, 87.

maintained that the presence of the Lord remains in the consecrated gifts, it has surrounded them with a certain reverential fear.[48] Since it is the whole, living Christ whom we receive in communion, he is worthy of adoration and therefore of adoration outside of the eucharistic celebration as well as within it. Thus Ratzinger wants to broaden the notion of "receiving" the Lord to include eucharistic adoration of the reserved sacrament. Churches that do not have tabernacles near the altar, accompanied by a perpetually burning light, run the risk of becoming museums, in his view. And so for him adoration signifies a certain prolongation of the eucharistic celebration in the space where the word is heard and the sacrifice offered. Thus he also stresses the corporeal dimension of the liturgy as well as its gift character. In a homily included in *God Is Near Us* and commenting on John Paul II's Holy Thursday letter of 1980 (*Dominicae Cenae*), Ratzinger goes so far as to suggest that while the Mass represents the encounter of the particular and the universal priesthood, eucharistic adoration reveals their "reciprocal compenetration."[49] I doubt that those who argue for change in the church's practice of ordination will find this idea comforting.

ASPECTS OF THE LITURGY

Ratzinger's eucharistic theology has specific consequences for the conduct of the liturgy. He has commented on almost every important aspect of liturgical celebration. Here we shall concentrate on:

1. Response to Traditionalists

2. The Liturgy of the Mass

3. Church Architecture (briefly) and Music

1. *Response to Traditionalist Arguments about the Mass*

We have already seen that Ratzinger has made an effort to present a balanced position on the question of the "for you and for all" (*pro multis*) of the Roman Canon. In *God Is Near Us* he takes up three objections to the Mass of Paul VI that have been made by traditionalists. The first has to do with the concept of "offering"; i.e., by changing the offertory rite of the Mass of the Roman Rite the reform has destroyed

---

[48] Ratzinger, *God Is Near Us*, 91.
[49] Ibid., 97.

its sacrificial character. Ratzinger responds by saying that the correct translation of *offerre* in Latin is not "to sacrifice" but rather "to bring" or "to present." He points to the fact that in the first millennium there were no offertory prayers of the type that were found in the later medieval Mass. In any case the true locus of sacrifice in the Mass is the word spoken in the eucharistic prayer.[50]

A second objection rejects receiving communion standing instead of kneeling and in the hand rather than on the tongue. Here Ratzinger first asks that priests exercise tolerance of both attitudes toward receiving communion. He proceeds to acknowledge that in the course of the first nine Christian centuries communion was received in the hand by people standing. It is impossible, he says, that the church received communion unworthily for nine hundred years.[51] He then proceeds to reflect on Cyril of Jerusalem's beautiful fourth-century description of receiving communion in the hand.

A third objection has been raised to the use of vernacular languages as opposed to Latin. Here Ratzinger points out that the Roman Church itself changed its liturgical language from Greek to Latin in the course of the third century when the language of the people changed. The word of God and the words of prayer need to be understood by people. This, for Ratzinger, justifies the use of the vernacular. At the same time he takes pains to insist that translations not be banal or pedestrian and that there is still a place for Latin in the liturgy. He makes the very valid point that the language of prayer transcends our normal rationality.[52]

2. The Liturgy of the Mass

One of the images Cardinal Ratzinger uses for the liturgical reform in general is that of a fresco that has been recently cleaned but is suffering from the damage wrought by air pollution.[53] The pollution stands for the anti-Christian elements in contemporary culture that threaten the church at its core. It is as if, mesmerized by the liturgical renewal, we have been lulled into a kind of ignorance or blindness to the insidious elements in the modern worldview.

[50] Ibid., 67.
[51] Ibid., 70.
[52] Ibid., 72–73.
[53] Ratzinger, *The Spirit of the Liturgy*, 8–9.

It is very interesting that Ratzinger criticizes attempts to return to a simple meal structure for the Eucharist on the basis of his reading of the Last Supper.[54] In his interpretation the Last Supper is not the first Eucharist, which could only be realized after the death and resurrection of the Lord.[55] What is important for Ratzinger is the dogmatic content of this meal, not its structure. In other words, the meal sacramentalizes Jesus' sacrifice by means of a *eucharistia*, the thanksgiving-sacrifice of the lips. Thus the early church needed to develop a liturgy on the basis of this content, not as an imitation of the Last Supper itself, which if it were a Passover meal could only be repeated once a year. He is certainly onto something here. One would have to say that the liturgy, if it represents anything, represents the paschal mystery, not the Last Supper.[56] Such an approach to the church's need to create a liturgy might lead Ratzinger in directions he does not want to go. It seems to me that Ratzinger's shock at liturgical abuses, not to mention his gloomy view of modern culture, prevents him from being able to appreciate this freedom in Christianity's development—at least as a principle for cultural adaption today. In any case, the need for creative adaptation in the early church provides Ratzinger with an avenue for one of his favorite criticisms of progressive liturgists—their "narrow view of Christian beginnings" that divorces the development of the church from Jesus.[57]

As we noted at the beginning of this section, Ratzinger has no desire to return simply to the pre–Vatican II liturgy. He certainly appreciates the Liturgy of the Word in the language of the people and is critical of

[54] Ratzinger, *Feast of Faith*, 66–67.

[55] Ibid., 40–44. In a postscript to this chapter Ratzinger commends the excellent work of Hartmut Gese, "The Origin of the Last Supper" (*Essays on Biblical Theology*, trans. Keith Crim [Minneapolis: Augsburg Press, 1981]) on the question of the thanksgiving sacrifice—*tōdah*—and its connection to the meal. It seems to me he is on target when he writes: "Structurally speaking, the whole of Christology, indeed the whole of eucharistic Christology, is present in the *tōdah* spirituality of the Old Testament." See my "Lo, the Full Final Sacrifice" (n. 31 above).

[56] In his address at Fontgombault he takes up the rather intemperate attack on the reform launched by the Lefbvreist Society of St. Pius X, *The Problem of the Liturgy Reform* (Kansas City: Angelus Press, 2001), which condemns the post–Vatican II reform for substituting "Paschal Mystery" for the traditional theology of eucharistic sacrifice. In kinder words Ratzinger demonstrates this to be nonsense; see "Theology of the Liturgy," 23–24; see also Duffy, "Benedict XVI and the Liturgy" (n. 12 above), 37.

[57] Ratzinger, *Feast of Faith*, 49.

the "Tridentines" who want to freeze the liturgy of the sixteenth century. At the same time he criticizes the *Missal of Paul VI* (1970) as a creation of professors rather than a liturgy that grew organically out of praying communities.[58] One of the more controversial aspects of Ratzinger's criticism of the post–Vatican II liturgy is his attitude toward proclamation of the eucharistic prayer. He finds the insistence on its being prayed aloud to be a misunderstanding of the notion of participation. In fact, he is critical of the very multiplication of eucharistic prayers because the new prayers have created an insatiable appetite for variety.[59] Clearly Ratzinger would have pursued a different direction for the reform of the liturgy.

3. *Church Architecture and Liturgical Music*

Of all the liturgical questions on which he has written, Cardinal Ratzinger has clearly created the most stir with his attitude toward the orientation of the priest-celebrant at Mass—an issue we shall also deal with in a separate chapter. To understand the stance he has taken, one must appreciate his theory of the development of church architecture. Basically he has accepted the theories put forward by Louis Bouyer in his famous *Liturgy and Architecture*.[60] Bouyer argued a direct link between the architecture of Jewish synagogues and the development of Christian church buildings, with the latter oriented toward the east instead of toward Jerusalem. In place of the ark containing the Torah, Christians set up the cross of Christ. Ratzinger sees in the "orientation" (literally east-facing) of Christian churches an attitude of eschatological expectation. The cross symbolizes the returning Christ, who will rise like the sun.[61] Thus the priest in offering the sacrifice faced east and the altar was placed near the eastern apse of the church building. Ratzinger emphatically insists that in the early church it was never a question of "facing the people" (*versus populum*) or not but rather one of orientation. Besides, it was never a question of the priest facing the other table participants *across* the table, since ancient dining

---

[58] Ibid., 86; see Ratzinger, *Spirit of the Liturgy*, 82.

[59] Ratzinger, *Feast of Faith*, 72–73; see also idem, *Spirit of the Liturgy*, 214–15.

[60] Louis Bouyer, *Liturgy and Architecture* (Notre Dame: University of Notre Dame Press, 1967).

[61] Ratzinger, *Spirit of the Liturgy*, 70. For a fine review of the state of the question see Jaime Lara, "*Versus Populum* Revisited," *Worship* 68 (1994): 210–21, and chapter 5 below.

custom had the most important person at the table sitting at the right hand of what we would call a C (the shape of the ancient Greek *Sigma*). In that sense, even in the understanding of the Eucharist as a meal, all faced in the same direction. Ultimately, with the development of eucharistic theology (and here Ratzinger insists that it is a development, not a decline), the tabernacle on the altar took the place of the cross as the eschatological symbol toward which prayer is directed.[62] Hence the importance for Ratzinger and the many who agree with him of the tabernacle centered in the sanctuary of a church.

For Ratzinger the position of the altar is "at the center of the postconciliar debate."[63] Having the priest face the people has caused a fundamental shift, essentially a novelty, in the meaning of the liturgy which now looks like a communal meal.[64] As we have seen above, he rejects this as a one-sided interpretation that fails to take the sacrifice aspect of the liturgy into account. To make matters worse, the liturgy now becomes primarily a matter of roles, since the priest's role has been so greatly accentuated and others need to have their functions too. The problem with all this for Ratzinger is that the liturgy devolves into a "self-enclosed circle" rather than worship directed toward God.[65] There is some accuracy to his criticism of a liturgy that has focused more and more on the role—and personality—of the priest. The great irony here is that in the pre–Vatican II liturgy the priest was *not* all that important (except when he sang badly).[66] The "success" of the liturgy had little to do with his personality, except for the fact that people might prefer the piety and devotion of one priest over another. Now, I would agree, too much can depend on the personality of the priest, who must exercise enormous self-discipline in not succumbing to the temptation to put himself forward.

In his reply to Pierre-Marie Gy, Ratzinger has recently reiterated that he does not necessarily want a return to the eastward position. He regards his own stance as rather nuanced. It involves three factors:

---

[62] Ratzinger, *Spirit of the Liturgy*, 85–91.

[63] Ibid., 71; see also Ratzinger, *New Song*, 78–93.

[64] Ratzinger, *Spirit of the Liturgy*, 77.

[65] Ibid., 80.

[66] A point made well by Ralph Kiefer in his commentary on the second edition of the General Instruction of the Roman Missal, *To Give Thanks and Praise* (Washington, DC: Pastoral Press, 1980), 98–99.

1. He thinks there should be a separate space for the proclamation of the Word.

2. In large churches where the apse altar is a great distance from the people, an altar should be constructed closer to them.

3. Altars need not be "turned around" again. Instead, the "liturgical East" can be symbolized by a cross in the center of the altar toward which both priest and people face.

He puts the last point this way: "To be able to fix our gaze, all of us together, on him who is the Creator, the one who receives us into the cosmic liturgy, and who shows us also the path of history—this is what would enable us to recover the dimension of deep unity that exists between the priest and the faithful within their common priesthood."[67] Elsewhere he had already regarded moving the cross on the altar to one side an absurd phenomenon in the liturgical reform.[68] I think it is fair to say, however, that he wishes that the altars had never been "turned around."

Liturgical music is obviously another subject of great importance in the post–Vatican II liturgical renewal, and Ratzinger has written a good deal about it. It should be noted that his older brother Georg, also a priest, was very active in the promotion of Gregorian chant. Each of Ratzinger's major books on the liturgy has a significant chapter or chapters on music.[69] His basic principles are laid out in his 1981 book, *The Feast of Faith*, in a chapter entitled "On the Theological Basis of Church Music." There he speaks frankly of the tension evident in the Vatican II Liturgy Constitution's section on liturgical music—a tension that, he observes, is usually resolved in favor of a banal kind of rationalism:

> The years which followed [the council] witnessed the increasingly grim impoverishment which follows when beauty for its own sake is banished from the Church and all is subordinated to the principle of "utility." One shudders at the lackluster face of the postconciliar liturgy as it has become, or one is bored with its banality and its lack of artistic standards.[70]

[67] Ratzinger, "Reply to Pierre-Marie Gy," 497–98, at 498.
[68] Ratzinger, *Spirit of the Liturgy*, 84.
[69] Ratzinger, *Feast of Faith*, 97–126; *New Song*, 94–146; *Spirit of the Liturgy*, 136–56.
[70] Ratzinger, *Feast of Faith*, 100.

Ratzinger goes on to speak of the struggle about the nature of church music within a number of significant theologians and pastors: Jerome, Augustine, Gregory the Great, and Thomas Aquinas. He notes the fact that Christian music took its inheritance more from the synagogue than from the Temple in the process of spiritualization that was characteristic of both Christianity and Rabbinic Judaism—hence the preference for the human voice over musical instruments. At the same time he insists on the aesthetic quality of liturgy that worships God by glorifying him: "'Glorification' is the central reason why Christian liturgy must be cosmic liturgy, why it must as it were orchestrate the mystery of Christ with all the voices of creation."[71]

He refers here to the work of his friend and *Communio* collaborator, Hans Urs von Balthasar, who has helped to make aesthetics a central category in contemporary theology. Because of these cosmic considerations Ratzinger insists that liturgical music must be more than merely functional. The category of "spiritualization," however, means that Christian worship must transform and purify music and is therefore always "critical of all ethnic music."[72] Clearly fearful of the seductive qualities of so-called pagan music, he associates it in particular with Africa. We shall return to his criticism of "rock" music, but note that a number of jazz composers (Duke Ellington, Dave Brubeck, Lalo Schifrin, Mary Lou Williams) have composed liturgical music that is both reverent and very contemporary. Jazz has African and Afro-Caribbean roots. It would be dreadfully narrow-minded to exclude it from Catholic liturgy. This is not to argue that any music at all is serviceable for Christian liturgy. All forms of music need to be properly contextualized by the liturgy. I tarry on this subject because we need to recognize that there is something we might well call a Eurocentric bias in Cardinal Ratzinger's thought. Much of what he has to say is very much tied up with a defense of traditional European civilization.[73]

Ratzinger also points out the necessity for a certain humility in church music—one that seeks edification more than applause.[74] He would, no doubt, be horrified by the many North American liturgical assemblies that burst into applause at the end of every liturgy! He

---

[71] Ibid., 115.

[72] Ibid., 118.

[73] Ibid., 125–26. We shall take up the question of the nature of chant and the texts of the traditional chants as they related to the liturgical cycle in a separate chapter.

[74] Ibid., 120.

concludes his reflections with a series of principles. Among these, perhaps most significant is his insistence that active participation (*actuosa participatio*) must not be limited to "doing" things but can also mean listening. To limit participation to the active is to give in to a superficial rationalism.[75]

Ratzinger continues his critique of "rock" and "pop" music in his 1995 *New Song for the Lord*. There he decries the stupor, ecstasy, and delirium characteristic of so much "Dionysian" contemporary music.[76] He makes the same kind of charge in his *Spirit of the Liturgy* where he claims that rock music is "the expression of elemental passions. . . . People are, so to speak, released from themselves by the experience of being part of a crowd and by the emotional shock of rhythm, noise, and special lighting effects . . . in the ecstasy of having all their defenses torn down, the participants sink, as it were, beneath the elemental force of the universe."[77] He would clearly be horrified by so-called Rave Masses that ape the drug-induced euphoria of all-night rock experiences. Frankly, it is difficult to imagine that rock music can be used with any credibility in Catholic liturgy—which is not to say that liturgical music cannot be upbeat. And perhaps it is my imagination that is at fault. I am sure there was a point in the late sixteenth and early seventeenth centuries when using stringed instruments for a Mass was equally unimaginable.

There are many positive aspects to Ratzinger's approach to liturgical music. He quotes with approval the lovely saying of St. Augustine: *Cantare amantis est* ("singing belongs to lovers"). Love is the source of the church's song.[78] There is a kind of restraint in liturgical music because it must proclaim the word of God. He cites Canon 59 of the fourth-century Council of Laodicea, which forbade the composition of nonbiblical song for use in church and then goes on to praise the purely vocal music of the Byzantine Church.[79] He knows, no doubt, that much of the music of the Byzantine tradition is nonbiblical hymnody—so much so that it tends to dwarf scriptural texts in terms of quantity.

---

[75] Ibid., 120–24.

[76] Ratzinger, *New Song*, 123. With this in mind I could only wonder what Pope Benedict XVI, the same man who made such criticisms as Joseph Ratzinger, was thinking when liturgical music that sounded very much like "Christian rock" was being sung at the Cologne World Youth Day.

[77] Ratzinger, *Spirit of the Liturgy*, 148.

[78] Ibid., 142.

[79] Ibid., 144–45.

Ratzinger sees the present moment as one of the great crises in the history of liturgical music. He does agree that a certain "cultural universalization" is needed and that modern classical music has retreated into a kind of ghetto. Ultimately he appeals for a kind of sobriety in liturgical music.[80] It is possible to agree with what he is driving at—liturgy should not collapse into a series of high emotional moments. At the same time there can be a kind of lusty enthusiasm in the singing of some of the great hymns of German and Welsh traditions, to give only two examples.

Finally, a word should be said about choirs and the use of Latin chants. Against a kind of "primitive actionism and prosaic pedagogical rationalism," Ratzinger considers the usefulness of choirs as beyond debate.[81] He also rejects a kind of "fanaticism about vernacular" that disallows the singing of music in Latin—after all, even the old Latin Mass contained texts in other languages, e.g., *Kyrie eleison*, *Hosanna*, *Alleluia*. He goes on to argue for the possibility (albeit not the necessity) of the choral singing of the *Sanctus* as opposed to the generally accepted liturgical principle that acclamations ought to be sung by the entire assembly. His argument is that since we are invited to join the praise of the heavenly choirs of angels, a choir is useful in transcending our own poor abilities and uniting us to the cosmos.[82] He also argues for the possibility (again, not the necessity) of splitting the *Sanctus* and *Benedictus*—that is, singing the latter after the institution narrative. Of course, this presupposes the silent recitation of the eucharistic prayer, an argument which, as we have seen, he has made elsewhere as well. His reasoning? "The *Sanctus* is ordered to the eternal glory of God; in contrast the *Benedictus* refers to the advent of the incarnate God in our midst. . . . For this reason the *Benedictus* is meaningful both as an approach to the consecration and as an acclamation to the Lord who has become present in the eucharistic species."[83]

If one grants the initial premise that silent recitation of the Canon is a good idea, it seems to me that the rest of Ratzinger's argument follows. After all, he says, Jungmann noted that the choral *Sanctus*/*Benedictus* extended the praise and thanksgiving aspect of the Eucharist. He also

[80] Ibid., 147–50.
[81] Ratzinger, *New Song*, 139. I might note here in passing that Ratzinger's own prose style and the technique of his translators are both refreshing and lively.
[82] Ibid., 141–42.
[83] Ibid., 144.

argues against limiting the singing of the *Agnus Dei* to the fraction rite, claiming that "only a completely fossilized archaism" would demand such a limitation.[84]

Cardinal Ratzinger's views on church architecture and liturgical music show how very far he is from the consensus about the nature of active participation that most liturgical scholars would support. This is not to say simply that he is wrong and they ("we" if I correctly place myself within this consensus) are right, but only to note that he has a very different vision of postconciliar liturgy.

POPE BENEDICT XVI AND *SACRAMENTUM CARITATIS*

Since the prolific critic of the liturgical reform, Joseph Ratzinger, has now become Pope Benedict XVI, it may be useful to examine his post-synodal exhortation, *Sacramentum Caritatis*, for its links to his previous writings. To begin with, post-synodal apostolic exhortations are by their nature somewhat problematic. The first such document to follow a synod was written by Paul VI in 1975 after the bishops' synod on evangelization.[85] Pope John Paul II continued this practice during his long pontificate, and now Benedict XVI has done the same. The nature of the document is problematic for two reasons. First, the synod does not get to produce its own summary of its results. Second, since the synod (even when it deals with a specific theme like the Eucharist) treats so many aspects of its theme that the document ends up as something of a "grab bag." This is certainly the case with *Sacramentum Caritatis*, which covers almost every conceivable theme with regard to the Eucharist in ninety-seven paragraphs.[86]

On the other hand, since this is the first time Benedict has dealt at any length with the subject of liturgy since becoming pope, the document is revelatory. One would almost have to wonder if the same man authored the criticisms of the reform that we have surveyed and also this papal exhortation. Then again, as a fine theologian Benedict understands well the difference between being a theologian (even as Prefect of the Congregation for the Doctrine of the Faith) and writing

---

[84] Ibid., 145.

[85] Pope Paul VI, *Evangelii Nuntiandi*, December 8, 1975, http://www.vatican.va/holy_father/paul_vi/apost_exhortations/documents/hf_p-vi_exh_19751208_evangelii-nuntiandi_en.html.

[86] For a sympathetic view see Andrew Cameron-Mowat, "Sacramentum Caritatis," *Pastoral Review* 3 (2006): 45–49, http://acameronmowatsj.com/Articles/Sacramentum%20Caritatis.pdf.

as Supreme Pontiff. Remember, this is the same person who, as Joseph Ratzinger, wrote the following:

> What happened after the Council was something else entirely: in the place of liturgy as the fruit of organic development came fabricated liturgy. . . . [the liturgical reform is] not a revival but a devastation . . . a liturgical devastation of frightful proportions.[87]
>
> I am convinced that the crisis in the Church that we are experiencing is to a large extent due to the disintegration of the liturgy . . . when the community of faith, the worldwide unity of the Church and her history, and the mystery of the living Christ are no longer visible in the liturgy, where else, then, is the Church to become visible in her spiritual essence? Then the community is celebrating only itself, an activity that is utterly fruitless.[88]

Here is what the Pope has to say about the liturgical reform in the 2006 post-synodal exhortation:

> If we consider the bimillenary history of God's Church, guided by the wisdom of the Holy Spirit, we can gratefully admire the orderly development of the ritual forms in which we commemorate the event of our salvation. From the varied forms of the early centuries, still resplendent in the rites of the Ancient Churches of the East, up to the spread of the Roman rite; from the clear indications of the Council of Trent and the Missal of Pius V to the liturgical renewal called for by the Second Vatican Council: in every age of the Church's history the Eucharistic celebration, as the source and summit of her life and mission, shines forth in the liturgical rite in all its richness and variety. . . . The difficulties and even the occasional abuses which were noted, it was affirmed, cannot overshadow the benefits and the validity of the liturgical renewal, whose riches are yet to be fully explored.[89]

In another place the Pope commends the catechetical work of those who make known "the current liturgical texts and norms, making available the great riches found in the *General Instruction of the Roman*

---

[87] From Joseph Ratzinger, Preface to the French edition of Klaus Gamber, *The Reform of the Reform*, cited in Roberto de Mattei, "Reflections on the Liturgical Reform," in Alcuin Reid, ed., *Looking Again*, 135, 141.

[88] Joseph Ratzinger, *Milestones: Memoirs 1927–1997* (San Francisco: Ignatius Press, 1987), 148–49.

[89] Pope Benedict XVI, *Post-Synodal Apostolic Exhortation Sacramentum Caritatis—on the Eucharist as the Source and Summit of the Church's Life and Mission*, 3.

Missal and the *Order of Readings for Mass*." In addition, he calls the new eucharistic prayers of the current Missal "noteworthy for their inexhaustible theological and spiritual richness."[90] He even makes an interesting suggestion about moving the greeting of peace to the juncture of the prayer of the faithful and the presentation of the gifts.[91] The suggestion is all the more remarkable since the peace has been placed before the reception of Holy Communion from the very earliest sources of the Roman Rite.[92]

On the other hand, the exhortation is consistent with a number of particular concerns that Pope Benedict had voiced as Joseph Ratzinger:

- avoiding putting the priest at the center of the celebration (23)

- care with regard to liturgical music and preference for Gregorian Chant (42, 62)

- the training of seminarians and priests to celebrate (the *Novus Ordo*) in Latin (62)

- the importance of adoration of the Blessed Sacrament (66ff.)

- the requirement that the placement of the tabernacle be readily visible to all who enter a church (69)

- receiving the Eucharistic liturgy as a gift and as the *actio Dei* whose "basic structure is not something within our power to change, nor can it be held hostage by the latest trends" (37).

One other issue that has serious theological consequences needs to be looked at: namely, the question of full, active, and conscious participation (*actuosa participatio*). Here the Pope is consistent with his earlier writing on the subject.[93] There is no antithesis between the proper art of celebration (*ars celebrandi*) and active participation (38). He further insists that participation does not mean "merely" external action but more profoundly refers to interior spiritual dispositions and "greater awareness of the mystery being celebrated and its relationship to daily life."[94]

---

[90] Ibid., 40, 48.

[91] Ibid., 49, n. 150.

[92] See Josef Jungmann, *Missarum Sollemnia: The Mass of the Roman Rite* (New York: Benziger Brothers, 1955), 2:321–32.

[93] E.g., Ratzinger, *The Spirit of the Liturgy*, 171–77.

[94] *Sacramentum Caritatis*, 52.

CONCLUSION

It has not been possible to cover every aspect of Joseph Ratzinger/ Pope Benedict XVI's contribution to the contemporary debate about the liturgy. For example, we have not dealt with his attitudes toward inclusive language in the liturgy—a subject on which he has had significant influence.[95] At any rate, this survey of a theologian who is a good example of the theological approach to criticizing the reform calls for some concluding observations.

1. Ratzinger's is an enormously rich theology characterized by an unswerving devotion to christocentricity as well as a cosmic and eschatological vision that transcends much of the subjectivism and individualism of modern culture.

2. At the same time he seems haunted by the Enlightenment and its privileging of historical-critical analysis. He makes a good deal of use of historical and exegetical writing but is very selective in his choice. As Gy points out in his review, Ratzinger's reliance on the tendentious work of Louis Bouyer does not show much historical sophistication.[96] The role that historical criticism plays in theology is, of course, one of the most contentious issues between supporters of the reform and the reform's critics.

3. Like Pope John Paul II, whom he served so well, Ratzinger has a very dour view of contemporary Western culture. There is a kind of "finger-wagging" tone to his writing and a somewhat romantic view of the liturgical glories of the past. Anyone familiar with his work will easily see the similarities (if not the influence) of his thought in John Paul II's encyclical on the Eucharist (*Ecclesia de Eucharistia*).[97]

4. At the same time, Joseph Ratzinger has raised important questions about the nature of active participation in the liturgy. He has thus demonstrated that it is possible to do "all the right things" in liturgy and not have its spirit at all. No liturgical/sacramental theology worth its salt can afford to forget that.

To this point we have surveyed three approaches taken by critics of the reform. One other remains: the critique from the point of view of sociology and anthropology, a critique that aims at the very principles on which *Sacrosanctum Concilium* was based.

---

[95] See the treatment in Allen, *Cardinal Ratzinger*, 192–98.
[96] Gy, "Esprit de la Liturgie," 428–29.
[97] "On the Eucharist in its Relationship to the Church," 17 April 2003.

Chapter Four

Liturgy as Ritual:
The Critique from Sociology and Anthropology

Another important avenue for the critique of the post–Vatican II reform of the liturgy has come from those who claim that on the whole it was sociologically and anthropologically naïve. In fact, naïveté is probably the most apt characterization of the reform from the point of view of the following authors. In one way or another all of them claim that the reformers were infatuated with accommodation to the modern just as it was losing its potency and giving way to postmodernity.

Among the critics from the social sciences, Victor Turner stands out as a highly respected social anthropologist, heavily used by liturgical scholars. In the mid-twentieth century Turner popularized the earlier "Rites of Passage" theory of Arnold van Gennep.[1] According to van Gennep traditional rites of passage take place in three stages: the initiate is separated from normal, everyday activity, e.g., the mother's hearth (separation); the initiate undergoes a period of trial and indoctrination, often sharing elements that make for solidarity (*communitas*), such as nudity or fasting or sleeplessness (liminality); finally, the initiate is rejoined to the group in a new status (re-aggregation). The liminal period creates a kind of anti-structure that is very different from the normal ways a society works. Clearly Turner's work has been very valuable to liturgical scholars who investigate rites such as marriage or the newly revived Rite of Christian Initiation of Adults.[2]

---

[1] Among his many works see *The Ritual Process: Structure and Anti-Structure* (Chicago: Aldine, 1969); *Dramas, Fields and Metaphors: Symbolic Action in Human Life* (Ithaca: Cornell University Press, 1975).

[2] E.g., Mary Collins, "Ritual Symbols and the Ritual Process: The Work of Victor W. Turner," *Worship* 50 (1976): 336–46.

Less appealing to mainline liturgical scholars was Turner's 1976 *Worship* essay, "Ritual, Tribal and Catholic."[3] There Turner, a Catholic, made clear his dissatisfaction with the recent reform of the liturgy. Here is his thesis:

> The traditional liturgy displayed an essential concern for proper form in the representations of sacral mysteries and the performance of sacred acts. . . . When men and women enter the "liminality," the tract of sacred space-time, which is made available to them by such a traditional liturgy, they cease to be bounded by the secular structures of their own age and confront eternity which is equidistant from all ages.
>
> These comparative considerations have induced me to regard certain features of the recent liturgical changes in Catholic ritual with a wary eye. In many ways depth has been abandoned for breadth, which is to say the spiritual for the material, or the historical for the ultramodern.[4]

Turner proceeds to explain what he means. The reform has surrendered to the spirit of the times, adopting an outdated functionalist (à la Emile Durkheim) approach to anthropology and seeking relevance, even going after fashions and fads. What he finds most lacking in the reformed liturgy is what he calls "flow," a term he borrowed from the social psychologist Mihalyi Cziksentmihalyi.[5] Flow refers to the state one achieves during activities at which one has become an adept, e.g., chess playing or rock climbing. This is a state of total involvement. Turner further relates this idea to the loss of ego and in this sense participation in sacrifice and the creation of *communitas*, his technical term for the solidarity often created by rites.[6] He continues:

> Formerly the flow ran deep; it was communion. Now, too often it is bubbles on the surface, transient communication. And what is being communicated is often relatively trivial information, in sermons, about current events, or may introduce elements from non-Catholic sources, presumably to further ecumenical ends. One advantage of the traditional Latin ritual was that it could be performed by the most diverse groups and individuals, surmounting their divisions of age, sex,

[3] Victor Turner, "Ritual, Tribal and Catholic," *Worship* 50 (1976): 504–26.

[4] Ibid., 523–24.

[5] He cites Mihalyi Cziksentmihalyi, *Beyond Boredom and Anxiety* (San Francisco: Jossey-Bass, 1975). See also idem, *Flow: The Psychology of Optimal Experience* (San Francisco: Harper, 1993) for a more popular exposition of the same ideas.

[6] Turner, "Ritual," 520–21.

ethnicity, culture, economic status or political affiliation. The liturgy stood out as a magnificent objective creation, a vehicle for every sort of Christian interiority. . . .

Now one fears that the tendentious manipulation of particular interest groups, prestigiously and strategically situated in the Church, is liquidating the ritual bonds which held the entire heterogeneous mystical body together in worship.[7]

Notice that Turner singles out "relevant" sermons in his barrage of criticism. And if there is any accuracy to his rhetoric, he unfortunately fails to sustain it with specific examples. Instead he offers the (relatively common in this group) complaint that the reforms appeal more to the cognitive than to the bodily aspect of human beings, a mistake in understanding how rituals work. He also adduces what has been called "the argument from tourism": one could go anywhere in the world and find a familiar Catholic ritual.[8] (This argument I somewhat cynically translate as: all must endure relatively unintelligible worship so that the few who have the resources to travel can feel comfortable.) In addition to offering few if any specifics with regard to the reforms, Catherine Bell has pointed out that Turner tends to de-contextualize and de-historicize ritual in his studies of the Ndembu of Zambia. From his writing, she claims, one would never even imagine that this tribe was living in a country (Northern Rhodesia becoming Zambia) that was experiencing enormous political and social upheaval.[9] In this response to Turner's famous and influential essay Bell also points out that he tends to make broad claims about the reformed Catholic liturgy without supporting them.[10] I would say that the force of Turner's critique lies more with his reputation as an anthropologist and influence among contemporary liturgical scholars than with his arguments.

David Torevell, while not an anthropologist, employs anthropological concepts in his critique of the reform, *Losing the Sacred*.[11] Fundamental to the argument of his work is the conviction that religion cannot thrive without a healthy and strong distinction between the sacred and the profane, a conviction he supports with appeals to

---

[7] Ibid., 525.

[8] Ibid., 512.

[9] Catherine Bell, "Ritual Tensions: Tribal and Catholic," *Studia Liturgica* 32 (2002): 16–17.

[10] Ibid., 22, n.15.

[11] David Torevell, *Losing the Sacred: Ritual, Modernity and Liturgical Reform* (Edinburgh: T&T Clark, 2000).

Emile Durkheim, Rudolf Otto, and Mircea Eliade.[12] He also appeals to Turner's notion of liminality as essential to the functioning of rites.[13] The basic thrust of his work is as follows:

> It is my contention in this book that the unique power and potential of ritualized liturgy to transform individual and collective identities and to reaffirm the values and beliefs on which a religious community is based, was forgotten about or underplayed in debates leading up to and beyond the reforms of the Second Vatican Council.[14]

Here we find the same basic critique we have already seen in Turner—but with a great deal more development. For example, Torevell spends a good amount of time dealing with modernity's flight from embodiment and into rationalism.[15] One of the results is that a liturgical reform that has absorbed (and I think "absorbed" is probably the best word here) the rationalist values of modernity will have an appeal to the middle class but not to working-class people.[16] For him the Enlightenment "turn to the subject" and the individualism so characteristic of modern society are inimical to the development of true liturgical reform.[17] He paints a picture of the premodern world as a society in which stability reigned and there was a great deal of clarity in religious affairs. In particular, priests were clearly agents of sacrifice:

> There was no imposing a new meaning onto liturgy with each perfor-mance (for example, by a group responsible for its preparation). It was simply an annual cycle of priestly-led repetitive acts of salvation, with the most important being a bloody act of sacrificial ritual—the Mass. But crucially, the order and meaning of the world was maintained by such an annual cycle of salvific rites.[18]

---

[12] Ibid., 2.

[13] Ibid., 40–42.

[14] Ibid., 11.

[15] Ibid. This is found in a very interesting chapter on "Modernity and Disembodi-ment" (80–115).

[16] Ibid., 163. Torevell is referring to a study by Anthony Archer, *The Two Catholic Churches: A Study in Oppression* (London: SCM Press, 1986). I do not know of any solid sociological studies along the lines of how the liturgical reform affected different social and economic classes, but they would certainly be enlightening.

[17] See e.g., 16, 117, 136–37. Note that we considered the same critique by Mannion in the introduction.

[18] Ibid, 91.

Now even granting the possibility that calling the Mass a "bloody" sacrifice is a misprint—since, however it is a sacrifice, the Mass is *not* a bloody but rather an *unbloody* representation of and participation in the sacrifice of the cross—Torevell here seems to betray a nostalgia for a simpler time when rites and the world they corresponded to were more stable. The result, I think, is a very unhistorical and ultimately unhelpful approach to liturgical reform. One of the reasons why liturgical reform became desirable was that the liturgy no longer seemed to "fit" into the eighteenth-century world (much less into that of the nineteenth, twentieth, and now the twenty-first centuries). This is not to say that the liturgy need not contain countercultural elements, for indeed Christian faith is always profoundly countercultural. Nor do I discount the importance of liminality, the necessity that liturgical rites be distinct from everyday life. We cannot, however, return to some mythical medieval society in which everyone knew his or (especially) her place; i.e., unless we want to relegate ourselves to becoming sectarian pockets in a wider world.

The role of the priest is emblematic of the problem. In his review of the Vatican II Liturgy Constitution Torevell states that "the priest as ritual expert was no longer acknowledged as being central to Christian worship."[19] Here he is manifesting the all-too-common tendency to treat ordained leadership and lay participation as a zero-sum game, an error the council documents avoid. It is true that *Sacrosanctum Concilium* and the landmark Constitution on the Church (*Lumen Gentium*) do begin a process of relativizing the hierarchical aspects of the church in light of the mission and identity of the whole people of God. And (frankly) in the years after the council there has been a good deal of confusion of roles among liturgical participants as well as in the precise ways that all of the faithful participate actively in the liturgy. This does not discount the ongoing requirement to think through the relationship between priest and people in the liturgy. It is certainly clear that we can no longer speak of the priest as "doing something" in the liturgy independently of the people of God.[20] The solution— theologically, anthropologically, and pastorally—has so far eluded us.

Torevell's position on the nature of ritual is clear:

---

[19] Ibid., 148.

[20] I have attempted to start thinking this through in a number of essays, among them "The Eucharist and Ministerial Leadership," in Judith Dwyer, ed., *Proceedings of the Catholic Theological Society of America* 52 (1997): 63–82; "The Priest as Sacra-

If as I have argued ritual action, as the basis of liturgy, is a highly stylised performance and consists in predictable stylistic repetition to maintain its form, then it follows that the subjective intentions of individual worshippers must always be subordinated to the objective world the liturgy endorses by its form. The distancing of a formalised drama of sacred action, free from any erratic interruptions emerging from the psyche of the worshipper, ensure its stability and power. Liturgical rites are far removed from quotidian occurrences by their location in a place set apart, their limited duration and their stylised action and speech which always follows a predetermined order and arrangement. . . . Contra this model, what emerged during the 1960's was an emphasis on the pastoral nature of liturgy underpinned by a more personalist, anthropocentric and individualistic approach to worship. The secular and theological culture of the time had clearly encouraged this far more rationalist, classificatory and subjective approach to worship. The challenge (never signalled at the time by Church reformers) was to meet the demands of pastoral liturgical sensitivity while preserving the liturgy of the Church as an objective ritual performance whose form, by its very nature, resisted alteration. It was not surprising that such a task proved increasingly difficult to achieve.[21]

I will agree that finding the correct balance between respecting the historical nature of the rites and being sensitive to actual pastoral needs remains elusive, but this is more of a problem of the practical implementation and performance of the reformed rites than it is of their construction.

Romano Guardini, one of the most significant leaders of the twentieth-century liturgical movement, once asked in an article: "Is the Contemporary Person Capable of Liturgy?" If modern people are capable of real liturgical participation, i.e., entering into the symbolic world the liturgy creates and nourishes (or better to speak theologically—that God creates and nourishes in and through the liturgy), then most of the sociological and anthropological critics do not think that modern conditions are ideal for such participation. That is why a sociologist like Kieran Flanagan is critical of the reforms themselves. Flanagan thinks the reforms suffered by coming along too early—too

---

mental Minister," in Donald Dietrich, ed., *Priests for the 21st Century* (New York: Crossroad, 2006): 19–32.

[21] Torevell, *Losing the Sacred*, 145.

soon, that is, for contemporary sociology to provide adequate tools for the liturgists to use.[22] He makes the following scathing indictment:

> What were the cultural assumptions used by liturgists in the past two decades in making alterations to forms of the rite? . . . an exercise in sociology of knowledge is required to investigate the indices used by liturgists that governed their expectations of rite. Many of their ideas were secular and ideological and owed little to either sociology or theology. The marginal position of liturgists within theology, and their clerical place on the edge of society, has often made them poor judges of what will convince in contemporary cultural circumstances. They managed to back modernity as a winning ticket, just at the point when it became converted into postmodernism. They found a solution in modern culture just when it failed in sociology.[23]

We have already noted the charge that liturgists were latecomers to modernity at the beginning of this chapter. But Flanagan's criticism is aimed not just at liturgists but at the Liturgy Constitution itself, which he accuses of having an "obsessive concern" with simplicity. As a result he argues that "the counterculture of the late sixties discovered an interest in romanticism and mystery that many were unable to find in the threadbare rites surrounding Vatican II."[24] Here he echoes a charge made by the historian James Hitchcock, who delights in the contradiction between the Harvey Cox who wrote *The Secular City* in 1965 and the Harvey Cox who wrote an almost diametrically opposed book, *The Feast of Fools*, just a few years later in 1971.[25] For Flanagan, those entrusted with reforming the liturgy were simply not aware enough of the "opacity of the cultural resources used to harness the holy."[26] In many ways the book becomes a plea for distance and objectivity especially on the part of liturgical actors who must ineluctably negotiate the ambiguities of rite. This is a somewhat fancy way of saying that liturgy needs to act as a screen on which a great variety of people can project their particular needs and concerns. Torevell raised

---

[22] Kieran Flanagan, *Sociology and Liturgy: Re-presentations of the Holy* (New York: St. Martin's Press, 1991), 10.

[23] Ibid., 42.

[24] Ibid., 38; cf. 52.

[25] James Hitchcock, *The Recovery of the Sacred* (New York: Seabury Press, 1974), 13; see also 22–23, 47.

[26] Flanagan, *Sociology and Liturgy*, 13.

the same issue in appealing to Roy Rappaport's distinction between the indexical (subjective) and canonical (official) meanings of ritual.[27] I have to agree that the problem with much contemporary liturgical performance (though certainly not necessarily with the structure and content of the reform itself) is with the over-verbalization of the rite (especially by means of commentary) on account of which people are not invited to enter into the liturgy on its own terms.

Perhaps to be self-consciously modern means that one cannot easily participate in a traditional ritual. Flanagan certainly sees difficulties here:

> The link between the sacred and the secular carries qualities of incommensurability. The religious rituals of Christianity have always displayed signs of contradictions to the surrounding cultural landscape. The improbable mysteries they display, the ambiguous and indeterminate qualities of their styles of enactment, all suggest they do not fit easily into the modern mind operating in advanced industrialised societies. The problem of incompatibility has been at the heart of efforts of liberal theologians to make religion consonant with the assumptions of contemporary culture.[28]

Another aspect of the difficulty may lie in the fact that the reforms brought attention to the liturgy itself, while the liturgy needs to point beyond itself. Flanagan wisely comments that

> liturgies operate best when they manage to make their social apparatus invisible and unsignified. When the social apparatus of rite is domesticated into a state of irrelevance, then liturgies achieve their highest degree of relevance, in theological and sociological terms. The limits of the form of the rite are treated in a way that marks them as incomplete and meaningless without reference to the limitless content they embody.[29]

I think he is correct in saying this, and he puts me in mind of the rather sarcastic comments made about liturgical reform (this time in the Church of England) by C. S. Lewis:

---

[27] Torevell, *Losing the Sacred*, 27, referring to Roy Rappaport, *Ecology, Meaning, and Religion* (Richmond, CA: North Atlantic Books, 1979).

[28] Flanagan, *Sociology and Liturgy*, 270.

[29] Ibid., 79.

I think our business as laymen is to take what we are given and make the best of it. And I think we should find this a great deal easier if what we were given was always and everywhere the same. To judge from their practice, very few Anglican clergymen take this view. It looks as if they believed people can be lured to go to church by incessant brightenings, lightenings, lengthenings, abridgements, simplifications, and complications of the service. And it is probably true that a new, keen vicar will usually be able to form within his parish a minority who are in favour of his innovations. The majority, I believe, never are. Those who remain—many give up churchgoing altogether—merely endure. Is this simply because the majority are hide-bound? I think not. They have a good reason for their conservatism. Novelty, simply as such, can have only an entertainment value. And they don't go to church to be entertained. They go to use the service, or, if you prefer, to enact it. Every service is a structure of acts and words through which we receive a sacrament, or repent, or supplicate, or adore. And it enables us to do these things best—if you like, it "works" best—when, through long familiarity, we don't have to think about it. As long as you notice, and have to count the steps, you are not yet dancing but only learning to dance. A good shoe is a shoe you don't notice. Good reading becomes possible when you need not consciously think about eyes, or light, or print, or spelling. The perfect church service would be one we were almost unaware of; our attention would have been on God. But every novelty prevents this. It fixes our attention on the service itself; and thinking about worship is a different thing from worshipping. . . . A still worse thing may happen. Novelty may fix our attention not even on the service but on the celebrant. You know what I mean. Try as one may to exclude it, the question "What on earth is he up to now?" will intrude. It lays one's devotion waste. There is really some excuse for the man who said: "I wish that the charge to Peter was "Feed my sheep"; not "Try experiments on my rats, or even, teach my performing dogs new tricks."[30]

Though certainly cranky, Lewis has a point. Good liturgy does not point to itself but ultimately to the one who is worshiped. There is some usefulness to rules and rubrics, after all. They help people to participate in a common activity and to be fairly sure that the liturgical ministers will not hijack the event for their own purposes.[31] Flanagan

---

[30] C. S. Lewis, *Letters to Malcolm, Chiefly on Prayer* (London: G. Bles, 1964), 4–5.
[31] Flanagan, *Sociology and Liturgy*, 153–55, 180.

concludes, speaking in the context of the more conservative direction liturgical legislation had taken during the papacy of John Paul II:

> It cannot be said that these liturgical reforms have stemmed the tide of secularisation or that they have reversed the decline in Church atten-dance over the past two decades. None of the constituencies the reforms were established to satisfy seem to feel their problems have been resolved; youth still claims to be 'bored', students are alienated, the middle classes remain divided and the working class is indifferent. There is a crisis in liturgy, because its sociological basis in a modern culture has never been properly examined or understood. Second thoughts have not yet cohered into a reconsideration of what has gone wrong. Rites no longer grip, symbols seem thin rather than thick and an unproductive uncertainty mixes with a disillusion at the outcome of the liturgical reforms. Too much got cast away in the decade follow-ing Vatican II.[32]

Now it is possible that Flanagan is correct, but with the exception of his analyses of choir members and altar servers he provides few specific analyses of the liturgical reforms themselves. It seems to me that a good sociological study of the liturgical reforms in the Roman Catholic and Anglican churches requires more thick description and less rhetoric. In any case, he questions the reform with regard to a number of crucial issues: simplicity, intelligibility, community, litur-gical agency, and participation. In each instance he finds the reform wanting—sociologically speaking.[33]

One of the critiques that followed quickly upon the reform was written by the St. Louis historian James Hitchcock. Although he is a historian, Hitchcock's criticism stays mainly in the area of anthropol-ogy—or at least the nature of ritual. Hitchcock seems to be more intent on criticizing the implementation of the reform than the reform itself. One needs to keep in mind the fact that Hitchcock's *The Recovery of the Sacred* was published in 1974 and therefore in the heyday of radical experimentation that followed immediately on the council. Some of his criticism is aimed at the reform itself, both (implicitly) the Liturgy Constitution and the postconciliar implementation by the *Consilium*.

---

[32] Ibid., 324–25.

[33] For a very able summary of Flanagan's rather opaque work, see Aidan Nichols, *Looking at Liturgy: A Critical View of Its Contemporary Form* (San Francisco: Ignatius Press, 1996), 58–67.

He summarizes the difference between the results of Vatican II and the pre–World War II liturgical movement in this way:

> (1) Rather than a desire to change the liturgy in order to show forth the "sacred mysteries" more effectively, it manifested deep suspicion of the mystical character of worship as a distraction from human problems. (2) Rather than emphasizing the timeless and perennially valid forms of the liturgy, it sought to bring it as much as possible into conformity with contemporary culture. (3) From a relationship of fundamental respect and obedience to church authorities, it began to conceive its role increasingly as one of divergence from officially prescribed forms. (4) From seeking forms of worship valid for the whole Church, it came to a preoccupation with liturgies usable only by special groups and an eager acceptance of the notion of "liturgical pluralism."[34]

I would be very surprised if any of the bishops or advisors involved in the implementation of the reform would recognize themselves in Hitchcock's first point. Rather, they were attempting to arrange for the celebration of the sacred mysteries in a way that was accessible to modern culture. One also needs to note that, instead of quoting the documents of the official reform, Hitchcock tends to cite the most liberal commentators, thereby setting up a kind of straw man. He is correct as to the second point. However, it is somewhat odd that a historian should fail to recognize that there was much change and development as well as continuity in liturgical forms. We have certainly seen a certain ahistorical bias among those who criticize the reform from the angle of anthropology and/or sociology. Perhaps it would be helpful to remind ourselves of the sea change that the philosopher-theologian Bernard Lonergan found in contemporary thought—between what he calls the changeless classicist point of view and the modern, which allows for historicity.[35] With regard to the second point, I would repeat that here Hitchcock is certainly not writing of the official reform but rather contending with those who took the

---

[34] Hitchcock, *Recovery of the Sacred*, 14.

[35] Bernard Lonergan, *Method in Theology* (New York: Herder & Herder, 1972), 124: "I must contend that classicism is no more than the mistaken view of conceiving that there is just one human culture. The modern fact is that culture has to be conceived empirically, that there are many cultures, and that new distinctions are legitimate when the reasons for them are explained and the older truths are maintained."

reform to mean that many forms of experimentation were now legitimate. Perhaps the coincidence of the reforms with the cultural instability of the late 1960s gave a good number of people the notion that reforming the liturgy meant that everything was fair game.[36] To be sure, paragraphs 37–40 of the Liturgy Constitution did give the warrant for further adaptation of the liturgy—under conditions that were controlled by the national episcopates. Here it seems that Hitchcock's main problem is not with the reform itself but with its implementation. The final point requires a complex response. If one accepts the point made by Lonergan with regard to classicist versus modern understandings of culture, one begins to realize that something significant happened after World War II that required Europeans (especially) to recognize that other cultures did not exist simply to be colonized but had deep values in their own right. Therefore, just as the Gospel had to be translated in the early centuries into Mediterranean culture and then subsequently in the Middle Ages to Northern European cultures, so now there were legitimate needs to translate the Gospel once more. Theologically this means accepting a certain pluralism. Hand in hand with theology goes the notion that liturgy will also manifest a good number of cultural markers (*lex orandi / lex credendi*). Of course, the most difficult decisions come with differentiating between "immutable elements, divinely instituted, and elements subject to change."[37]

Hitchcock does make some interesting observations with regard to those to whom the reform—or at least more radical elements of experimentation—appealed most. They were most enthusiastic at first and then quickly tired of the reforms—either out of boredom or from the fact that they were not radical enough.[38] This claim is similar to the one made by Flanagan and Archer that the reforms appealed to the educated middle class and not to the working class for the most part. For Hitchcock the liturgical reform, like all such movements, became a full-fledged revolution only after a certain liberalization occurred.[39] This is to say that a reform only really becomes a revolution when it

---

[36] Hitchcock, *Recovery of the Sacred*, 130.

[37] SC §21. I would submit that no one has come up with a really satisfactory formula for this differentiation. I have tried a scheme—Core, Code, Culture—in "The Changing World of Liturgy: The Future of Anglican Worship," *Anglican Theological Review* 82 (2000): 65–81.

[38] Hitchcock, *Recovery of the Sacred*, 28–29, 106.

[39] Ibid., 105, 78.

becomes subject to the "revolution of rising expectations." The models are of course the French Revolution and the Russian Revolution, and these are bound to cause some alarm, especially among the religiously minded. At the same time, how could people have conceived further reform and renewal of the liturgy had their imagination not been enabled by the notion that some change in the church's liturgical life was possible?

With regard to the ritual nature of liturgy itself, Hitchcock proposes the following principle:

> Sacred rituals cannot be reformed substantially without serious disloca-
> tion in the society whose symbols they are.
>
> Those for whom traditional symbols have the deepest meaning tend
> to be those most deeply affected by change. This can take the form,
> either of liturgical conservatism, as the individual perceives that the
> alteration of the symbols will have profound effects on the lives of
> those concerned, or of liturgical radicalism stemming from the same
> perception.[40]

He goes on to argue that the post–Vatican II reform was badly handled for a number of reasons. People were not adequately consulted with regard to their desires and needs; they were insufficiently educated; change came from the top down; reforms were introduced in dribs and drabs; the rationale for the various changes was unclear; there were no stable books (missals/hymnals) to help people through the change.[41] These criticisms are fair enough as far as they go. They would be persuasive in favor of not launching the reform in the first place. However, *change was needed*; it was needed because the pre–Vatican II liturgy was indeed a relic of a bygone age, a relic that had its beauty to be sure, but had been frozen mainly for very unliturgical reasons—the polemical stance that the church found itself taking with regard to the Protestant Reformation and then the Enlightenment and then the cultural changes that came with the Industrial Revolution and the upheavals of the nineteenth and early twentieth centuries. It was the cumulative effect of these cultural changes that made a radical reform of the liturgy desirable.

Hitchcock by no means opposes all of the reforms. He applauds the increased level of participation by the laity as well as the introduction

[40] Ibid., 132.
[41] Ibid., 133.

of the vernacular, not to mention the reformed Holy Week rites and the contextualization of baptism within the celebration of the Eucharist. He realizes (remember, this book was published in 1974) that it will take a good many years before we know how the reform has been received.[42] On the other hand, he laments the loss of Latin in the liturgy: "The association of the Latin language with the timeless, mysterious, and traditional aspects of worship is so profound that no fully adequate translation of it into the vernacular is possible."[43]

Now, "adequate" is a concept that would be difficult to define precisely in this context, but his point is well taken. Even the elegant sixteenth-century translations of prayers from the Roman Missal into English by Thomas Cranmer are subject to the same critique. Perhaps this is why it became more and more obvious that the corpus of prayers that was mined from the pre–Vatican II *Missale Romanum* as well as the rich medieval Sacramentary tradition would not be adequate to the church praying in English—or Spanish—or Tagalog. We shall take up the question of liturgical language and translation further in the next chapter. For now, suffice it to say that Hitchcock is correct about this: translating the liturgy into the vernacular inevitably brought about profound changes in the perception of what it means to worship God as Roman Catholics.

I will tarry on one more anthropological point Hitchcock makes. He is concerned that the reformed liturgy inspired a certain "poverty of gesture."[44] We found the same concern with embodiment characteristic of Torevell's critique. It is also characteristic of the implicit critique of the reform (one often appealed to) by Mary Douglas. Douglas found that the abandonment of the Friday abstinence from meat (not a liturgical reform, to be sure) was devastating to rank-and-file Irish Catholics in England.[45] She was also strongly critical of the anti-ritualism and carelessness about strong boundaries she found typical of contemporary Roman Catholicism.[46] I think it is true that there was a certain period of infatuation with ideas and concepts in the late 1960s and the 1970s. Robert Hovda was surely correct when he wrote (with regard to liturgical vesture):

---

[42] Ibid., 134–35.
[43] Ibid., 136.
[44] Ibid., 140.
[45] Mary Douglas, *Natural Symbols* (New York: Random House, 1970), 37ff.
[46] Ibid., 19, 51.

Like so many sense experiences that rationalist types dismiss as trivial, liturgical vesture has a considerable impact on the feelings of the assembly as a whole as well as on those exercising a particular role of leadership. Anyone who contrary to the most elementary human experience, persists in the stubborn conviction that ideas, points, arguments are the stuff that move human beings, is natively unfit for liturgical leadership, if not for liturgical life.[47]

There has been a neglect of gesture in the past thirty years or so, and the loss or diminution of some gestures led people to find other gestures otiose (e.g., the triple crossing of oneself during the introduction of the gospel, or bowing at the words "By the power of the Holy Spirit . . ." in the Nicene Creed, or genuflecting at those words on Christmas and the Solemnity of the Annunciation). This is not to say that we must simply return to former practices. But there is need for a new "choreography" of the liturgy in the sense of conscious and intentional use of the body.

* * *

We have now completed our survey of the various approaches to the critique of the reform. At this point there remain a number of important issues that are being contested today. The next chapter will deal with them.

[47] Robert Hovda, "The Vesting of Liturgical Ministers," in John Baldovin, ed., *The Amen Corner* (Collegeville, MN: Liturgical Press, 1994), 219.

Chapter Five

Major Issues

The previous chapters of this book have considered the various approaches with which the liturgical reform following the Second Vatican Council (and indeed the conciliar constitution itself) has been criticized. Several important issues are still hotly contested today, and any book of this sort would be deficient if they were not dealt with. Obviously it is not possible to provide an exhaustive treatment for any of the following issues, but I would hope that we can see the value of the reform—as well as the need to respond to its critics—in these areas.

The first issue is that of church architecture, especially the arrangement of the altar and position of the priest-presider, but also the placement of the tabernacle for the reservation of the Blessed Sacrament. The second issue is that of liturgical language: both the principles upon which the vernacular was introduced into the Roman liturgy and the issue of the style of translation to be employed. A third item of concern is liturgical music, in terms of both text and style. Finally, no book that deals with criticisms of the reform can avoid the subject of Pope Benedict XVI's July 2007 *Motu Proprio, Summorum Pontificum* (=SP).

1. LITURGICAL ARCHITECTURE AND THE ORIENTATION OF THE PRIEST

There is no questioning the fact that Roman Catholic churches built after Vatican II tend to look very different from those built before the Council. This is because (1) they are no longer visually focused on a tabernacle set on a shelf just above the middle of the altar and (2) the altar itself is not attached to the church's "east" wall. (I am going to use the liturgical convention by which the "east" signifies the position against the church's wall, whether or not this is truly the geographical east. Thus "the eastward position" of the priest will mean that he is facing in the same direction as the assembly.) Moreover, many pre–Vatican II churches were renovated in such a way that the formerly central tabernacle was moved either to a side altar or to a chapel separate from the body of the church.[1] In renovated churches the main altar was detached from the east wall or a new one was placed closer to the space for the assembly.[2] Often churches were arranged so that the seating for the assembly was either U-shaped or fanned in a semicircle around the sanctuary. In 1978 in the United States, the Bishops' Committee on the Liturgy issued a document, *Environment and Art in Catholic Worship*, that outlined the renewed understanding of church architecture and furnishing.[3] This latter document itself came in for a good deal of criticism on the basis of its perceived liberal and "modernist" bias.[4]

With regard to the placement of the tabernacle the controversial section reads as follows:

> The celebration of the eucharist is the focus of the normal Sunday assembly. As such, the major space of the church is designed for this *action*. Beyond the celebration of the eucharist, the Church has had a most ancient tradition of reserving the eucharistic bread. The purpose of this reservation is to bring communion to the sick and to be the object of private devotion. Most appropriately this reservation should be designated in a space designed for individual devotion. A room or chapel specifically designed and separate from the major space is important so that no confusion can take place between the celebration

---

[1] See *GIRM* 314–15. Paul Cavendish has kindly pointed out that the 1917 Code of Canon Law had required only that the tabernacle be kept on the most decorated altar in the church and that, in theory at least, altars were to be freestanding.

[2] *GIRM* 299, originally in *Inter oecumenici* 91 (1964) = *DOL* 383.

[3] USCC, Bishops' Committee on the Liturgy, *Environment and Art in Catholic Worship (EACW)*, in *The Liturgy Documents*, Vol. 1 (3rd ed. Chicago: Liturgy Training Publications, 1991), 313–40.

[4] See, e.g., Steven Schloeder, *Architecture in Communion* (San Francisco: Ignatius Press, 1998); Michael Rose, *Ugly as Sin: Why They Changed Our Churches and How We Can Change Them Back Again* (Manchester, NH: Sophia Institute Press, 2001). "Modernist" is a term that can have several meanings. It can often refer to the theological movement (represented by, e.g., Alfred Loisy and George Tyrrell) condemned in the early twentieth century by Pope Pius X. Unless otherwise noted I will use it to mean the spare (sometimes severe) twentieth-century artistic style in architecture and music.

of the eucharist and reservation. Active and static aspects of the same reality cannot claim the same human attention at the same time.[5]

It is not very difficult to understand why this section would wave a red flag in front of those who were unhappy with the reform in the first place. Critics denied the assertion that the reserved sacrament represented a static aspect of the Eucharist and appealed to centuries of devotion that associated the reserved sacrament with the altar.[6] Indeed, in the words of Louis Bouyer, the Baroque Catholic church building had become a throne room for the Blessed Sacrament. American liturgists, church architects, and liturgical design consultants countered by citing the *General Instruction of the Roman Missal*. The most recent edition of the *GIRM*, however, weakens the earlier statement:

GIRM 2nd edition 1975	GIRM 3rd edition 2002
§276 Every encouragement should be given to the practice of eucharist reservation in a chapel suited to the faithful's private adoration and prayer. If this is impossible because of the structure of the church, in accordance with the structure of each church and legitimate local customs, the Most Blessed Sacrament should be reserved in a tabernacle in a part of the church that is truly noble, prominent and readily visible, beautifully decorated suitable for prayer . . . and reserved at an altar or elsewhere, in keeping with local custom, and in a part of the church that is worthy and properly adorned.[7]	§315 Consequently, it is preferable that the tabernacle be located, according to the judgment of the diocesan Bishop, a. either in the sanctuary, apart from the altar of celebration, in a form and place more appropriate, not excluding on an old altar no longer used for celebration; b. or even in some chapel suitable for the faithful's private adoration and prayer and organically connected to the church and readily visible to the Christian faithful.

[5] *EACW* §78. Emphasis in original.

[6] See, e.g., James Hitchcock, "Saint Nowhere's," *Adoremus Bulletin* 3/6 (September 1997): http://www.adoremus.org/9-97St.%20Nowhere.html; Denis McNamara, "Can We Keep Our Churches Catholic?" *Adoremus Bulletin* 4/1 (February/March 1998): http://www.adoremus.org/98-03_mcnamara.htm.

[7] In the endnotes the *GIRM* cites the Instruction *Eucharisticum Mysterium* (1967), §§53–54 (= DOL 1281–82) and *Inter oecumenici* 95 (= DOL 387).

One does not need to be very astute or perceptive to see the difference in spirit between these two editions of the *GIRM*. Taking their cue from this change, the American bishops issued a new statement on church building, renovation, and decoration—this time as a document not of the Bishops' Committee on the Liturgy, but of the whole national episcopal conference. The relevant section of *Built of Living Stones* reads:

> 73. The place of reservation should be a space that is dedicated to Christ present in the Eucharist and that is designed so that the attention of one praying there is drawn to the tabernacle that houses the presence of the Lord. . . .
> 74. There is [*sic*] a number of possible spaces suitable for Eucharistic reservation. . . .[8]

The document goes on to explain that the placement of the tabernacle is the responsibility of the diocesan bishop. As a consequence more bishops are insisting on churches built with the tabernacle on a perpendicular axis with the center aisle or at least in a chapel that is readily visible from the main body of the church. What to make of the debate behind these changes? In the first place it should be clear that the reservation of the Blessed Sacrament is an important aspect of any Catholic church building. Obviously the chapel for eucharistic reservation should be easily accessible from the church. However, it does seem that to insist that it be readily *visible* smacks somewhat of the "argument from tourism" I criticized in the previous chapter. How Catholics will work out the place of reservation for the Blessed Sacrament will be closely tied to the disposition of the next question.

Time and again as one reads the critics, one finds something like:

> The reform of the Roman rite of Mass after Vatican II initiated many changes to Catholic worship. Perhaps the most conspicuous shift, along with the introduction of the vernacular, was the adoption of Mass being celebrated "facing the people," which has become an almost universal practice in the Latin Church.[9]

---

[8] USCCB, *Built of Living Stones: Art, Architecture and Worship* (2000), §§73–80: http://www.usccb.org/liturgy/livingstones.shtml#chaptertwoc. The entire section is much longer than the space devoted to reservation of the Blessed Sacrament in *EACW*.

[9] Uwe Michael Lang, "The Direction of Liturgical Prayer," in idem, ed., *Ever Directed Towards the Lord: The Love of God in the Liturgy of the Eucharist Past, Present,*

As we have already noted in dealing with the critiques of Klaus Gamber (chapter 2) and Joseph Ratzinger/Pope Benedict XVI (chapter 3), this is a very live issue in the discussion of contemporary Catholic liturgy. The first document to mention a freestanding altar was the postconciliar instruction *Inter oecumenici* (1964):

> The main altar should preferably be freestanding to permit walking around it and celebration facing the people. Its location in the place of worship should be truly central so that the attention of the whole congregation naturally focuses there.[10]

The latest expression of the same idea can be found in the *General Instruction of the Roman Missal*, as follows: "The altar should be built apart from the wall, in such a way that it is possible to walk around it easily and that Mass can be celebrated at it facing the people, which is desirable whenever possible."[11]

The *General Instruction*'s decided preference for celebration facing the people (*versus populum*) has been questioned recently. Christopher Cullen and Joseph Koterski argue that the Latin should be translated differently and that this sentence really says that it is preferable that the altar be separated from the wall, not that Mass be celebrated facing the people. The argument hangs on the translation of *quod* in the following sentence: "*Altare maius exstruatur a parietate seiunctum, ut facile circumiri et in eo celebratio versus populum peragi possit*, quod expedit ubicumque possibile sit."[12]

It is possible that the *quod* phrase is in apposition to the idea of an altar separate from the wall. But the much more likely translation would have this phrase modify the idea of celebration *versus populum*. Cullen and Koterski have two arguments to counter this. First, this paragraph is located in the section on the disposition of the church building (*GIRM*, chapter 5) not the chapter on celebration of the

---

and Hoped For (Edinburgh: T&T Clark, 2007), 90. This essay is an abbreviated form of his longer argument in *Turning Towards the Lord: Orientation in Liturgical Prayer* (San Francisco: Ignatius Press, 2004), with a foreword by the then Joseph Cardinal Ratzinger. I am grateful to Paul Cavendish for pointing out how frequently *versus populum* celebration was practiced in the 1940s and 1950s.

[10] *Inter oecumenici* 91 (= DOL 383).

[11] *General Instruction of the Roman Missal* (2002), §299.

[12] *GIRM*, §299. Emphasis supplied.

Eucharist (chapter 4). Second, they point to the occasions in the description of the celebration of the Eucharist in which the orientation of the priest is mentioned explicitly. The first is the instruction that the priest, after washing his hands, comes to the center of the altar and "turning towards the people" says the invitation: *Orate, fratres*.[13] The second comes when the priest invites the people to communion. The *GIRM* explicitly says he should face the people. In the next paragraph it directs him to turn toward the altar to receive communion.[14] Cullen and Koterski argue that these references mean that the *GIRM* presumes celebration *ad orientem* and not *versus populum*.[15] These paragraphs could just as well be construed as insisting that the priest is turned toward the people at certain moments, *even when* the Eucharist is celebrated *ad orientem*. Otherwise one would have to wonder why the ambiguity in §299 is let stand.

The question remains: What is the warrant for *versus populum* celebration? It has commonly been accepted that in primitive Christianity the priest faced the assembly while praying. Recent studies, however, have shown that the idea of facing the people in prayer was not nearly as important as the question of orientation: i.e., facing the geographical east. This is made abundantly clear by Marcel Metzger's 1971 review article contesting the findings of Otto Nussbaum in *Der Standort des Liturgen am christlichen Altar vor dem Jahre 1000*, an important study that supported the idea of *versus populum* celebration in the early and medieval church. In a careful examination of the archaeological and literary evidence, Metzger shows that the overwhelming concern of the early church was with geographical orientation.[16] In his own review of the evidence Uwe M. Lang relies heavily on the work of Metzger. In addition—and more recently than Metzger—Jaime Lara has come to a similar conclusion about the importance of orientation. He does show that seeing what the priest was doing was not a major issue one way or the other for the early and medieval church. On the other hand, there is some evidence for *versus populum* celebration when the apse was "occidented" (i.e., when it faced west) as in some

---

[13] *GIRM*, §146.

[14] *GIRM*, §§157–158.

[15] Christopher Cullen and Joseph Koterski, "The New IGMR and Mass *versus populum*," *Homiletic and Pastoral Review* 101 (2001): 51–54.

[16] Marcel Metzger, "La Place des Liturges a l'Autel," *Revue des Sciences Religieuses* 45 (1971): 113–45.

Roman basilicas. There is also artistic evidence for people moving to the "other side" of the altar and looking at the priest during the eucharistic prayer. Lara also finds some examples of experimentation with *versus populum* celebration in sixteenth-century Spain and New Spain.[17]

Some scholars like Louis Bouyer and Klaus Gamber have argued that in cases where the apse faced west and the priest faced the doors of the church over the altar (as at St. Peter's in Rome) the people actually faced east along with him.[18] We clearly do have evidence of the people being commanded to turn east in both the Byzantine and North African traditions.[19] In my opinion it is not really possible to know for sure whether the people actually turned to face east during the eucharistic prayer or whether the command was a spiritual exhortation along the lines of "Lift up your hearts."

Another line of reasoning with regard to the direction of priest and people at prayer has to do with how the prayer is directed—or perhaps better, how people perceive it is directed. Ratzinger argues strongly for an eschatological orientation in prayer, symbolized by the crucifix on the "eastern" wall or the tabernacle, as was the practice after the sixteenth century.[20] At the very least he wishes there to be a cross on the altar (even when the Eucharist is celebrated *versus populum*) that can serve as a focus for prayer. Lang echoes the concern of Cardinal Christoph Schönborn that the liturgy be celebrated *obviam Sponso*—facing the Bridegroom, i.e., Christ.[21] Ratzinger had criticized the Mass facing the people in that it represents a "closed circle," i.e., according to him it conveys a wholly immanent understanding of what is happening, a festive communal banquet rather than the celebration of the

[17] Jaime Lara, "*Versus Populum* Revisited," *Worship* 68 (1994): 210–21.

[18] Louis Bouyer, *Liturgy and Architecture* (Notre Dame: University of Notre Dame Press, 1967), 55–56; Klaus Gamber, *Liturgie und Kirchenbau: Studien der Geschichte des Meßfeier und des Gotteshauses in der Frühzeit*. Studia patristica et liturgica 6 (Regensburg: Pustet, 1976), 23–25. Both are cited in Uwe Michael Lang, "The Direction of Liturgical Prayer," in idem, ed., *Ever Directed Towards the Lord*, 97–98. Lang also cites Cyrille Vogel's opposition to the notion that people would have turned their backs to the altar: "L'orientation vers l'Est du celebrant et des fidèles pendant la celebration eucharistique," *L'Orient Syrien* 9 (1964): 26–29.

[19] Lang, "Direction of Liturgical Prayer," 95.

[20] Ratzinger, *Spirit of the Liturgy*, 81–84.

[21] Lang, "Direction of Liturgical Prayer," 93–94.

eucharistic sacrifice.[22] The person, even the personality, of the priest achieves thereby a dominance it never had hitherto. This is a somewhat telling point since everyone has had experiences of priests who make themselves and their personalities the center of the celebration.

How to sort all this out? First, it seems to me that historical honesty requires us to admit that the idea that the early liturgy was habitually celebrated *versus populum* was mistaken (at least as far as prayer was concerned—only traditionalist extremists want the Word to be proclaimed in the old-fashioned manner). Second, it must also be admitted that the priest can "hijack" the liturgy and that the celebration can seem to be purely horizontal. Third, we need to acknowledge that it has never been forbidden to celebrate the liturgy with the priest facing the liturgical east—even in the *Missal of Paul VI*.

On the other hand, Jaime Lara makes a good point when he claims: "Today with our twentieth-century sensibilities, we are asking different questions of liturgical space than in previous ages."[23] He goes on to ask whether the cosmic symbolism of the east (i.e., the rising Sun) makes much sense in a world flooded with artificial light. Second, we need to ask ourselves why the "turning of the altars" was accepted so quickly and so effortlessly. People clearly have the sense that they are now offering the Eucharist together with the priest. *Versus populum* celebration helps people to understand the "we" of traditional liturgical prayer: i.e., that the priest is voicing the prayer of the entire church and the community that is assembled.

My suspicion is that the sense of the Christian faithful supports the celebration of Mass facing the people and that efforts at "re-orienting" churches will not be successful. In any case, a most sensible statement about the position of the priest is found in a response by the Congregation for Divine Worship and the Discipline of the Sacraments to a question as to whether *versus populum* celebration was made mandatory by the third edition of the *GIRM*. After explaining that the *versus populum* position is not mandatory but is preferable, the document states:

> However, whatever may be the position of the celebrating priest, it is
> clear that the Eucharistic sacrifice is offered to the one and triune
> God and that the principal, eternal, and high priest is Jesus Christ,

[22] Ratzinger, *Spirit of the Liturgy*, 80.
[23] Lara, "*Versus Populum* Revisited," 220.

who acts through the ministry of the priest who visibly presides as his instrument. The liturgical assembly participates in the celebration in virtue of the common priesthood of the faithful which requires the ministry of the ordained priest to be exercised in the Eucharistic synaxis. The physical position, especially with respect to the communication among the various members of the assembly, must be distinguished from the interior spiritual orientation of all. It would be a grave error to imagine that the principal orientation of the sacrificial action is towards the community. If the priest celebrates *versus populum*, which is legitimate and often advisable, his spiritual attitude ought always to be *versus Deum per Iesum Christum* (towards God through Jesus Christ), as representative of the entire Church. The Church as well, which takes concrete form in the assembly which participates, is entirely turned *versus Deum* (towards God) as its first spiritual movement.[24]

The Congregation puts it well. Whatever the stance of the priest, both priest and people need to be oriented toward God in prayer.[25]

2. LANGUAGE: THE USE OF THE VERNACULAR AND THE DEBATE OVER TRANSLATION

A second set of issues that remains contested today centers around the language of the liturgy. We shall deal first with translation of the liturgy into the vernacular and then with the contemporary debate over the process and result of translations (those into English at any rate), pausing briefly to deal with the selection of prayers themselves. The twentieth-century discussion about whether the liturgy should be translated into the vernacular has been well and thoroughly chronicled elsewhere.[26] Most of the council fathers certainly recognized the need to have the readings for Mass translated and read at the appropriate time in the liturgy. Steps had also been taken before the council to translate the *Roman Ritual* (for the celebration of the sacraments)

---

[24] CDWDS, "Response to Questions on the new General Instruction of the Roman Missal," 2000, quoted in Lang, *Turning Towards the Lord*, 26–27. I am grateful to my student, Joseph Villecco, for first alerting me to this document.

[25] I realize that this begs a number of questions, especially with regard to eucharistic sacrifice. I will deal with them in the final chapter.

[26] Keith Pecklers, *Dynamic Equivalence: The Living Language of Christian Worship* (Collegeville, MN: Liturgical Press, 2003).

into various modern languages. The Liturgy Constitution's statements on the question of translation are quoted frequently by the critics:

§36. (1) The use of the Latin language, with due respect to particular law, is to be preserved in the Latin rites.

(2) But since the use of the vernacular, whether in the Mass, the administration of the sacraments, or in other parts of the liturgy, may frequently be of great advantage to the people, a wider use may be made of it, especially in readings, directives and in some prayers and chants. Regulations governing this will be given separately in subsequent chapters.

(3) These norms being observed, it is for the competent territorial ecclesiastical authority mentioned in Article 22:2 to decide whether, and to what extent, the vernacular language is to be used. Its decrees have to be approved, that is, confirmed, by the Apostolic See. Where circumstances warrant it, it is to consult with bishops of neighboring regions which have the same language.

. . .

§54. A suitable place may be allotted to the vernacular in Masses which are celebrated with the people, especially in the readings and "the common prayer," and also, as local conditions may warrant, in those parts which pertain to the people, according to the rules laid down in Article 36 of this Constitution.

Nevertheless care must be taken to ensure that the faithful may also be able to say or sing together in Latin those parts of the Ordinary of the Mass which pertain to them.

Wherever a more extended use of the vernacular in the Mass seems desirable, the regulation laid down in Article 40 of this Constitution is to be observed.[27]

As I have mentioned, the critics do not tire of pointing out that Vatican II did not specifically intend that the whole liturgy be translated into the vernacular languages. How then can one defend the decision to do so? In his description (and defense) of the liturgical reform Annibale Bugnini takes pains to show why and how SC's prescriptions with regard to the vernacular eventually became a

---

[27] The same recommendation with regard to the vernacular is given for the sacraments (SC 63) and the Divine Office (SC 101).

liturgy translated entirely into modern languages.[28] In the first stage of the reform, with regard to the Eucharist the vernacular could be used for the readings, prayer of the faithful, ordinary chants (e.g., *Kyrie*, *Sanctus*), the proper chants, acclamations, greetings and dialogues, the Lord's Prayer with its introduction and embolism, and the three "presidential prayers" (e.g., Opening Prayer).[29] By the next year eighty-seven episcopal conferences had requested the use of texts in the vernacular. Everything was able to be translated except for the preface and the Roman Canon and the majority of the Rites of Ordination. But, as Bugnini points out, once the preface dialogue and *Sanctus* were prayed/sung in the vernacular, it made little sense to leave the preface in Latin. More and more conferences asked for the preface as well as the Roman Canon to be translated into the vernacular. By 1966, just a year after the end of the council, it was clear that a majority of episcopal conferences wanted the entire eucharistic liturgy in the vernacular.[30] Rendering the whole liturgy in the vernacular was not the plot of some devious "experts" who wished to force their own version of reform on the church. The pressure came from the various conferences of bishops throughout the world who were concerned with active participation in liturgical celebration—the same bishops who had voted for SC. Bugnini goes on to defend the idea that rendering the whole liturgy in the vernacular can be justified as a broad interpretation of SC §§36 and 54.[31]

In addition, Pope Paul VI showed great sensitivity when he said in 1969, just prior to the introduction of the new Order of Mass on 30 November, the first Sunday of Advent:

> Clearly the most noticeable new departure is that of language. From now on the vernacular, not the Latin, will be the principal language of the Mass. For those who appreciate the beauty of Latin, its power and

---

[28] The battle over who would have the final say in translations is documented anew in Piero Marini, *A Challenging Reform: Realizing the Vision of the Liturgical Renewal*, Mark Francis, John Page, and Keith Pecklers, eds. (Collegeville, MN: Liturgical Press, 2007), especially chapter 1.

[29] By April 21, 1964; see Annibale Bugnini, *The Reform of the Liturgy 1948–1975* (Collegeville, MN: Liturgical Press. 1990), 101.

[30] Ibid., 104–09. That permission was granted in 1967.

[31] Ibid., 110–13, especially 111, where he quotes the report to the council by Bishop Jesús Enciso Viana (Mallorca).

aptness to express the sacred, substitution of the vernacular certainly represents a great sacrifice. We are losing the idiom of the Christian ages; we become like profane intruders into the literary sanctuary of sacred language; we shall lose a large portion of that wonderful and incomparable artistic and spiritual reality, Gregorian chant. We indeed have reason for sadness and perhaps even for bewilderment. What shall we put in the place of this angelic language? *We are sacrificing a priceless treasure. For what reason? What is worth more than these sublime values of the Church? The answer may seem trite and prosaic, but it is sound because it is both human and apostolic.* Our understanding of prayer is worth more than the previous, ancient garments in which it has been regally clad. Of more value, too, is the participation of the people, of modern people who are surrounded by clear, intelligible language, translatable into their ordinary conversation. If our sacred Latin should, like a thick curtain, close us off from the world of children and young people, of work and the business of everyday, then would we, fishers of men, be wise to allow it exclusive dominion over the speech of religion and prayer?[32]

This splendid paragraph demonstrates Paul VI's deep commitment to the radical reform of the liturgy that was needed toward the end of the twentieth century. He obviously knew well that many people would find the new liturgy—and especially the use of the vernacular throughout—difficult. But in the pastoral judgment of this pope the pain that was experienced by leaving behind the treasure of the Latin liturgy was worth it because of the value of enabling people to understand their worship of God. We shall return to the question of the limits of intelligibility in the final chapter, but for now it should be clear that in the minds of the reformers putting the whole liturgy into the vernacular was a fulfillment and not a betrayal of the council.

The question of the style of translation has also been the subject of much discussion over the past several years. In a somewhat laconic sentence Bugnini writes: "The problem of translation was the first and

---

[32] Pope Paul VI, "Address to the general audience, on the new *Ordo Missae*, 26 November 1969 (= DOL 212). Emphasis supplied. I am grateful to Marc Reeves, SJ, for pointing me to this source. See also two other addresses by Paul VI in *DOL* 113:787 and 116:815. I am grateful to John Page for pointing me to these latter allocutions.

most troublesome of the liturgical reform."[33] In the first place mixed commissions (i.e., joining the forces of various national episcopates that shared a common language) needed to be put in place. This turned out to be somewhat easier for the French-, German-, and English-speaking worlds than for other regions. This section will deal with the principles of translation in general and then the fate of translation in the English-speaking world in particular.

The story of general principles might be called "A Tale of Two Instructions." The first instruction with regard to translation was entitled *Comme le prévoit* (January 1969)[34] and was timed to coincide with the publication of the Roman Missal. There are several major principles operative in this instruction. The liturgical text is clearly considered a medium of spoken communication:

> To achieve this end, it is not sufficient that a liturgical translation merely reproduce the expressions and ideas of the original text. Rather it must fully communicate to a given people, and in their own language, that which the Church by means of this given text originally intended to communicate to another people in another time. A faithful translation, therefore, cannot be judged on the basis of individual words: the total context of this specific act of communication must be kept in mind, as well as the literary form proper to the respective language. (6)

The theory of translation this represents has been called "dynamic equivalence." Therefore it is as concerned with the receiver as it is with the original text. In other words, how is this text going to make sense (in an oral/aural fashion) for the listeners? This approach gave translators great leeway in fashioning texts and inspired avoiding a wooden literalism when translating (11–13). The instruction also insisted on common usage, i.e., everyday language (15). Care is taken that sacramental formulae (consecratory prayers, eucharistic prayers) be translated with less freedom than the proper prayers of the Sacramentary (30–31). The spirit of the instruction is nicely summed up as follows:

---

[33] Bugnini, *Reform of the Liturgy*, 233.

[34] *Consilium, Instruction Comme le prévoit, on the translation of liturgical texts for celebrations with a congregation, 25 January 1969* (= DOL 123). I will cite the paragraph numbers for the document in parentheses in the text for the sake of convenience. See Bugnini, *Reform of the Liturgy*, 236–38, for further commentary.

The prayer of the Church is always the prayer of some actual community, assembled here and now. It is not sufficient that a formula handed down from some other time or region be translated verbatim, even if accurately, for liturgical use. The formula translated must become the genuine prayer of the congregation and in it each of its members should be able to find and express himself or herself. (20)

Just how much has changed since 1969 will soon be evident. Formed during the council, the International Commission on English in the Liturgy (ICEL) has been responsible for liturgical translations in the English-speaking world ever since. ICEL produced its translation of the Sacramentary (= Roman Missal) within four short years of the appearance of the Latin typical edition. Soon after the dismissal of Archbishop Bugnini and the Vatican's change of liturgical course in 1975, the new curial congregation started shifting to a more cautious mode.[35] ICEL then began to experience some opposition from those who opposed the idea of inclusivity with regard to liturgical language. Through all of this time, however, ICEL's officials were able to continue a dialogue with the CDWDS.

Dialogue ended and the crisis came to a head with the Vatican's strong rejection in 1997 of the ICEL Psalter (1995), which had greatly reduced male references to God as well as to human beings. The year 1997 also saw the beginning of the end for ICEL as it had operated since its inception during the council. Under the new prefect of the Congregation for Divine Worship and the Discipline of the Sacraments, Cardinal Jorge Medina Estevez, the national episcopal conferences received an astoundingly harsh rejection of ICEL's translation of the second typical edition of the ordination rites. As Wilkins points out, the Vatican response listed 114 difficulties with the translation and added that the list was not exhaustive.

Since 1981, ICEL had also been involved in a fresh translation of the Roman Missal (Sacramentary).[36] The various national episcopal

---

[35] These developments are detailed by John Wilkins, "Lost in Translation: The Bishops, the Vatican, and English Liturgy," *Commonweal* 132/21 (December 2, 2005): 12ff. The following narrative takes most of its facts from Wilkins, although I can attest to some of the events myself.

[36] The Lectionary had never been part of ICEL's brief. In the interests of transparency I should mention that I served on ICEL's Advisory Committee from 1994 until its demise and on its subcommittee on Translation and Revision from 1995.

conferences had all approved the Sacramentary by the mandatory two-thirds vote by 1998 (the targeted date for completion had been 1992–1993.[37] That same year in June the new American representative to ICEL, Cardinal Francis George (Chicago), represented Cardinal Medina and the Congregation's position that ICEL had gone off the rails and needed to change. ICEL was forced to make significant changes in its staff, to dismiss the majority of its advisors, and to adopt statutes acceptable to Rome. The longtime executive secretary, Dr. John Page, an American, was dismissed and replaced by Rev. Bruce Harbert from England. The 1997/98 ICEL Sacramentary was deemed unacceptable by the CDWDS and a new instruction on translation, *Liturgiam Authenticam* (LA), was published on March 28, 2001.[38]

Liturgiam Authenticam is deliberately intended to replace *Comme le prévoit* as the standard for translation.[39] It calls for thorough scrutiny in the context of this work, since in many ways it shows that the critics of the reform have now become the proprietors of the church's liturgy. The rationale given for this instruction is that thirty years of experience have shown the need for a new approach (7). The subtext of the document seems to be that many modern translations have weakened or departed from the faith of the Catholic Church and a faithful rendering of the Latin originals, hence the call for liturgical books that are "marked by sound doctrine, which are exact in wording, free from all ideological influence . . ." (3). It does not take much imagination to realize that "ideological" here refers to a desire on the part of contemporary translators (and their episcopal conferences) to respect the progress made in ecclesiology by Vatican II and to be attentive to the requirements of inclusive language in a world in which the male gender can no longer be considered normative for human beings.

According to LA, another problematic aspect of contemporary translations makes the biblical readings as well as prayers into "a sort of mirror for the interior dispositions of the faithful; rather, they

---

[37] For this and many other important details I am indebted to Dr. John Page, who so kindly reviewed my manuscript and kept me from making a number of egregious errors.

[38] CDWDS, *Liturgiam Authenticam: On the Use of Vernacular Language in the Publication of the Books of the Roman Liturgy, Fifth Instruction on the Implementation of the Constitution on the Sacred Liturgy* (Washington, DC: USCCB, 2002). Paragraph numbers will be cited in parentheses.

[39] See the commentary by Anthony Ward, "The Instruction 'Liturgiam Authenticam': Some Particulars," *Ephemerides Liturgicae* 116 (2002): 197–221.

express truths that transcend the limits of time and space" (19). Here as elsewhere in the document the framers pose a rather dubious either/or. Clearly, timeless and transcendent truths need to be expressed in language that can be affectively apprehended by people living in a particular time and place—whether in Latin or in contemporary vernaculars. The instruction describes the very laudable goal of translations "characterized by the kind of language which is easily understandable, yet which at the same time preserves these texts' dignity, beauty, and doctrinal precision" (25). Who could possibly disagree? At the same time, many of the principles that are further enunciated make it difficult to hold intelligibility and precision in healthy tension. Bishop Donald Trautman has been a strong critic of the resulting translations into English, which tend to archaize in their pursuit of a more literal rendering of the prayer texts.[40] Take, for example, the following differences in the second eucharistic prayer and the Creed:

	Eucharistic Prayer II	Nicene Creed
1969 *Missale Romanum*	*Haec dona ergo quaesumus, Spiritus tui rore santifica . . .*	*. . . consubstantialem Patri. . . . Et incarnatus est de Spiritu Sancto ex Maria Virgine*
ICEL 1973 translation	Let your Spirit come upon these gifts to make them holy . . .	. . . one in being with the Father . . . by the power of the Holy Spirit he was born of the Virgin Mary
Proposed translation	Make holy these gifts, we pray, by the dew of your Holy Spirit.	. . . consubstantial with the Father . . . by the Holy Spirit was incarnate of the Virgin Mary

In both cases the proposed translation is much closer to the original Latin in syntax and vocabulary. But do the proposed changes make for formulas that can be picked up aurally? Texts in liturgy are, after all, oral/aural communication. The proposed translation is also the result of obedience to LA's desire for a "sacred style," one that uses words and expressions "which differ somewhat from usual and everyday

[40] Donald Trautman, "The Relationship of the Active Participation of the Assembly to Liturgical Translations," *Worship* 80 (2006): 290–309, at 292.

speech" (27; see also 47). This notion of a sacral vernacular is highly problematic, as Peter Jeffery has shown in his devastating analysis of LA.[41] Among other things Jeffery demonstrates quite convincingly that the liturgy itself never really affected popular language.[42] It is also quite clear from the history of liturgical Latin that traditional attempts at translation eschewed the sacred vocabulary of the surrounding (pagan) culture while striving for a somewhat elevated style of language. In doing so they did create a kind of sacral language of their own. Christine Mohrmann, one of the foremost Christian Latinists of the twentieth century, put it this way: ". . . from the very earliest times, Christians sought for prayer forms which were far removed, in their style and mode of expression, from the language of everyday life. This tendency was combined with a conscious striving after sacral forms of expression."[43] A number of critics have pointed to the unsatisfactory register of the English used in the ICEL translations of the 1970s.[44] As Aidan Kavanagh once said of the 1973 ICEL translation of the Sacramentary: "liturgical English is presently a pidgin form of the language possessing all the stylistic flair of a wet potato chip."[45] For example, Eamon Duffy is very critical of the tendency to reduce divine agency (thus leaning toward Pelagianism) in the 1973 ICEL Sacramentary. He admits that the texts proposed for the 1998 Sacramentary represent an improvement, especially in that they tend to do a better job of catching the wordplay of the Latin orations. Here is an example:

[41] Peter Jeffery, *Translating Tradition: A Chant Historian Reads* Liturgiam Authenticam (Collegeville, MN: Liturgical Press, 2005): "the most ignorant statement on liturgy ever issued by a modern Vatican congregation" (p. 9) and "Since LA is full of misstatements about the Roman liturgical tradition, those who wrote and approved it are simply in no position to judge whether a practice or text is Roman or not" (p. 17).

[42] Ibid., 93.

[43] Christine Mohrmann, *Liturgical Latin: Its Origins and Character* (London: Burns and Oates, 1957), 26.

[44] E.g., Aidan Nichols, *Looking at Liturgy: A Critical View of Its Contemporary Form* (San Francisco: Ignatius Press, 1996), 100–102; Eamon Duffy, "Rewriting the Liturgy: The Theological Implications of Translation," in Stratford Caldecott, ed., *Beyond the Prosaic: Renewing the Liturgical Movement* (Edinburgh: T&T Clark, 1998), 97–126.

[45] Aidan Kavanagh, "Liturgical Business Unfinished and Unbegun," *Worship* 50 (1976): 356.

Latin Text: Roman Missal 1969, Eleventh Sunday of the Year

> *Deus, in te sperantium fortitudo, invocationibus nostris adesto propitius, et, quia sine te nihil potest mortalis infirmatas, gratiae tuae praesta semper auxilium, ut, in exsequendis mandatis tuis, et voluntate tibi et actione placeamus. Per . . .*

1973 ICEL Sacramentary	1998 ICEL proposed Sacramentary, as quoted in *Progress Report on the Revision of the Roman Missal* © 1988, ICEL
Almighty God, Our hope and our strength, without you we falter. Help us to follow Christ and to live according to your will. We ask this through our Lord Jesus Christ, your Son, who lives and reigns with you and the Holy Spirit, one God, for ever and ever.	O God, the strength of all who hope in you, accept our earnest prayer. And since without you we are weak and certain to fall, grant us always the help of your grace, that in following your commands we may please you in desire and in deed. We ask this through our Lord Jesus Christ, your Son, who lives and reigns with you in the unity of the Holy Spirit, God for ever and ever.

Few people involved with translation thought the 1973 texts stood the test of time. That is why a new project of translation was initiated in 1981. The resulting 1997/98 translation is quite clearly more faithful to the Latin original, and quite proclaimable at the same time. LA is also insistent on the retention of words the ICEL translators have deemed superfluous because they belong more to the Latin rhythm or *cursus* than to the content of the prayer (55). A typical Latin opening prayer (collect) will employ a phrase like: *Da, quaesumus, omnipotens Deus*. . . . ICEL's tendency has been to translate it as: "Almighty God, grant that. . . ." It would seem that LA would insist on something like "Grant, we pray, Almighty God, that. . . ."

One of the most contentious and problematic examples given by LA is the translation of the phrase *et cum spiritu tuo*, which is given in the current ICEL (and ecumenical English language) texts as "and also with you" (56). I part company with probably the majority of my colleagues in agreeing that "and with your spirit" would be a better translation. It is slightly more elevated and elegant and makes it clear that we are using ritual language. Moreover, with the notable exception of Portuguese (which renders the phrase with "he is in our midst"!), the other modern Western European languages all use the more formal phrasing, equivalent to "and with your spirit." On the other hand, I would not opt for changing this response without wide consultation and agreement with other churches and ecclesial communions who employ "and also with you."[46] I will have more to say about ecumenism, the critics, and the liturgical reform in the final chapter. A further concern of the instruction is the employment of sacral rather than secular terms. An unfortunate example, cited by Trautman, is the insistence on using "chalice" instead of "cup" for *calicem* in the translation of the Eucharistic Institution Narrative. Surely the fourth-century framers of the Roman Canon intended *calix* to mean "cup" rather than "chalice" in that particular context. Will the liturgy really become more reverential because of the use of pointless archaisms? A last example is LA's directive to translate the beginning of the Nicene Creed with "I believe" instead of the current "We believe" for the Latin *Credo*. Of course, *Credo* is a singular form, but as Peter Jeffery has shown, the Latin liturgical tradition has allowed for the use of the plural (after all, the original Greek was *pisteuomen*—"we believe"). Moreover, as Jeffery also points out, the use of the plural in the Nicene Creed is not at all as radical as the 2002 *Missale Romanum*'s addition of "one" to the beginning of the Apostles' Creed: "I believe in [*one*] God."[47]

Another delicate subject raised by LA is that of inclusive language. Although the instruction recognizes the difficulty posed by those languages that seem to make formerly generic terms (like "man") restricted to one gender, it opts for the retention of exclusive terms and for catechesis to the effect that they do not really mean what everyone understands by them. So they reject strategies like:

> the systematic resort to imprudent solutions such as the mechanical substitution of words, the transition from the singular to the plural,

[46] A spirited criticism of recent Roman actions with regard to the liturgy was given by David Holeton, an Old Catholic professor in Prague, in his 2007 Presidential Address for the international ecumenical Societas Liturgica. This address will be published in *Studia Liturgica* 38 (2008).

[47] Jeffery, *Translating Tradition*, 18–22. There is something like a slogan war going on with regard to the term. One group of priests, dissatisfied with the earlier ICEL translations in the U.S., calls itself "Credo," while another, consisting of more progressive liturgists, calls itself "We Believe." Transparency requires that I declare that I am a member of the latter group.

the splitting of the unitary collective term into masculine and feminine parts, or the introduction of impersonal or abstract words, all of which may impede the communication of the true and integral sense of a word or an expression in the original text. (31)

This directive does read like a tortuous attempt to avoid inclusive language, and one has to wonder whether the desire to avoid inclusive language has more to do with the fear that recognizing women is the camel's nose under the tent with regard to women's ordination rather than with a desire to be more accurate or faithful in translating texts.[48] Finally, LA §104, which denies the right to propose translations to episcopal conferences, seems directly to contravene SC §36:3–4, which puts the responsibility squarely in the hands of those conferences. It was quite clear from the very beginning of the implementation of the reform in 1964 that the Vatican wanted to reserve the right of final approval of any texts to itself. But this move, which makes it possible for the Vatican itself to propose translations, is a radical departure from the former translation policy.[49]

Liturgiam Authenticam is certainly a very different document both in style and content from *Comme le prévoit*. Its ideals are good, and many of them had already been implemented in the second generation of ICEL texts. At the same time, a slavish application of its principles, especially with regard to accounting for every syntactical element, will not lead to felicitous translations in modern languages.

There is another issue which merits at least some attention. We should not ignore the fact that even the Latin texts that make up the *Missal of Paul VI* have been criticized. In a series of articles Lauren Pristas has set out to question the principles upon which the various presidential prayers (opening prayer, prayer over the gifts, prayer after communion) were chosen and edited in the *Missal of Paul VI*.[50] Her basic premise is that André Dumas, OSB, and the committee

---

[48] I should make it clear that Peter Jeffery disagrees that the avoidance of inclusive language is a main motivation of LA: *Translating Tradition*, 105.

[49] Marini, *Challenging Reform*, 22–27. There are also a number of restrictions put on the "mixed commissions" like ICEL by the instruction.

[50] Lauren Pristas, "Theological Principles that Guided the Redaction of the Roman Missal (1970)," *The Thomist* 67 (2003): 157–95; eadem, "The Orations of the Vatican II Missal: Policies for Revision," *Communio* 30 (2003): 621–53; eadem, "*Missale Romanum* 1962 and 1970: A Comparative Study of Two Collects," *Antiphon* 7 (2002): 29–33.

responsible for these prayers (*Coetus* 18 *bis* of the *Consilium*) were driven by an inappropriate desire to accommodate to the signs of the times. Using a series of examples from Dumas' own presentation of the selecting and editing of these prayers,[51] she questions, for example, whether or not prayers for royal saints (Henry, Louis of France) should be updated to suit a more modern mentality.[52] To quote her in full:

> Dumas' consistently reiterated concern that the liturgy "be accommodated to the modern mentality" raises the question of whether the primary referent governing the work of the reformers was, in fact, the modern person, or, to express the same possibility in a somewhat different way, whether the reformers understood the task of reform to consist in reshaping the liturgy according to the suppositions of the modern age as they perceived them.[53]

Two comments are in order. First, since the reform was clearly intended to update anachronistic aspects of the Roman liturgy (SC 23, 50) it was certainly part of the brief of the reformers that they select and edit prayers to suit the changes in theology and spirituality experienced in the late twentieth century. Any other course of action would have been irresponsible. Therefore when more positive motivations are substituted for a rather negative spirituality, the reformers were performing their task. Second, it is clear that Dumas' intention was not merely to accommodate a modern mentality, but rather to balance it with respect to the tradition. In the very essay she translates, he states:

> In the liturgical renewal, from the beginning the revisers regarded concern for the truth and simplicity to be particularly indispensable so that the texts and rites might be perfectly—or at least much better—accommodated to the modern mentality to which it must give expression *while neglecting nothing of the traditional treasury to which it remains the conduit.*[54]

---

[51] André Dumas, "Les oraisons du nouveau missel romain," *Questions Liturgiques* 25 (1971): 263–70.

[52] Pristas, "Redaction," 173–75.

[53] Ibid., 185.

[54] André Dumas, "The Orations of the Roman Missal," as translated in Pristas, "Orations," 633. Emphasis supplied.

Clearly, then, at the very least the aim of Dumas, his committee, and the *Consilium* as a whole was to update the presidential prayers while at the same time showing reverence for tradition. At times this meant that they would substitute phrases or patch together elements from several prayers (centonization). A fair survey of all the prayers of the 1970 Missal will show that the priority of divine grace, the Catholic theological "accent" of cooperation with that grace, and the need to avoid the sinful aspects of the world are all amply represented.[55] Therefore Pristas' insinuations that there may be a theological error at the very heart of the reform,[56] or that at times formulae give way to "Protestant sacramental thought,"[57] or that Dumas' work represents a "rather cavalier approach to tradition,"[58] are, to my mind, without merit. As far as texts are concerned, one must consider not only the presidential prayers but also the immensely enriched corpus of eucharistic prefaces as well as the prayers *ad diversa* (for particular needs) that were added to the traditional Roman Missal.

3. LITURGICAL MUSIC

This section is a good example of fools rushing in where angels fear to tread. I cannot pretend to survey, much less analyze, the contemporary critique of liturgical music, but since the issue is so central both to liturgical renewal and to the concerns of the critics, I do need to make several observations.

First, the critics always take note of the fact that as far as musical style is concerned Gregorian chant is given pride of place in all of the pertinent documents.[59] But this preference for Gregorian chant has been replaced by other styles of music in the liturgy. Indeed, the crucial move, according to the Hungarian critic and musicologist Laszlo Dobszay, was to allow for the substitution of any other content besides the traditional chants to be found in the Roman Rite. He calls

---

[55] See, e.g., the fine study by Gerard Moore, *Vatican II and the Collects for Ordinary Time: A Study in the Roman Missal (1975)* (San Francisco: Catholic Scholars Press, 1998).

[56] Pristas, "Redaction," 186.

[57] Ibid., 192.

[58] Pristas, "Orations," 653.

[59] E.g., SC 116; *Musicam Sacram* (5 March 1967) 4b (= DOL 508) merely mentions Gregorian chant as one of the forms of sacred music—although it is still expected that normally the liturgical texts (e.g., the Introit) will be used; see §32.

this "the anthrax in the envelope."[60] He continues by citing the 1967 Instruction *Musicam Sacram*:

> In some places there exists the lawful practice, occasionally confirmed by indult, of substituting other songs for the Introit, Offertory, and Communion chants in the *Graduale Romanum*. At the discretion of the competent territorial authority this practice may be retained, on condition that the songs substituted fit in with those parts of the Mass, the feast, or the liturgical season. The texts of such songs must also have the approval of the same territorial authority.[61]

Worse still, for Dobszay, was the *GIRM*'s direction that the chants from the Proper might be taken from the Roman Gradual or the Simple Gradual—or "some other appropriate song" (*vel alius aptus cantus*).[62] The objective nature of the liturgy is thus destroyed in favor of pastoral needs and personal taste. As he writes: ". . . henceforth chant does not have a role in the self-explanation of the liturgy. More rudely put: the chant is no longer an integral part of the liturgy."[63] To this he contrasts SC's statement of the integral relation between the

---

[60] Laszlo Dobszay, *The Bugnini-Liturgy and the Reform of the Reform* (Front Royal, VA: Catholic Church Music Associates, 2003), 88.

[61] Sacred Congregation of Rites, Instruction *Musicam Sacram* (1967), §32.

[62] Dobszay, *Bugnini-Liturgy*, 87. The reference is to the 1975 (2nd) edition of the *GIRM*. The 2002 edition has the following adaptation for the U.S. version: "In the dioceses of the United States there are four options for this Entrance Chant: (1) the antiphon from the *Roman Missal* or the Psalm from the *Roman Gradual* as set to music there or in another musical setting; (2) the seasonal antiphon and Psalm of the *Simple Gradual*; (3) a song from another collection of psalms and antiphons, approved by the Conference of Bishops or by the diocesan Bishop, including psalms arranged in responsorial or metrical forms; (4) a suitable liturgical song similarly approved by the Conference of Bishops or by the diocesan Bishop" (48). The United States Bishops have published a new directory for liturgical music: *Sing to the Lord: Music in Divine Worship* (Nov. 14, 2007). The .pdf file is at http://www.usccb.org/liturgy.

[63] Dobszay, *Bugnini-Liturgy*, 89. At points Dobszay can be rather harsh: "And yet one reads glowing reports about how good and warm-fuzzy even the very highest prelates feel today at hearing the juvenile music which resounds in the Masses of young people! Such is the real value of the vague "principles" which do not go beyond *quaedam sanctissima verba*, venerable but absolutely ineffective verbiage" (p. 91; see also 97). I must admit to wondering how Pope Benedict XVI reacted to the very pop music sung at the World Youth Day Mass in Cologne in 2005—especially since he has himself been such a strong critic of popular music in the liturgy.

chant and the liturgy—"as sacred song, closely bound to the text, it forms a necessary or integral part of the solemn liturgy" (SC §112). His presumption is of course the traditional connection of the chants with the readings of the Roman Rite lectionary throughout the liturgical year whereby a Sunday could be known by its introductory chant, e.g., *Resurrexi* (Easter Sunday), *Rorate coeli* (4th Sunday of Advent), or *Invocabit* (1st Sunday of Lent). This situation has changed (lamentably as far as he is concerned) with the introduction of the three-year cycle of Sunday readings. Indeed, Dobszay's argument only holds if one insists on the integrity of the pre–Vatican II liturgy with the chants associated with the one-year lectionary. I choose the word "associated" deliberately since very often the chants were not necessarily chosen to correspond so much to the liturgical readings as they were appropriate to the Roman stational church employed on that day: e.g., *Laetare Jerusalem* for the Fourth Sunday of Lent, which took place at Rome's Church of the Holy Cross in Jerusalem.[64]

This is not to say that there is some merit in employing the older chant texts either in Latin or the vernacular from time to time. In other words, there is some middle ground between insisting that the pre–Vatican II liturgy of the Mass be retained and the wholesale rejection of all its traditional parts. The wise master can draw both old and new from the storehouse (Matt 13:52). Another aspect of Dobszay's argument relates to who sings the chants of the Proper. As he puts it:

> Neither history, nor the nature of the liturgy, nor the norms of the Church or of the Council, nor even the postconciliar regulations vindicate the need for having the Proprium sung by the entire congregation. . . . General congregational participation is a good thing—but only if the content, the message of the liturgy is not sacrificed on the altar of "active participation," for that would mean that the Greater is being sacrificed for the sake of the Lesser in importance.[65]

It is very difficult to imagine the current eucharistic liturgy of the Roman Rite without the people being encouraged to sing at times like the entrance rite and the procession for communion. *GIRM* §48

---

[64] For further examples see John F. Baldovin, *The Stational Character of Christian Worship: The Origin, Meaning and Development of Stational Liturgy in Jerusalem, Rome and Constantinople*. Orientalia Christiana Analecta 228 (Rome: Pontifical Institute for Oriental Studies, 1987), 153–58.

[65] Dobszay, *Bugnini-Liturgy*, 108.

certainly provides for this possibility, but it is the last of the options offered. A solution, as I will attempt to outline it in the final chapter, can be found in the choice of the music to be sung and not (exclusively) retaining the old chants in Latin or the vernacular. To give him his due, Dobszay does not argue simply for a wholesale return to the old chants, which he admits would be unrealistic. Some adaptation would be required, even in his proposal.[66]

On the other hand, Dobszay is certainly correct in pointing out the important relationship between what is sung and the content of the liturgy. An Old Testament professor of mine never tired of saying that the best commentary on Scripture was Scripture itself: in other words, how parts of the Bible related to each other. The same can be argued for the liturgy.

In addition there is plenty of room for criticism of contemporary liturgical music. It makes an easy and convenient target for the critics. For example, Aidan Nichols laments:

> The Second Vatican Council renewed the pledge of the early-twentieth-century popes to the chant and to the polyphony that can be regarded as the authentic continuation of its qualities in the specifically choral tradition, but to no avail. The scores of chant books and polyphonic settings were cleared out of the choir lofts and dumped in used bookstores, where astute entrepreneurs were more than willing to exploit them, having grasped (as one commentator has put it) their ability to comfort the afflicted.[67]

Nichols and people like him tend to write as though every pre–Vatican II liturgy was gorgeously sung as at the London Oratory, the Jesuit Farm Street Church, or Corpus Christi and St. Ignatius Loyola in Manhattan. We must keep reminding ourselves that the chants and polyphonic settings that are the subject of such rhapsodizing by the critics were very rarely heard in the pre–Vatican II church. Of course, the musical nostalgia we have been considering is closely linked to a desire to return to the so-called Tridentine Mass. To that subject we now turn.

---

[66] Ibid., 189.

[67] Nichols, *Looking at Liturgy*, 106. He is citing Thomas Day, *Where Have You Gone, Michelangelo? The Loss of Soul in Catholic Culture* (New York: Crossroad, 1993), 33. Day is of course well known for his earlier book, *Why Catholics Can't Sing: The Culture of Catholicism and the Triumph of Bad Taste* (New York: Crossroad, 1991).

4. *SUMMORUM PONTIFICUM* AND THE USE OF
THE 1962 *MISSALE ROMANUM*

On July 7, 2007 Pope Benedict issued a *motu proprio* entitled *Summorum Pontificum* (SP), liberalizing the permission to use the Missal of 1962, i.e., the last edition of the Roman Missal before the Second Vatican Council. This decision was greeted with great enthusiasm by those who want to return to the older rite of the Mass. Since they are among the primary (but certainly not the only) critics of the reform it is necessary to deal with the pope's decision as one of the "major issues" treated in this chapter.

Pope Benedict decrees that individual priests may celebrate the Eucharist according to the Missal of 1962 whenever they celebrate without a congregation.[68] A good deal of confusion has been wrought by the denial of permission to celebrate according to the Missal of 1962 on any day except during the Triduum. Obviously this does not refer to parishes or religious communities that are celebrating the pre–Vatican II liturgy, but rather to solitary celebrations, which should not take place during the Triduum in any case. Parish communities where "a group of the faithful attached to the previous liturgical tradition exists stably" may use the old Mass. They may even use the former liturgy for any of the sacraments with the exception of ordinations. (Ordinations are not specifically mentioned, but their omission seems significant.) One wonders whether the pope and his advisors considered the difficulty in the difference between the "form" or essential sacramental formula in the older and newer rites of Confirmation. Mainly for historical and ecumenical reasons Paul VI made a somewhat radical decision to change the traditional form of the sacrament in his Apostolic Constitution introducing the new rite. His formal decree reads: "The sacrament of confirmation is conferred through the anointing with chrism on the forehead which is done by the laying on of the hand, and through the words: Be sealed with the gift of the Holy Spirit [*Accipe signaculum doni Spiritus Sancti*]."[69] The earlier form of the sacrament had been "I sign you with the sign of the cross and confirm you with the chrism of salvation in the name of the

---

[68] SP, art. 2. In itself the practice of private or solitary Mass should be a somewhat problematic notion. It certainly does not seem to be encouraged by the church's present norms; see *GIRM* §254.

[69] Pope Paul VI, Apostolic Constitution *Divinae consortium naturae*, 15 August 1971 (= *DOL* 303).

Father and of the Son and of the Holy Spirit." The difference between the forms by which this sacrament is administered is difficult to reconcile with the assertion of Benedict XVI that we now have one Roman Rite with two "uses." At least in the Middle Ages a "use" like the Sarum (Salisbury) Use in England was a variation on the Roman Rite. Considering the pre– and post–Vatican II Roman liturgies as "uses" certainly stretches the meaning of the term.

Moreover, Benedict asserts that the former liturgy was never abrogated. This was clearly not the mind of Paul VI as Andrew Cameron-Mowat and Nathan Mitchell have very ably demonstrated. In his Apostolic Constitution introducing the Missal of 1969, Paul VI clearly intended to abrogate the older rite, allowing only for elderly priests who had difficulty in accepting the new liturgy to celebrate in private.[70] Then again, in 1984 and 1988 Pope John Paul II extended the use of the pre–Vatican II liturgy, but with major restrictions. He did not claim that the earlier liturgy had not been abrogated.[71] Cameron-Mowat asks a number of important questions that arise from allowing an ordinary and extraordinary use of the Roman Rite:

> What will happen, say, if parishes decide to reject the forthcoming translation of the liturgy into the vernacular? Does this Motu Proprio set a precedent for parishes with "1970 vernacular usage" and others with "2008 vernacular usage"? Will the 2008 translation become the "ordinary" one and the 1970 one "extraordinary"? As female altar servers were permitted by canon law, does that mean they may not be excluded from the 1962 rite? Are communicants barred from receiving under both species at these celebrations?[72]

Some of this is tongue-in-cheek of course, but the confusion that could possibly come about with two "uses" is a real possibility.

---

[70] Andrew Cameron-Mowat, "*Summorum Pontificum*: A Response," *The Pastoral Review* 4 (2007): 4–11, at 6; Nathan Mitchell, "The Amen Corner: "Summorum Pontificum," *Worship* 81 (2007): 552–58.

[71] As the church's supreme legislator, the pope is of course free to legislate as he wishes in a matter like this, but even a pope cannot make something false true. I was recently asked at a talk whether the indult allowing the use of the older liturgy given to the bishops of England and Wales did not show that the old rite had never been suppressed. Of course the questioner proved my point. The fact that indults were granted means that Paul VI had definitely suppressed the pre–Vatican II rite.

[72] Cameron-Mowat, "Response," 10.

Moreover, I find it somewhat troubling that the pope does not take pains to insist that those who adopt the Missal of 1962 should be clear about their allegiance to church teaching, in this case Vatican II. One would not normally expect a requirement of that kind in a liturgical document, but clearly many who wish for a return to the older form of the Roman Rite do in fact reject the documents of the Second Vatican Council. Pope Benedict's accompanying letter to the bishops of the world is an attempt to allay some disquiet but, at least in my opinion, not a very successful one. While I can heartily agree that much confusion would be avoided were the *Missal of Paul VI* to be "celebrated with great reverence in harmony with the liturgical directives" and that "this will bring out the spiritual richness and the theological depth of the Missal," it does seem that such confusion would have been better avoided if Pope Benedict had made that the focus of his decree rather than the restoration of the pre–Vatican II liturgy. Many people have not accepted the Second Vatican Council and the renewal and reform of the church that have sprung from it. This document will only give them hope that the last forty years can be reversed.

All this being said, it does not seem to me that the movement to return to the pre–Vatican II liturgy will amount to much.[73] The possibility of participating in a "Tridentine Mass" will attract the curious for a while, but interest will quickly wane.[74] There seems something rather postmodern about the whole phenomenon—what the post-modernists like to call "bricolage," a little of this and a little of that. It is also characteristic of a consumerist society in which such rites are taken out of their pre–Vatican II context to satisfy what Nathan Mitchell has called "commodified nostalgia."[75]

I am sure that a good number of people (both those who remember it with affection and those who have never experienced anything like it) will find a well-produced Solemn High Mass according to the 1962 Missal aesthetically and emotionally quite pleasing. But at this point a

---

[73] For a similar judgment see Mitchell, "Amen Corner," 549.

[74] Dobszay points out (*Bugnini-Liturgy*, 151) that the 1962 Missal is not identical with the Tridentine Missal. He also correctly observes, as do others, that "Tridentine Mass" is something of a misnomer since the *Missal of Pius V* (1570) was not really anything very new but rather a cleaned-up version of the medieval liturgy.

[75] Mitchell, "Amen Corner," 563. Mitchell is inaccurate on two points, however. First, SP 9 does not allow the use of the pre–Vatican II ordination rites, 558 n. 19. Second, SP 2 does not exclude the celebration of the Triduum in the old rite (p. 564), but rather the private celebration of the old rite during the Triduum.

Mass like that is just that—a production—and it is not possible to re-produce the religious or cultural world in which it expressed the worship of Catholics. Ultimately even the critics of the liturgical reform will not find the pre–Vatican II liturgy compelling—if only because the vast majority of Roman Catholics will continue to employ the "ordinary use." I am guessing, of course. But my suspicion is that except for a tiny minority the future of Roman Catholic liturgy does not lie with the pre–Vatican II rites. Where then might it lie? The final chapter of this book is an attempt to answer that question in light of the critique we have surveyed.

Conclusion: A Way Forward

In the previous chapters of this book I have tried to lay out the substance of the various critiques launched at the reform of the liturgy that followed Vatican II—and indeed the critics of the council's Constitution on the Sacred Liturgy itself. The aim of this final chapter is twofold. First I will summarize and respond to various features of the criticisms we have seen. I will do this by responding to a series of questions. Second, I will suggest some paths for the way forward, since the reform of the liturgy is far from complete.

A. RESPONDING TO THE CRITICS

1. *Is the criticism of the reforms uniform?*

By now the answer to this question should be rather obvious. By no means are all of the critics on the same page. Therefore it is necessary to develop a kind of typology of the critique.

A. EXTREME TRADITIONALISTS

This group of critics denies many of the principles of *Sacrosanctum Concilium*. It includes the Society of St. Pius X,[1] Alcuin Reid, Didier Bonneterre,[2] and Michael Davies. A number of monasteries like Fontgombault and Barroux in France are adherents of this approach. At times these critics express their disquiet even with the breviary reform of Pius X. They want to cast the entire reform in doubt because of the extraordinary value and doctrinal security of the pre–Vatican II rites—not only the Eucharist but all the sacraments. These people are no doubt enthusiastic about Pope Benedict XVI's *motu proprio, Summorum Pontificum*, because they think that once the faithful have

---

[1] See their book, *The Problem of the Liturgical Reform: A Theological and Liturgical Study* (Kansas City: Angelus Press, 2001).

[2] Didier Bonneterre, *The Liturgical Movement: From Dom Gueranger to Annibale Bugnini* (Kansas City: Angelus Press, 2002).

a chance to experience the pre–Vatican II liturgy they will flock to it. It would be very surprising were this to happen.

B. PROPONENTS OF "REFORMING THE REFORM"

The majority of the critics we have dealt with would fall more or less within this category—for example, Klaus Gamber, Joseph Ratzinger/Pope Benedict XVI, James Hitchcock, Kieran Flanagan, and the authors represented in Thomas Kocik's *The Reform of the Reform?*[3] These critics do not necessarily reject Vatican II or its Liturgy Constitution. One qualification: a number of them (including Flanagan) think the council Fathers were naïve with regard to ritual anthropology. Rather, they argue that the *Consilium* that actually produced the reformed liturgies after the council went well beyond its brief and did not give the church a liturgy that was *organically* related to the previous rites. They all willingly acknowledge the necessity of some kind of reform, but usually they argue for a return to the "eastward" position of the priest celebrant, for a much greater use of Latin (neither of these is actually forbidden by the reformed books), a reduction in the number of eucharistic prayers, and the return to a one-year cycle for the Sunday lectionary. In some ways these "reformers of the reform" have already gained a significant foothold in the Vatican, as can be witnessed in documents like the Fourth Instruction on the Liturgy (*Varietates Legitimae*—on inculturation), the Instructions *Liturgiam Authenticam* and *Redemptionis Sacramentum*. This is one of the areas in which a comprehensive rather than narrowly contentious understanding of history can be helpful, as I have tried to elucidate elsewhere.[4]

C. THE REFORM WAS POORLY IMPLEMENTED

A last group consists of critics who object not so much to the reforms as they exist "on the books" as to the way they were implemented. This group includes Denis Crouan, Francis Mannion, and many who are dissatisfied with the current state of liturgical architecture and liturgical music. Mannion's own preferred category, "recatholicizing the reform," aptly characterizes this group who hope for a greater interiorization of the liturgy. My own proposals will come closest to those of this group.

[3] Thomas Kocik, *The Reform of the Reform? A Liturgical Debate: Reform or Return?* (San Francisco: Ignatius Press, 2003).

[4] See my essay, "The Usefulness of Liturgical History," appended to the body of this book. See also Robert Cabié, "La Place de l'Histoire dans les Etudes Liturgiques," *Ecclesia Orans* 23 (2006): 321–35.

Most of the issues we shall deal with in the following pages are raised by the second group—those who question the liturgy produced by the *Consilium*.

2. *Was the reform a Trojan Horse for ecumenism?*

The story of the Trojan Horse is familiar from Homer's *Odyssey* and Vergil's *Aeneid*. The Greeks tricked the Trojans into accepting a horse as a gift and a sign that they had accepted defeat and had withdrawn their siege of the city. The gift was a trick, of course, because the horse was hollow and insinuated Greek troops inside the walls of Troy. Just so, it seems that most of the critics object to the post–Vatican II liturgical reform on the basis that it has "Protestantized" the Catholic liturgy. For those who oppose the development of mainstream Catholic theology in the twentieth century this is probably an accurate observation. Vatican II was made possible by the recognition that many of the church-dividing issues of the past could be overcome in a new non-polemical atmosphere and on the basis of renewed studies in Scripture and church history.

When one reads many of the critics one has the impression that the very word "Protestant" is sufficient to discredit an idea, just as the word "Communist" or "Marxist" discredited many proposals having to do with social justice during the 1950s. Frankly, the moves to allow the vernacular in the liturgy, to open further the treasury of Sacred Scripture, to permit communion under both kinds, to talk about the eucharistic sacrifice in terms of memorial, and to reimagine the ministerial priesthood and the role of the assembled baptized faithful are all "concessions" to insights of the Protestant Reformation. It is useless to excoriate the Council of Trent for being polemical. That was the religious and theological world of the sixteenth century. On the other hand, it is wrong in the twentieth or twenty-first century not to admit the valid insights that have come to us from the various Protestant traditions. Some critics want to treat religious ideas and practices like a zero-sum game. That is immature. We shall revisit this topic under the fourth point, on the theology of the paschal mystery.

3. *Did the liturgical reform betray the Catholic tradition?*
Was it an exercise in antiquarianism?

Much of chapter 2—on the historical approach to the critique—centered on this question. A number of critics, including Gamber, Ratzinger, and Reid, point out that SC §23, which asks for an organic development of liturgical forms, was not adequately respected. So much depends here on how one construes the liturgical tradition. If one compares the Missal of 1962 with the Missal of 1969 or the pre– and post–Vatican II ordination rites, for example, one may conclude that the reform was a radical departure from the organic development of the tradition. Balancing this is a view of the tradition as a whole—including an appreciation of the liturgies of the Christian East. In many of the critics I find on the whole that there is a tendency to idolize the Roman Rite—that is, to substitute reverence for the Roman tradition as we have known it since the Middle Ages for reverence for God and the increase of faith, hope, and charity. The framers of the renewal were clearly working from a different understanding and an appreciation of the tradition as a whole.

Was this antiquarianism, as so many have charged? I understand antiquarianism as an attempt to re-create the past for its own sake. In this sense the reform was not an exercise in antiquarianism but a (more or less successful) attempt to retrieve those elements of the tradition (such as worship in a language that is understandable) with a view toward greater participation in the mysteries of the faith. There is obviously in this project some judgment of the medieval development of the liturgy, especially with regard to the relationship between the ordained and the rest of the assembly. One cannot argue that authentic tradition is fixed at a certain point—say in the early Middle Ages—and that everything that comes later can or should be discarded. That would be to fall prey to the "genetic fallacy" that only what is earliest is best.

If by "the Catholic tradition" one insists on understanding the condition of Catholicism immediately prior to Vatican II, then the reform can look like a betrayal. If one looks at the tradition as a whole, on the other hand, then far from being a betrayal, it is an enrichment.

4. *Is a theology of the paschal mystery really Catholic?*

I have singled out a particular critique for comment here. The Society of St. Pius X (the schismatic group who are followers of the late Archbishop Marcel Lefebvre) has published a strong attack on the reform in a book titled *The Problem of the Liturgical Reform*.[5] Here dissatisfaction with the liturgical reform is squarely focused on what the

[5] See n. 1.

(anonymous) authors perceive as the theological underpinning of the whole enterprise, namely the theology of the paschal mystery. For them, to consider the whole paschal mystery (= the passion, death, resurrection, and ascension of Christ) rather than focusing on Christ's redemptive Passion is a betrayal of classic Catholic theology. Indeed, it leads to a denial of Catholic faith because it ultimately denies the doctrine of Christ's vicarious satisfaction for sin by his death. The authors seem to be completely innocent of twentieth-century theological discussion on the nature and meaning of the atonement, insisting on a purely "Anselmian" reading of vicarious satisfaction.[6] The more positive note brought in by the theology of the paschal mystery is responsible for a theology underlying the structure (i.e., the elimination of the old offertory prayers) and content of the new rite, a rite that in their opinion therefore downplays the doctrine of eucharistic sacrifice. The eucharistic sacrifice can only be adequately understood (for them) by affirming the visible sacrifice in the double consecration of the bread and the wine, i.e., in the separation of the transubstantiated body and blood. That such a theology of sacrifice has been largely discredited throughout the twentieth century (long before Vatican II) seems not to worry these authors in the least.

The Problem of the Liturgical Reform is an extremely useful book, not because its authors are correct, but because nowhere else have I seen what is stake with the post–Vatican II reform of the liturgy so clearly outlined and so well understood. Their understanding of the Mass as sacrifice relates primarily to the application of the merits of Christ with a view to the remission of sin and especially the temporal punishment due to sin—both for the living and for the dead. In the theology of the paschal mystery—and especially in the mystery-presence theology of Dom Odo Casel vindicated in SC—they see a much more positive presentation of how the events of our salvation are continually made present in the sacraments. Nothing seems to escape their attention: the concept of mystery, the role of the Trinity in the sacraments, the nature of grace, the meaning of representation (*repraesentare*), the biblical and patristic notion of memorial, the analogical meaning of the word "sacrament," the nature of Scripture vis-à-vis the magisterium. All of these factors are problematic in the new rite. And of course, given their theological presuppositions, elements like the importance of

---

[6] *The Problem of the Liturgical Reform*, 85–88.

Scripture in and of itself and as a vehicle of the presence of Christ are truly disturbing. In addition, they consider the role of the priest celebrant as found in the new rite very problematic. They take issue both with the *GIRM* and with the *Catechism of the Catholic Church* (and indeed the Constitution on the Church, *Lumen Gentium*), all of which contextualize the role of the priest within the assembly of the baptized.[7]

In all of this they are completely on target. That is, these are the issues that are at stake in the reform of the liturgy. The reformed liturgy does represent a radical shift in Catholic theology and piety. But their charge is that it also departs from orthodox Roman Catholic doctrine, and here I must disagree. In fact, I see in their work a tendency to what could be called "creeping doctrinalization"—a tendency to mistake theological positions for the church's doctrinal affirmations. A case in point is their insistence that "satisfaction for sin" can only be understood within an Anselmian theological framework, since this is the theology behind the *Roman Catechism*'s treatment of the subject.[8] (It is somewhat ironic that the authors wish to dogmatize the *Catechism of Trent = Roman Catechism* while at the same time being highly critical of the current *Catechism of the Catholic Church*.) Aside from taking issue with the Mystery-presence theology of Odo Casel, they show no interest in other theologies of atonement and eucharistic sacrifice proposed during the twentieth century, e.g., in the work of Maurice de la Taille, Anscar Vonier, or Eugene Masure. What is more, they could well profit from some of the contemporary work done on Christ's sacrifice by theologians who have been influenced by the thought of René Girard, including S. Mark Heim, Stephen Finlan, and Robert Daly.[9]

---

[7] Ibid., 19–26.

[8] Ibid, 85–86.

[9] S. Mark Heim, *Saved from Sacrifice* (Grand Rapids: Eerdmans, 2006); Stephen Finlan, *Problems with Atonement* (Collegeville, MN: Liturgical Press, 2005); Robert Daly, "Robert Bellarmine and Post-Tridentine Eucharistic Theology," *Theological Studies* 61 (2000): 239–60; idem, "Sacrifice unveiled or sacrifice revisited: Trinitarian and liturgical perspectives," *Theological Studies* 64 (2003): 24–42; idem, "Images of God and the Imitation of God: Problems with Atonement," *Theological Studies* 68 (2007): 36–51. I have tried to make sense of eucharistic sacrifice on the basis of the liturgy itself; see John F. Baldovin, *Bread of Life, Cup of Salvation: Understanding the Mass* (Lanham, MD: Rowman & Littlefield, 2003), 151–70, and in my "Lo, the Full Final Sacrifice: On the Seriousness of Christian Worship," *Antiphon* 7 (2002): 51–56.

Another example of "creeping doctrinalization" is their insistence that the only doctrinally sound understanding of eucharistic sacrifice is that of the double consecration—i.e., the separation of the Body and Blood of Christ.[10]

That the theology of the paschal mystery—which by no means denies the salvific death of Christ but rather puts it within the context of the whole salvation event—is central to the church's contemporary understanding of the work of Christ is clear from these authors' dissatisfaction with its use by Pope John Paul II and the *Catechism of the Catholic Church*.[11] That centrality is affirmed by Joseph Ratzinger, who insists (explicitly against these same authors) that the event of salvation is a unity and is appropriately called the paschal mystery.[12] It would be difficult to find a notion more central, indeed essential, to the foundations of the liturgical reform.

The authors of *The Problem of the Liturgical Reform* seem to be opposed to every innovation in theology since the late 1940s and the era of *La Nouvelle Théologie*. One can agree with their complete rejection of modern theology, of course, but I think that the price is very high indeed.

5. *Has the didactic aspect of the reformed liturgy triumphed over the latreutic?*

While this way of formulating the question might seem strange, it strikes at the heart of the debate over the reformed Roman Catholic liturgy. Aidan Nichols is representative of a number of the critics in framing the question as follows: "Is the Liturgy primarily latreutic, concerned with the adoration of God, or is it first and foremost didactic or edificatory, the conscious vehicle of instruction of individuals and the upbuilding of a community?"[13]

---

[10] It is true that Pius XII had insisted on this understanding of eucharistic sacrifice in *Mediator Dei* (1947) §115.

[11] For John Paul II see, e.g., Apostolic Letter *Vicesimus Quintus Annus* (on the 25th anniversary of the promulgation of the conciliar constitution, *Sacrosanctum Concilium*, on the Sacred Liturgy), 1988 (http://www.vatican.va/holy_father/john_paul_ii/apost_letters/documents/hf_jp-ii_apl_04121988_vicesimus-quintus-annus_en.html).

[12] Joseph Ratzinger, "Theology of the Liturgy," in Alcuin Reid, ed., *Looking Again at the Question of the Liturgy with Cardinal Ratzinger: Proceedings of the July 2001 Fontgombault Liturgical Conference* (Farnborough: St. Michael's Abbey Press, 2003), 33–34.

[13] Aidan Nichols, *Looking at Liturgy: A Critical View of Its Contemporary Form* (San Francisco: Ignatius Press, 1996), 32; similarly John Parsons, "A Reform of the

Now of course the answer is that the question is badly put. Is it really a matter of either/or? After all, SC speaks of the purpose of the liturgy as the glorification of God and the sanctification of the human race (§§7, 10). The operative word in Nichols' question is "primarily." I think it is safe to say that the liturgy is primarily about glorifying God (with the caveat that it is always God's act first), but at the same time I want to recognize that the conciliar constitution affirms that one cannot disassociate the latreutic and didactic elements of the liturgy. Our growth in holiness and our acknowledgment of the holiness and glory of God need to go hand in hand. In this sense it is important to emphasize the fact that the liturgy *always has a didactic and edificatory aspect* in addition to a latreutic one. Mistakes are made when the didactic element overwhelms the latreutic. As Robert Taft puts it, when people tell him they do not go to church because "they don't get anything out of it," he responds that what one "gets out of it" is "the inestimable privilege of worshiping Almighty God."[14] Ratzinger is after a similar target when he speaks of the liturgical "turn toward entertainment":

> . . . the liturgy is not a show, a spectacle, requiring brilliant producers and talented actors. The life of the liturgy does not consist in "pleasant" surprises and "attractive" ideas but in solemn repetitions. It cannot be an expression of what is current and transitory, for it expresses the mystery of the Holy. Many people have felt and said that liturgy must be "made" by the whole community if it is really to belong to them. Such an attitude has led to the "success" of the liturgy being measured by its effects at the level of spectacle and entertainment. It is to lose sight of what is *distinctive* to the liturgy, which does not come from what *we do* but from the fact that something is *taking place* here that all of us cannot "make."[15]

Doubtless Ratzinger is correct about the contemporary tendency to make liturgy into spectacle and to make it "interesting." James

Reform?" in Thomas Kocik, *A Reform of the Reform?*, 219.

[14] Robert Taft, "Sunday in the Byzantine Tradition," in idem, *Beyond East and West: Problems in Liturgical Understanding* (2nd rev. ed. Rome: Pontifical Oriental Institute Press, 2001).

[15] Joseph Ratzinger (with Vittorio Messori), *The Ratzinger Report: An Exclusive Interview on the State of the Church* (San Francisco: Ignatius Press, 1985), 126–27, cited in Kieran Flanagan, *Sociology and Liturgy: Re-presentations of the Holy* (New York: St. Martin's Press, 1991), 54. Emphasis in original.

Alison makes a similar point with regard to what he names the "un-Nuremberg" nature of authentic Christian liturgy, for he contrasts the growth in holiness that Christians achieve from true worship with great spectacles like the Nazi Nuremberg rallies documented in Leni Riefenstahl's film, *Triumph of the Will*.[16] I will return to the notion of "something taking place" in the second part of this chapter.

Let me add one other note with regard to the didactic aspect of liturgy. It is related to the question of translation and understanding we looked at in chapter 5. One of the pitfalls of translating the liturgy into the vernacular has been the tendency to think that everything that is prayed must be readily and easily understood. On one level, of course, this is true. On the other hand, we should not forget that we are trying to articulate our relation to the Divine Mystery, understood not as a puzzle to be solved, but as Karl Rahner put it so well, an unfathomable richness that can never be fully appreciated.[17] It is not so much that employing the vernacular has enabled us to understand the Absolute Mystery who is God as that we now can appreciate the depth of our not understanding.

As Louis-Marie Chauvet put it so well, "now we understand that we do not understand."[18]

6. *What is the meaning of active participation* (participatio actuosa)?

Another frequent topic among the critics has been the meaning of the phrase "active participation." The critics love to point to the Latin *participatio actuosa* and to insist that *actuosa* does not mean external activity but rather an internalized engagement with the liturgical action. At the risk of being obvious, one needs to point out several things.

1. The phrase first appeared in Italian as *participazione attiva* in Pius X's *motu proprio, Tra le sollecitudini*. In that context it is quite clear that the pope was trying to promote more external participation in the liturgy.

---

[16] James Alison, "Worship in a Violent World," *Studia Liturgica* 34 (2004): 133–46.

[17] Karl Rahner, "The Concept of Mystery in Catholic Theology," *Theological Investigations* IV (London: Darton, Longman and Todd, 1966), 36–73.

[18] Louis-Marie Chauvet, *Symbol and Sacrament: A Sacramental Reinterpretation of Christian Existence*, trans. Patrick Madigan and Madeleine E. Beaumont (Collegeville, MN: Liturgical Press, 1993), 326–30.

2. The phrase "full, conscious, and active participation" in SC §14 echoes and repeats what has already been said in §11: "it is also their (pastors') duty to ensure that the faithful take part fully aware of what they are doing, actively engaged in the rite, and enriched by its effects."

Only a foolish person would try to argue that such participation need not also be accompanied by a deep and internalized spiritual engagement in the rite. It is ridiculous to argue that everyone in the assembly needs to be doing everything all of the time. But it would be equally foolish to imagine that such internal commitment and engagement are not related to people actually participating in the liturgy with their voices and bodies.

7. In what would a remedy consist? What would provide a "reform of the reform"?

Certainly one of the phrases most frequently employed by the critics has been the idea of a "reform of the reform." It has been championed by Klaus Gamber, Joseph Ratzinger, Joseph Fessio, Aidan Nichols, Laszlo Dobszay, Thomas Kocik, the Adoremus Movement in general, and others. Each of these critics proposes a program for reforming the reform, and all of the programs share a family resemblance. In this final section of this part I would like to take a look at one of these proposals.

Much of Thomas Kocik's book, *The Reform of the Reform?* consists of a debate between a proponent of the "reform of the reform" party and a traditionalist who insists on returning to the pre–Vatican II Missal *tout court*. Both can agree on the following diagnosis, however:

> Massive ignorance about the fundamental nature of the Mass; the precipitous decline in the rate of Mass attendance everywhere since 1965; loss of belief in the Real Presence of Christ in the Blessed Sacrament; the removal of tabernacles and the destruction of communion rails; the replacement of the altar with a table; doctrinally ambiguous and offensively banal prayers; the manipulation of the liturgy for every conceivable personal, ideological, and political agenda (feminism, fuzzy ecumenism, and so on); an archaizing and sometimes neo-gnostic tendency toward arcane rites and equally abstruse language to accompany them ("scrutinies," "mystagogy," "catechumenate"); the diminution of the priest's role in the face of new lay "ministries" (extraordinary minister of the Eucharist, among others) and the (allegedly) consequent dearth of priestly vocations; the wholesale

abandonment, almost overnight, of a centuries-old sacred language and musical patrimony; the glorification of the profane ("folk" Mass, "rock" Masses, liturgical dance)—these are the fruits of a sweeping revolution that occurred in the wake of Vatican II.[19]

Needless to say, this is a sweeping indictment of the reform. What remedies are sought? Kocik provides a number of appendices. Among them is a proposal for a reform of the reform by Brian Harrison. It is based on the arguments of Klaus Gamber, which we surveyed in chapter 2. Here is what he proposes:[20]

- The retention of Latin for everything in the Mass except for the readings, prayer of the faithful, and proper prayers and chants (Collects, Introits, etc.)

- Retention of only the Roman Canon—somewhat adjusted to include an epiclesis and with a sung doxology and elevation at the end. Also some of the signs of the cross removed

- Retrieval of all the offertory prayers of the 1962 Missal

- Return to the proper prayers of the 1962 Missal

- Offertory prayers and Roman Canon recited in a low voice

- Communion to be received kneeling and on the tongue

- Elimination of extraordinary ministers of the Eucharist, a practice he calls the "clericalization" of the laity

- Eastward orientation of the priest

As I have already stated, these eight proposals are fairly representative of what most of the critics think would be a better eucharistic liturgy. Let us address them one by one:

1. We have already seen that, within a few years of the council, the vast majority of the world's bishops were requesting that the entire liturgy be translated into the vernacular. With the exception of some of the Ordinary texts, e.g., the Creed or *Lamb of God*, the

---

[19] Kocik, *Reform of the Reform?* 14–15.

[20] Brian Harrison, "Postconciliar Eucharistic Liturgy: Planning a 'Reform of the Reform,'" in Kocik, *Reform of the Reform?* 170–93.

Latin texts would be well beyond the reach of most congregations. At the same time, for the sake of tradition, and in multilingual and multinational assemblies, it would be helpful for everyone to learn some of these basic Latin chants as well as some traditional hymns like the *Salve Regina* and *Pange Lingua*. It can be very stirring to sing *Credo III* or the Lord's Prayer in an international setting.

2. It is true that SC did not envisage multiple eucharistic prayers in the reformed rite. But once again, the experience of the *Consilium* showed that "tinkering" with the Roman Canon (about which a great deal of dissatisfaction had been expressed) was not going to be sufficient. In any case we are seeing that in practice only two of the prayers of the current Sacramentary get a good deal of use (Eucharistic Prayers II and III). However much professional liturgists may lament this development (and I do, since some of the prayers, e.g., for reconciliation and for special occasions, are excellent) there is a kind of evolutionary development of liturgical practice that will win out.

3. With good reason Josef Jungmann referred to the old offertory prayers as a kind of jungle. They certainly (and confusingly) repeated the ideas of the Canon and communicated a notion of individual priestly offering (prayers said in the first-person singular) which I think one would be hard put to defend in terms of the proper role of the ordained minister. Of course, the role of the priest is precisely one of the most contested issues in contemporary sacramental/liturgical theology. I would maintain that we are far from finding a satisfactory theological approach to exactly how the priest functions ministerially at the liturgy, especially if we deem it important that the whole church offers the eucharistic sacrifice.[21] While one might complain that using the late-seventh-century *Ordo Romanus Primus* (which has no prayers between the

---

[21] I have made various attempts to address this issue: lately, "Liturgical Presidency: The Sacramental Question," in Eleanor Bernstein, ed., *Disciples at the Crossroads: Perspectives on Worship and Church Leadership* (Collegeville, MN: Liturgical Press, 1993), 27–44; "The Eucharist and Ministerial Leadership," in Judith Dwyer, ed., *Proceedings of the Catholic Theological Society of America* 52 (1997): 63–82; "Developing a Solid Eucharistic Theology of the Anaphora," *Liturgical Ministry* 14 (2005): 113–19; "The Priest as Sacramental Minister," in Donald Dietrich, ed., *Priests for the 21st Century* (New York: Crossroad, 2006), 19–32.

Creed and the prayer over the gifts) is an exercise in antiquarianism, the current rite does help to clarify the basic four-action shape of the liturgy:

Taking	—	*Presentation of Gifts*
Blessing	—	*Eucharistic Prayer*
Breaking	—	*Fraction*
Giving	—	*Communion*

4. Harrison refers to the study of Anthony Cecada, which found that the 1970 Missal retained only 17 percent of the prayers of the older rite.[22] We have already seen a similar criticism in chapter 5 when we analyzed the contribution of Lauren Pristas. It is certainly the case that the framers of the new rite intended to soften the harshness of some of the prayers of the older Missal. Harrison puts it this way:

> Instead of these timeless and essential aspects of catholic doctrine and spirituality, we have been given a liturgy that to an alarming extent reflects the naïve and transient optimism of the 1960's: consciousness of sin, guilt, enemies, and judgment had to yield to that "insight" of popular modern psychology that reassures us all: "I'm OK, you're OK."[23]

Now, this is good rhetoric but a very poor reading of the current Sacramentary, which (whatever its faults) does not represent a theology that stems from pop psychology. How can one accuse either the framers of the Missal itself or its translators of giving in to a pop-psychology mentality when we hear prayers like:

Prayer over the Gifts	Second Sunday of Advent
Lord, we are nothing without you. As you sustain us with your mercy, receive our prayers and offerings . . .	*Placare, Domine, quaesumus, nostrae precibus humilitatis et hostiis, et, ubi nulla suppetunt suffragia meritorum, tuae nobis indulgentiae succurre praesidiis.* [a prayer taken from the older *Missale Romanum*]

---

[22] Anthony Cecada, *The Problem with the Prayers of the Modern Mass* (Rockford, IL: Tan Books, 1991), cited in Brian Harrison, "Postconciliar Eucharistic Liturgy," 189.

[23] Harrison, "Postconciliar Eucharistic Liturgy," 190.

Or

Opening Prayer	Twenty-First Sunday in Ordinary Time
Father, help us to seek the value that will bring us lasting joy in this changing world. In our desire for what you promise make us one in mind and heart . . .	*Deus, qui fidelium mentes unius efficis voluntatis, da populis tuis id amare quod praecipis, id desiderare quod promittis, ut, inter mundanas varietates, ibi nostra fixa sunt corda, ubi vera sunt gaudia.*[24]

5. Harrison also criticizes the "constant patter of words" in the new liturgy. This is the reason he gives for proposing the quiet recitation of the prayers of the offertory and the Roman Canon. While it would be a good thing if more assemblies paid attention to the recommendation for a greater use of silence as the *GIRM* recommends (§45), reciting the eucharistic prayer silently or in a low voice contradicts the whole ethos of the reform. It could only make sense if one accepted the rationale for retaining only the Roman Canon and for the priest adopting the eastward position.

6. The recent CDWDS instruction *Redemptionis Sacramentum* (§§88–96) has addressed the question of the reception of holy communion at great length. It manifests a clear concern on the part of the Vatican and others that appropriate reverence is not always shown in receiving the sacrament.[25] But it also makes clear that there are legitimate options that may be adopted. One can agree wholeheartedly with Harrison and other "reformers of the reform" that

[24] See the treatment of this text (originally from the Old Gelasian Sacramentary [ms. Vat. Reg. 316]) by Gerard Moore, *Vatican II and the Collects for Ordinary Time: A Study in the Roman Missal* (San Francisco: Catholic Scholars Press, 1998), 268–80. Moore has found that thirty-one of the thirty-four came from traditional sources: twenty-five from the *Missal of Pius V* and six from the ancient Sacramentary tradition: see 668. To be sure, there are some adaptations to the prayers that would fall under Harrison's criticism of softening the notions of sin and guilt.

[25] I would observe, however, that the direction to communicants that they bow before receiving the Body of Christ or Precious Blood has not proven to be easily adopted. In fact, for most people it seems embarrassingly awkward. See the commentary by Anthony Ward, "The Discipline of the Eucharist: The Instruction 'Redemptionis Sacramentum,'" *Ephemerides Liturgicae* 118 (2004): 209–43.

greater reverence should be shown in receiving holy communion without insisting that communion be received on the tongue and in the kneeling posture. At the same time, I will acknowledge the need to find a better approach than the assembly line we currently employ in most Catholic churches.

7. Critics of the reform like to point to the use of extraordinary ministers of communion as an example of the "clericalization" of the laity. We see here once again a good amount of disagreement about the appropriate role of the ordained minister. For some, it makes a great deal of sense for priests and/or deacons who have not participated in a particular Eucharist to be called in at communion time in order to distribute holy communion. Extraordinary ministers are in the strictest sense of the word "extraordinary." On the other hand, others (I would include myself) understand that the integrity of a particular worshiping assembly makes it inappropriate to "import" ordained ministers into a service in which they have not participated. There is no question that the reformed Roman Catholic liturgy has represented a welcoming of lay ministers in the celebration of the Eucharist. Needless to say, all are not ministers in the same way—there are appropriate and differentiated roles—but all are truly celebrants of the liturgy.

8. We have considered the question of the eastward position in the last chapter. There I suggested that the CDWDS recommendation in its 1999 letter is the most apt response to those who are dissatisfied with *versus populum* celebration: i.e., the focus of celebration should be the Lord who gathers us together.

That point leads us to propose a vision of the continuation for the liturgical reform.

B. A WAY FORWARD

Writing a book is a kind of education. One hopes to have learned something in the course of trying to communicate to others. I certainly hope that this book is no exception. Writing these chapters has deepened my appreciation for the scheme outlined by Francis Mannion in the introduction and convinced me that the way forward in liturgical reform depends mainly on his fifth category—"Recatholicizing the Reform." The current state of Roman Catholic liturgy—in the United States at least—does not call for a return to Latin or the eastward position or a restriction on the use of lay liturgical ministers, much less on a radical reform of the current three-year lectionary or the elimination of post–Vatican II eucharistic prayers. On the other hand, neither does it call for the kind of free experimentation that became common in the late 1960s and the 1970s. Rather, today a deeper appreciation, savoring if you will, of the liturgy is a requirement for going forward. It is possible that I am wrong, of course, and that the correct way forward is to adopt the popular elements to be found in the megachurches or in youth-oriented liturgies. It is difficult to argue with success, but it seems to me that the gains of going in that direction will be ephemeral and will also be unfaithful to the rich tradition of Catholic worship. At the same time, those committed to liturgical renewal must realize that (in the words of a European liturgist friend in conversation several years ago) after forty years we have not yet succeeded in communicating to the vast majority of Catholics the meaning and importance of communal worship. The suggestions that follow are meant to help in that vital task.

I agree with Kevin Seasoltz's recent comment that: "the major liturgical issue facing the church today is not the structure or style of the eucharistic ritual and the form it takes . . . but rather the nature of the communities that celebrate the eucharist with their visions, their goals and their everyday practices."[26]

1. *Receiving the liturgy as a gift*

If I were to argue only one point in this concluding section, it would be that we need to understand that the liturgy is first and foremost God's act—a gift—and only secondarily something that we do. It has become very popular to parrot the etymology of the word "liturgy" as "the work of the people." This is true—but incomplete. The origin of the term has more to do with what we would normally call benefaction. A liturgy in the Greek world was first *a work done for the people*—a public service, like putting a fountain in a town square. The priority of God's action/gift in the liturgy is affirmed by the Christian theology of grace, which insists on God's prior action in saving us. It is signified in the universal pattern or dynamic of the liturgy, which has now been happily clarified in the structures of the reformed rites. That dynamic

---

[26] R. Kevin Seasoltz, *God's Gift Giving: In Christ and Through the Spirit* (New York: Continuum, 2007), 239.

consists in gift/response and is most clearly manifest in the structure: word/action. The reason why the word is proclaimed before we cele- brate the Eucharist is that what comes from God as nothing that we can earn or deserve must precede our doing anything ritually. Such an anti-Pelagian stance on the part of the liturgy has been, is, and always will be profoundly countercultural and acts as a roadblock to the cleverest and most attractive ideas we are able to come up with.

How can we combat the narcissistic notion that liturgy exists primarily for us to "get something out of it" if we do not recognize in a profound way that in worship God lays a claim on us, that in this sense liturgy is first and foremost a duty? Isn't this why the Byzantine Divine Liturgy is so attractive and compelling? No one would dare think that it is primarily a human construction.

Now then, what to do with the historical-critical enterprise of the last four centuries, an enterprise by which we have discovered just how very much of human culture, historical and geographical circum- stances, not to mention human talent and ingenuity, have contributed to the liturgy? We know very well, as Aidan Kavanagh used to say, that liturgy did not "just fall down from heaven in a glad bag." We can very often trace the roots and evolution of liturgical forms and at times see how historical circumstances have radically changed them.[27] In other words, we know that liturgical rites have cross-fertilized and that they have undergone significant change over the centuries. In addition, we know that theology must always be an enterprise of interpretation. Doctrine gives us the grammar of theology, but not theology itself. It must always be interpreted in specific contexts. At the same time as one accepts this fact, one recognizes how deeply the critics of the reform are wedded to an ahistorical understanding of Christian faith and therefore practice. But it is precisely out of a historical appreciation of theology and liturgy that the impetus for a reform of the liturgy arose.

How then to receive the liturgy as a gift? How to accept the liturgy as something that is not quite the work of our own hands? There is no easy and simple answer to this question. One of the difficulties raised

---

[27] See, e.g., the work of James C. Russell, *The Germanization of Early Medieval Christianity: A Sociohistorical Approach to Religious Transformation* (New York: Oxford University Press, 1994); and Yitzhak Hen, *The Royal Patronage of Liturgy in Frankish Gaul to the Death of Charles the Bald (877)* (London: Boydell Press [Henry Bradshaw Society], 2001).

by the influential postmodern philosopher Jacques Derrida has been the impossibility of a true gift—i.e., a gift that is wholly and completely altruistic—even from the hand of God. A number of philosophers and theologians, notably Jean-Luc Marion and John Milbank have attempted to respond. In fact, for Marion, God as gift is crucial to a new appreciation of both God and Eucharist,[28] but the liturgy itself demands the kind of second naïveté that Paul Ricoeur wrote of when dealing with the symbolism of evil. If one merely stays at the level of a system of symbols, argues Ricoeur, one can have a kind of truth as inner coherence. If, however, one asks the question of belief—even after a critique of symbols—one must opt for a kind of second naïveté that wagers the truth behind this system.[29] Similarly, the liturgy will remain a tool to be manipulated if we do not wager the fact that it is ultimately a gift from God. The same is true of Scripture, whose content and structural dynamic lies at the source of Christian worship.[30] True worship requires a suspension of disbelief and a willingness to accept what one is given.[31] C. S. Lewis put it very well, even if in curmudgeonly fashion, in the passage from *Letters to Malcolm* cited in chapter 4. Given the fact that so much of postindustrial society is consumer oriented, it is only natural that many (if not most) people have come to expect "what they want" out of liturgy. I am convinced that this factor, rather than some romantic dream of a once-satisfying pre–Vatican II liturgy, is what accounts for the steep decline in church attendance among Roman Catholics. Combined with the loss of the conviction that the vast majority of people are going to hell (and I might very easily be one of them), a consumerist mentality toward religion accounts for many people simply opting out of faithful or regular

---

[28] The bibliography on this subject is large. See, e.g., Jacques Derrida, *The Gift of Death* (Chicago: University of Chicago Press, 1995); Jean-Luc Marion, *Being Given: Toward a Phenomenology of Givenness* (Stanford: Stanford University Press, 2002); John Milbank, "Grace: the Midwinter Sacrifice," in idem, *Being Reconciled: Ontology and Pardon* (London: Routledge, 2003), 138–61. The discussion is very ably summarized in Seasoltz, *God's Gift Giving*, 4–15.

[29] Paul Ricoeur, *The Symbolism of Evil* (Boston: Beacon Press, 1967), 352–54.

[30] See the excellent argument for "juxtaposition" as a basic principle in both the Bible and liturgy in Gordon Lathrop, *Holy Things: A Liturgical Theology* (Minneapolis: Fortress Press, 1993).

[31] This is, of course, extremely difficult for people who work in the field of liturgy, in particular for parish liturgy coordinators who often seem to think the church's liturgy is simply not enough to justify their existence without extensive tinkering.

churchgoing. I wonder too if we haven't preached the Gospel too well. In other words, when people hear what kind of faith, hope, and love the Gospel really requires, they decide that this is not the sort of religion that is going to meet their needs.[32]

I am not arguing that Christian faith and specifically Catholic worship does not meet very profound human needs. But if we fall prey to the Instrumentalist Fallacy that the liturgy is primarily about our finding our needs met, then we can never really accept the liturgy for what it is: God's work first. The rest is all specifics.

2. *The liturgical role of the priest/ministers*

Surely at this point people must be tired of liturgists saying that the talk-show host approach to Catholic worship is inappropriate if not downright subversive of liturgy's intent. I think it is repeated so often because it remains so problematic. What remedy might be found?

I have become convinced that exhortation to priests and others who have speaking roles in the liturgy more often than not falls on deaf ears. "Yes, I know exactly what those liturgists are talking about. That talk-show business has no place in liturgy. Now, of course, the people need me to explain the rites to them and set the scene for the day's readings or to introduce myself if I am a stranger to this particular assembly." Since well over half (I am being very conservative here) of priests cannot seem to understand how to use the facultative moments of introduction in the liturgy (introduction to the Mass, to the readings, and to the eucharistic prayer), my suggestion would be not to allow any ad lib remarks during the eucharistic liturgy, except of course for the homily, announcements, and prayer of the faithful. The French sacramental theologian Louis-Marie Chauvet puts the thrust of my proposal in a nutshell when he says: "The basic law of liturgy is not 'say what you are doing,' but 'do what you are saying.'"[33] Imagine how incongruous one would find it if the priest began the Divine Liturgy of St. John Chrysostom with "Good morning. I'm Father George and I want to welcome you here today." Why is it that we are not quite so astonished when this is done in the Roman Rite?

[32] On consumerism in contemporary American religion see the fine study of Vincent Miller, *Consuming Religion: Christian Faith and Practice in a Consumer Culture* (New York: Continuum, 2005).

[33] Louis-Marie Chauvet, *Symbol and Sacrament: A Sacramental Re-reading of Christian Existence* (Collegeville, MN: Liturgical Press, 1995), 326.

Naturally my proposal would involve a change in the rubrics as well as the *General Instruction* and the *Praenotanda* to the other sacraments, but it would have two major salutary effects:

1. Much of the discomfort felt by the critics (but not limited to them) with the reformed liturgy has come from its performance. Were the liturgy to achieve some real stability by the elimination of off-the-cuff remarks and invitations, this would go a long way toward alleviating this situation.

2. Realizing that we cannot do catechesis during the liturgy itself may well force us to work harder to find appropriate ways to catechize the community. It has been my frequent observation that the liturgy is unable to sustain the catechetical and community-building weight that has been put on it.

My proposal could be read as a rejection of the whole project of inculturation. It is not. Inculturation is a serious process and decisions about how to properly inculturate need to take place mainly at the level of national episcopal conferences and not in parish meeting rooms.[34] For example, the proposed ICEL Scripture-related Collects for the three-year liturgical cycle were an excellent attempt to inculturate liturgical language. Moreover, I hope that my proposal can help to limit liturgies that are often dubious exercises in self-congratulation.

3. *Liturgy's aesthetic dimension*

Much of what I have just been discussing relates to the verbal, even intellectual, dimension of the liturgy. In particular it has been intended as an antidote to the didacticism and over-verbalization that is sometimes the target of the critics of the reform.

In chapter 5 we surveyed some of the criticism with regard to liturgy and church architecture and especially the position of the priest at the altar. These are related issues, of course, since many of the Catholic churches constructed over the past forty years are simply not

---

[34] I very much like the approach of Catherine Bell: "Inculturation is invoked so frequently now and with such an aura of settled liberal consensus about it, that I sometimes wonder if I still know what it means. One recent argument suggested that inculturation must go deeper, to appropriate and endow elements of the local culture with Christian meaning and make them part of Christian worship." "Ritual Tensions: Tribal and Catholic," *Studia Liturgica* 32 (2002): 26. Her reference is to Dennis Smolarksi, *Sacred Mysteries: Sacramental Principles and Liturgical Practice* (New York: Paulist, 1995), 10.

suited to *versus orientem* celebration (much less the celebration of the Missal of 1962). On the other hand, the attempt to create spaces that promote communal celebration has not always been felicitous. Many (but certainly not all) of the recent churches are far too comfortable to convey the tension involved in worshiping the God who is at once transcendent and immanent. To put it baldly: we need to stop designing churches that look like slightly out-of-date living rooms. Aidan Kavanagh said it well in one of his grammatical rules of liturgy: "Churches are not carpeted."[35]

Another crucial aesthetic element is liturgical music. Thomas Day's *Why Catholics Can't Sing* was pretty much dismissed out of hand by the American liturgical establishment when it appeared in 1990, but

[35] Aidan Kavanagh, *The Elements of Rite: A Handbook of Liturgical Style* (New York: Pueblo, 1982), 21. See his "Elementary Rules of Liturgical Usage" no. 6: "Raw space becomes liturgical place through the change his (Christ's) presence by grace, faith, and sacrament causes. Liturgical place is thus not a monument to the pastor's tastes, or the locale in which the assembly feels most comfortable. Jesus Christ's incarnate presence caused notable discomfort even for those who loved him best, and he is reported to have resorted to violence on one occasion when faced with the obduracy of the temple clergy's tastes. Liturgical place belongs to the assembly only because the space it occupies is first his. He alone makes it a place by specifying its meaning as distinct from all others. To this specification the assembly can only be obedient; for it the assembly can only pray even as it cooperates with him by faith in its specification.

What the church building shelters and gives setting for is the faithful assembly, the Church, in all its rich diversity of orders from catechumen to penitent, from youngest server to eldest bishop. As it meets for worship of the Source and Redeemer of all, the assembly is the fundamental sacrament of God's pleasure in Christ on earth. The Eucharistic food and drink are the sacred symbol of this ecclesial reality, which Paul simply calls Christ's Body. Christian instinct has been to house this assembly as elegantly as possible, avoiding tents, bedrooms, and school basements. . . .

The strong and elemental openness of liturgical place makes for dynamism and interest. It is a vigorous arena for conducting public business in which petitions are heard, contracts are entered into, relationships witnessed, orations declaimed, initiations consummated, vows taken, authority exercised, laws promulgated, images venerated, values affirmed, banquets attended, votes cast, the dead waked, the Word deliberated and parades cheered. It is acoustically sonorous, rarely vacant of sound or motion. It possesses a certain disciplined self-confidence as the center of community life both secular and sacred. It is the Italian piazza, the Roman forum, the Yankee town green, Red Square moved under roof and used for the business of faith. It is not a carpeted bedroom where faith may recline privately with the Sunday papers" (15–17).

not all of his observations were off target. Toward the end of the book he insists that there will be no decent liturgical music unless pastors take an active interest in it. He is right. If we are to have liturgies in which the music truly fits the celebration (as opposed to singing merely what people like), then pastors must take an active role in the selection of that music. There is a catch. The pastors would have to know something both about liturgical music and about liturgy. This requires the kind of adequate seminary training (and continuing education) that we are far from achieving, at least as far as I can tell. It should go without saying that such a program also requires adequately trained and adequately compensated liturgical musicians.

I would not argue for eliminating metrical hymnody in favor of chant at points in the liturgy where Scriptural texts (mostly psalm verses) have been provided. Some critics of course make that case.[36] The recent U.S. Bishops' document, "Sing to the Lord," does offer helpful guidelines, among them:

> Church legislation today permits an option the use of vernacular hymns at the Entrance, Preparation of the Gifts, Communion, and Recessional. Because these popular hymns are fulfilling a properly liturgical role, it is especially important that they be appropriate to the liturgical action.[37]

At the same time this document makes it clear that approval of hymns, songs, and acclamations for use in the liturgy is entrusted to the local bishops of those dioceses where liturgical music publishers are based (§108). Such supervision is appropriate since what is sung in the liturgy rivals Scripture readings, liturgical texts, and homilies in terms of what people actually take from their experience of worship. The new document provides rather good guidelines for the choice of music in various parts of the Eucharist, other sacraments, and the Liturgy of the Hours. Somehow, without turning to draconian measures, more assistance is needed in helping liturgical musicians and pastors decide what is appropriate for an entrance procession, for example, as opposed to the communion procession.

---

[36] It is also made by someone I would not consider a critic, Kevin Irwin, in his *Context and Text: Method in Liturgical Theology* (Collegeville, MN: Pueblo, 1993), 235–46.

[37] USCCB, *Sing to the Lord: Music in Divine Worship*, Nov. 14, 2007, 115 = http://www.usccb.org/liturgy/SingToTheLord.pdf.

Things are not quite as bad as in 1976 when Aidan Kavanagh wrote: "Most of the music currently done in the liturgy is stunningly immodest and stunningly bad."[38] At the same time the reform and renewal of Catholic liturgy can greatly benefit from more serious attention paid to the training of pastors and musicians.

CONCLUSION

I am convinced that, through the nineteenth- and twentieth-century liturgical movement, the Liturgy Constitution of the Second Vatican Council, and the reform and renewal of Roman Catholic liturgy that followed, God has brought great blessings to the church, enabling and encouraging millions of people to appreciate and deepen their faith and the Christian living that springs from its celebration. We owe a great debt, I believe, to Pope Paul VI and Annibale Bugnini in particular, but also to those dozens of scholars and pastors who worked so tirelessly for liturgical reform. Of course no such monumental undertaking can be without its flaws, and in some ways forty years is too short a time to judge its success or failure. In this book I have tried to listen to the many voices that in various ways have criticized the Vatican II liturgical reform. I hope I have treated them with the respect they deserve, for surely, like the reformers, they have the good of God's people at heart. (From time to time one unfortunately does not detect the same presupposition among the critics with regard to those entrusted with the reform.) In these pages I have also tried to reflect appreciatively on those areas where the critics need to be heeded. Let me end, then, with a caution and two convictions.

The caution: it is very important when comparing the pre– and post–Vatican II liturgy to try to make the comparison as fair as possible. Of course one can easily see the flaws in a fifteen-minute pre–Vatican II Low Mass said entirely in Latin when compared to a carefully prepared post–Vatican II eucharistic liturgy in which all the proper ministerial roles have been employed and the people have learned to participate with mind, heart, voice, and body. At the same time it is easy to ridicule a poorly prepared, self-congratulatory post–Vatican II liturgy in which very few participate actively when compared to a beautifully sung and aesthetically powerful example of

---

[38] Aidan Kavanagh, "Liturgical Business: Unfinished and Unbegun," *Worship* 50 (1976): 354–64, at 357.

a pre–Vatican II Solemn High Mass. All too often that is the level at which comparisons are made. They are, to say the least, unhelpful.

A first conviction: with regard to the church's worship there is no going back. Antiquarianism can take many forms and today it seems often to assume that of a nostalgia for a beautiful medieval dream of a liturgy, a liturgy that took place in the Ages of Faith. That world—and therefore that liturgy—are gone. It will do no good to try to retrieve them. What we can do, must do, is the painstaking and patient work of translating and creating texts and fashioning and preparing liturgical services that truly nourish the people of God today.

The second conviction reiterates my first point in this section. I believe that it is of the utmost importance that we concentrate on the liturgy as God's gift to us and that we find more and better ways to cooperate in receiving this gift. After all, in the liturgy we receive nothing less than divine life, a life meant to be shared with the world. What better gift can there be than that? And what better reason is there to put our energies into receiving that gift well and responding to it in our daily lives, so that we might become reflections of the world's true light, Jesus Christ.

The Uses of Liturgical History
(Berakah Response)[1]

In his recent *hommage* to Romano Guardini, *The Spirit of the Liturgy*, Cardinal Joseph Ratzinger (now Pope Benedict XVI) offered a severe critique of liturgical historians. I will let him speak for himself. The context is his argument about the position of the priest vis-à-vis altar and people:

> As I see it, the problem with a large part of modern liturgiology is that it tends to recognize only antiquity as a source, and therefore normative, and to regard everything that developed later, in the Middle Ages and through the Council of Trent, as decadent. And so one ends up with dubious reconstructions of the most ancient practice, fluctuating criteria, and never-ending suggestions for reform, which lead ultimately to the disintegration of the liturgy that has evolved in a living way.[2]

This is a serious indictment of the kind of work many liturgical historians do. Given the author's present ecclesial role, his critique seems all the more pressing today. I propose to address it in this essay. Does the work of modern liturgiology really romanticize the early church in a way that treats all subsequent development as mistaken? And has the modern study of the liturgy really led to a disintegration of an organically evolved liturgy? Ratzinger is representative of a large number of critics of the liturgical reform in the Roman Catholic Church that followed Vatican II. I have reviewed his criticisms as well as those of Catherine Pickstock and Klaus Gamber elsewhere.[3] But the list of

---

[1] Published as "The Uses of Liturgical History," *Worship* 82 (2008): 2–18, and previously as "The Usefulness of Liturgical History," *Proceedings of the North American Academy of Liturgy* (2007): 18–32.

[2] Joseph Ratzinger, *The Spirit of the Liturgy*, trans. John Saward (San Francisco: Ignatius Press, 2000), 82.

[3] John F. Baldovin, "Catherine Pickstock and Medieval Liturgy," in Clare V. Johnson, ed., *Ars Liturgiae: Worship, Aesthetics and Praxis: Essays in Honor of Nathan D. Mitchell* (Chicago: Liturgy Training Publications, 2003), 55–74; "Klaus Gamber

serious critics is fairly long. It includes, among others, Eamon Duffy, John Bossy, Francis Mannion, Jonathan Robinson, Denis Crouan, and Alcuin Reid. There are, no doubt, a number of similar critiques launched at the contemporary reforms in other churches as well, but I have not been able to investigate them. Suffice it to say that the issues facing standard contemporary liturgiology are common to historians of the liturgy whatever their affiliation. It seems to me that these authors cannot simply be dismissed as cranks or restorationists.

Therefore the first aim of this essay is to evaluate this critique of liturgical historians as antiquarians. A second aim is to reemphasize the importance, actually the indispensability, of liturgical history by recalling some of the major contributions to the study and practice of liturgy over the past century. Third, I want to discuss an area in which ongoing historical research may have a major impact on theology and practice today.

IS LITURGICAL HISTORY AN EXERCISE IN ANTIQUARIANISM?

I am not trying to argue that the historical work that informed the contemporary liturgical reforms is unproblematic. Let me give one example. In the course of his magisterial treatment of the development of the Roman Eucharist, Joseph Jungmann has this to say about the Mass at the end of the Middle Ages:

> The designation of the fourteenth and fifteenth centuries as the "autumn of the Middle Ages" (Huizinga) proved to be exceptionally apt in the history of the liturgy and not least in that of the Mass. There is indeed a rich and manifold growth, as we have just seen exemplified in church music. New forms, new inferences are continually being developed. But the inferences are developed only from what is at hand. There is no cutting back to the living roots, no springing forth of new, healthy growths. Scholastic theology produced nothing for the liturgy of the Mass or for a better understanding of it. So the forms appear overripe, the growth becomes dry and withered.[4]

---

and the Post-Vatican II Reform of the Liturgy," *Studia Liturgica* 33 (2003): 223–39; "Cardinal Ratzinger as Liturgical Critic," in Maxwell Johnson and Edward Phillips, eds., *Studia Liturgica Diversa: Essays in Honor of Paul F. Bradshaw* (Portland: Pastoral Press, 2004), 211–28.

[4] Joseph A. Jungmann, *Missarum Sollemnia: The Mass of the Roman Rite*, trans. Francis A. Brunner (New York: Benziger Bros., 1951) 1:127–28.

This analysis and statements like it are typical of Jungmann's historiography. As Ratzinger noted in the passage I cited above, Jungmann and others (like Theodor Klauser) were convinced that the Middle Ages saw a considerable decline in the fortunes of Christian liturgical celebration—and in theologizing about it. To give another example, Jungmann wrote about connecting gifts of Christian charity to the offerings made at the eucharistic celebration "in an age which was liturgically alive."[5] The clear implication is that at a certain point liturgical development ceased, i.e., it died. Contrast Jungmann's assessment with that of English historian John Bossy in his 1985 book, *Christianity in the West 1400–1700*:

> Despite the complaints of liturgists and reformers, it was not a contradiction that mass should be offered by the priest alone, in a ritual language, largely in silence and partly out of sight, and yet embody or create the sense of collective identity. In that respect it represented Durkheim's identification of the sacred with the collective. It represented something else where, as B. L. Manning put it, it possessed the "human interest" of engaging with the socially particular as well as with the general: it performed the dramatic coup of eliciting the supernatural out of the mundane. We need not suppose that congregations were ignorant of what the priest was doing at the altar, if only because his performance was so frequently criticized. The average parishioner, who would probably not be up to that, nevertheless knew what he needed to know. He knew that the priest was making sacrifice and satisfaction for the living and the dead; he knew that he would make God actually present in the Host before consuming it. If he was not a heretic or unbeliever he knew that this extraordinary event represented the best thing that could have happened in the universe, a deliverance from the powers of evil, a reconciliation of God and man from which any amount of consequential good might follow, in this world and the next.[6]

Now there is revisionist history at its best—at least in terms of prose. (Let me hasten to add that every good historical investigation is at least to some extent revisionist. Otherwise it is mere repetition of what has already been written.) Bossy's implication is clear. Liturgists and

[5] Ibid., 2:3.
[6] John Bossy, *Christianity in the West 1400–1700* (New York: Oxford University Press, 1985), 67.

reformers, those who were the architects of the post–Vatican II liturgy (I should say "liturgies" because all the reforms share the same or similar intellectual pedigree, for example, the widespread acceptance of Gregory Dix's fourfold shape of the eucharistic liturgy)[7] as well as those who have supported those reforms with scholarship, teaching, and pastoral application—all those people are inspired by a poor understanding of the development of liturgical history. Bossy's position is fairly representative of revisionist historians.

As another example, take this crucial and oft-cited statement about the principles of reform in the Vatican II Constitution on the Liturgy: "In the reform of the liturgy, therefore, the following general norms are to be observed. The rites should be marked by a noble simplicity; they should be short, clear, and unencumbered by useless repetitions; they should be within the people's powers of comprehension and as a rule not require much explanation."[8]

The principles of simplicity, brevity, clarity, and the avoidance of repetition are the result of historical investigations since the sixteenth century (but especially in the twentieth century) that unearthed accretions to the liturgy in an attempt to uncover more pristine forms. Forty years later one can legitimately ask, as Catherine Pickstock does rather severely, what precisely constitutes unnecessary repetition?[9] She has some very interesting criticisms of the Mass of Paul VI.[10] And I think that to a certain extent she is correct, for we can admit to a certain naïveté with regard to some anthropological dimensions of worship, such as the usefulness of repetition (e.g., litanies), without discounting the historical project behind contemporary liturgical reforms. Witness Jungmann's understanding of his own project as he summarizes the introduction to the first volume of *Missarum Sollemnia*: "It is the task of the history of the liturgy to bring to light these ideal patterns of past

---

[7] See John F. Baldovin, "The Liturgical Movement and Its Consequences," in Charles Hefling and Cynthia Shattuck, eds., *The Oxford Guide to the Book of Common Prayer: A Worldwide Survey* (New York: Oxford University Press, 2006), 249–60.

[8] Second Vatican Council, Constitution on the Sacred Liturgy (*Sacrosanctum Concilium*), §§33–34, in *The Liturgy Documents: A Parish Resource* (4th ed. Chicago: Liturgy Training Publications, 2004) 1:10.

[9] Catherine Pickstock, *After Writing: On the Liturgcial Consummation of Philosophy* (Oxford: Blackwell Publishers, 1998), 186–90.

[10] I have tried to assess them elsewhere. See n. 2.

phases of development which have been hidden in darkness and whose shapes are all awry."[11]

Is this antiquarianism, by which I mean the search for the past in a (vain) effort to repeat it? This cannot be the task of the liturgical historian, for as Robert Taft has put it memorably: "The purpose of this history is not to recover the past (which is impossible), much less to imitate it (which would be fatuous), but to understand liturgy which, because it has a history, can only be understood in motion, just as the way to understand a top is to spin it."[12]

Taft's approach is clearly not antiquarianism, nor is it romanticizing the early church, as in Ratzinger's criticism, but rather the ongoing attempt to understand how Christian worship developed in the various contexts it called home.

We must be careful, however, not to privilege any one period or locality in our historical reconstructions. I used to labor under the conviction that the fourth century represented a kind of pinnacle of liturgical development, after which everything went downhill. Who could not love the wonderful descriptions of the pilgrim Egeria? Or the elegant Anaphora of Saint Basil—especially in its Alexandrian form? Or the liturgy as it seems to have been in the homilies of those great fourth-century mystagogues: John Chrysostom, Cyril of Jerusalem, Ambrose of Milan, and Theodore of Mopsuestia? But good liturgical history avoids such simplifications. Paul Bradshaw disabused me of my reverence for the fourth century with his incisive analysis of precisely what did change at that point. He describes the rosy picture that many paint of the post-Constantinian developments and goes on to add:

> many of the fourth century liturgical developments were the responses of a church which had already passed its peak, and was experiencing the beginnings of decline, and was trying to do something to stem the

[11] Jungmann, *Missarum Sollemnia* 1:5. See also the introduction entitled "History, the Present, and the Future," in idem, *The Early Liturgy: To the Time of Gregory the Great*, trans. Francis Brunner (Notre Dame: University of Notre Dame Press, 1959), 1–8. See similarly another extremely influential work, Theodor Klauser, *A Short History of the Western Liturgy: An Account and Some Reflections*, trans. John Halliburton (2nd ed. New York: Oxford University Press, 1979), 1–3.

[12] Robert Taft, *Beyond East and West: Problems in Liturgical Understanding* (2nd revised and enlarged ed. Rome: Edizioni Orientalia Christiana/Pontifical Oriental Institute, 1997), 192.

tide. Unfortunately, all too often the "something" that was then done unwittingly carried within it seeds of further destruction rather than the solution that would preserve the glories of the past.[13]

This is not to say that the third century—or the second or the first—represents a golden age of Christian worship. There is no period to go back to and imitate: not fourth-century Jerusalem, or seventh-century Rome, or tenth-century Constantinople, or fourteenth-century Salisbury or sixteenth-century Geneva, for that matter. The task is to understand liturgical forms as they develop in their particular historical contexts. Each period produces the liturgies it needs, but I maintain that there are liturgical forms that can be recaptured at least as general models for contemporary worship. The eucharistic liturgy described in *Ordo Romanus Primus*, for example, cannot and should not be reproduced today—especially not with all those notaries, chamberlains, and other assorted ecclesiastical court officials doing God-knows-what in the course of the liturgy. At the same time, that description of the liturgy did provide a kind of template for the Mass of Paul VI (and a number of other contemporary eucharistic liturgies) because, among other things, the basic clarity of its lines, the extent of participation by the faithful (e.g., in the procession of the gifts), and the audibility of the eucharistic prayer all recommended themselves to a twentieth-century adaptation of the liturgy. Let me hasten to add that in raising up the liturgy of *Ordo Romanus Primus* as a kind of model I also want to agree with Anscar Chupungco, who understood the first generation of liturgies produced after the council as a kind of bare-bones reform that still required quite a bit of inculturation.[14] Let me turn then to the question of what liturgical history has to offer.

HOW IS LITURGICAL HISTORY USEFUL?

David Tracy has argued that the best contributions of modern systematic theology have been hermeneutical in nature. He puts it this way: "The heart of any hermeneutical position is the recognition that all interpretation is a mediation of past and present, a translation

[13] Paul F. Bradshaw, "The Effects of the Coming of Christendom on Early Christian Worship," in Alan Kreider, ed., *The Origins of Christendom in the West* (Edinburgh: T&T Clark, 2001), 270.

[14] Anscar Chupungco, *Liturgies of the Future: The Process and Methods of Inculturation* (New York: Paulist Press, 1989), 3–23.

carried on within the effective history of a tradition to retrieve its sometimes strange, sometime familiar meanings."[15] Tracy proceeds to say that in making these assertions he is attempting to argue for a "non-classicist notion of the classic." The theologians he holds up as modern candidates for classical status were all involved in the retrieval of classics: Rahner and Lonergan of Aquinas, Tillich and Bultmann of Luther, Barth of Calvin, and Reinhold Niebuhr of Augustine.[16]

A non-classicist approach to liturgical history is precisely what is required today. By this I mean a history that does not idolize frozen moments in the tradition but rather (as with Taft's understanding of the purpose of liturgical history) tries to understand how this important monument of the way we worship came about and how it relates to other aspects of belief and practice. Tracy is dealing with classic texts, but we need to remind ourselves that the study of the liturgy is not the study of texts alone. What are, strictly speaking, liturgical texts do not by any means tell the whole story. Even when one can piece together a sacramentary, lectionary, calendar, and ordo, one does not have the historical phenomenon of a liturgy. To get the full picture requires some understanding of art and architecture, music (which is admittedly very difficult for Christian liturgy up to the ninth century), and social history. Recently, in his brilliant and scathing indictment of Morton Smith's *Secret Gospel of Mark*, Peter Jeffery has underlined the inadequacy of dealing with texts alone when it comes to liturgical history. He calls for a threefold analysis: of the text, of the liturgy as act, and that yielded by ritual criticism.[17]

I attempted to provide this kind of picture of liturgical context in *The Urban Character of Christian Worship*, especially when I wrote:

> The fact that liturgy is always culturally conditioned has been insufficiently appreciated until modern times. The discipline of sacramental theology was able to ignore the importance of liturgical celebrations until liturgiology became a science in its own right. Thus, there was little attention paid to the comparative study of various liturgies in

---

[15] David Tracy, *The Analogical Imagination: Christian Theology and the Culture of Pluralism* (New York: Crossroad, 1981), 99.

[16] Ibid., 104.

[17] Peter Jeffery, *The Secret Gospel of Mark Unveiled: Imagined Rituals of Sex, Death, and Madness in a Biblical Forgery* (New Haven: Yale University Press, 2007), 55–60. Jeffery refers to the work of Lawrence Hoffman, *Beyond the Text: A Holistic Approach to Liturgy* (Bloomington: Indiana University Press, 1987).

various times and places as a means of understanding the nature and meaning of worship. But the meaning of Christian worship is not to be found in an abstract notion of the essence of a sacrament, but rather in the gradual unfolding of the historical celebration of the sacraments, i.e., in the history of the liturgy itself.[18]

What is more, no one can pretend to have the last word. For example, the Australian expert on John Chrysostom, Wendy Mayer, took my work a step further in an excellent analysis of the use of the sea in Constantinople's stational liturgy.[19] Another example: in the recent fifth volume of his monumental history of the Liturgy of St. John Chrysostom, in his treatment of the fraction rite and the commixture of water and wine, Robert Taft accepted Pierre Nautin's argument that the *fermentum* in fifth-century Rome did not refer to presbyters placing the consecrated bread they received from the papal Mass into wine that had already been consecrated (in the eucharistic prayer). Nautin argued that the presbyters themselves were receiving communion in the neighborhood churches (*tituli*) while they were busy about other kinds of Sunday services for catechumens and penitents. Taft's careful scholarship prompted me to review the dossier of material on the subject. At first I was convinced that the commonly accepted opinion (which I had followed in my book, *The Urban Character of Christian Worship*) was correct, and that, since even Homer nods, Taft might be wrong. In the end, after reviewing the evidence and several other important studies, I came around to Taft's position—at least more or less—and was convinced that the presbyters were not actually celebrating the Eucharist but rather presiding over communion services in the neighborhood churches.[20]

Projects like these are not work for antiquarians but for those convinced that the past of Christianity has much to offer to its present. That work is also never quite completed—as though once we have

[18] John F. Baldovin, *The Urban Character of Christian Worship: The Origins, Development and Meaning of Stational Liturgy*. Orientalia Christiana Analecta 228 (Rome: Pontifical Oriental Institute Press, 1987), 254.

[19] Wendy Mayer, "The Sea Made Holy. The Liturgical Function of the Waters Surrounding Constantinople," *Ephemerides Liturgicae* 112 (1998): 459–68.

[20] See Robert Taft, *A History of the Liturgy of St. John Chrysostom*. Vol. V: *The Precommunion Rites*. Orientalia Christiana Analecta 261 (Rome: Pontifical Oriental Institute Press, 2000), 413–26; John F. Baldovin, "The Fermentum in Fifth Century Rome," *Worship* 79 (2005): 38–53.

arrived at a definitive history we can then do an adequate theology. No, the work of liturgical history is unending (i.e., those of us who do liturgical history for a living have hope of future employment), because new situations will always prompt us to ask new questions of the material of history, which means that there will never be a final and complete theology or a final and complete liturgical reform either.

So liturgical history remains useful for several reasons. The first is that no one pretends to invent tradition anew, even when some radically new ways are employed to communicate and celebrate religious faith. To be religious is to have a tradition, and to have a tradition is to need somehow to understand its ongoing relevance. Second, liturgical history remains relevant because we do not cease to have pressing questions to bring to the past. So, for example, when a scholar like Andrew McGowan reviews the data from the early church on the celebration of wine-less Eucharists, new perspectives for the understanding of the broader tradition are opened up.[21] When Gabriele Winkler studies the anointings in the Syriac tradition, she finds that the earliest patterns suggest a baptismal theology significantly at odds with the accepted paschal theology that is much in vogue today.[22] In a similar fashion, the research done by Paul Bradshaw, Maxwell Johnson, and Edward Phillips on the *Apostolic Tradition* should make it very difficult for theologians and reformers alike to make facile claims about that important document—especially when it comes to Christian initiation and the nature of the eucharistic prayer.[23]

A further testimony to the relevance of liturgical history may be found in the work of the North American Academy of Liturgy itself. Anyone who peruses the *Proceedings* will find that only three out of twenty seminar groups are explicitly devoted to the study of liturgical history, but a closer investigation of the *Proceedings* for 2006, for

[21] Andrew McGowan, *Ascetic Eucharists: Food and Drink in Early Christian Meals* (Oxford: Clarendon Press, 1999); more recently, "Food, Ritual, and Power," in Virginia Burrus, ed., *A People's History of Christianity 2: Late Ancient Christianity* (Minneapolis: Fortress Press, 2005), 145–64.

[22] Gabriele Winkler, "The Original Meaning of the Prebaptismal Anointing and Its Implications," in Maxwell Johnson, ed., *Living Water, Sealing Spirit* (Collegeville, MN: Liturgical Press, 1995), 58–81.

[23] Paul Bradshaw, Maxwell Johnson, and L. Edward Phillips, *The Apostolic Tradition: A Commentary*. Hermeneia (Minneapolis: Fortress Press, 2002); see John F. Baldovin, "Hippolytus and the Apostolic Tradition: Recent Research," *Theological Studies* 64 (2003): 520–42.

example, will reveal that nine out of sixty-one presentations (outside of the three history seminars) dealt with explicitly historical topics.

This leads to several reflections. On the one hand, there can be little doubt that the dominance liturgical history once held in the field of liturgical studies is long gone. But, on the other hand, I would want to argue that responsible historical scholarship is needed to ground the historical claims we inevitably make when analyzing common worship. As Kathleen Hughes has written in an essay about the work of Jungmann:

> The Church is filled with pastoral liturgists today who have lost their theological moorings and have become liturgical dilettantes. Jungmann's method of doing pastoral liturgy challenges liturgists today to ground their convictions in meticulous research into the long and rich tradition of the Church's corporate prayer, and to recognize, at every step, the multiple factors that produced the liturgy in possession at the time of the council and the equally complex reality of the liturgy as it unfolds in the political and cultural context of our day.[24]

Such scholarship has become all the more important at a time when further reforms, for example, the current project of translating the third edition of the *Missal of Paul VI*, rely on differing readings of history. In particular I am referring to the debate over the nature of translation and of liturgical language, which often comes down to one's understanding of the intent of the people who formulated the first Christian Latin liturgical texts. Were they aiming for a sacral language or not?[25]

I need to add that vigilance about our historical claims is always necessary. In 1986 Thomas Talley published his research on the origins of the liturgical year.[26] In this groundbreaking book he questioned any number of popularly held historical assumptions, e.g., the theory that the date of the Roman liturgical celebration of Christmas had its origins in a reaction to a pagan festival, the *Natalis Solis Invicti*. The nature of

---

[24] Kathleen Hughes, "Meticulous Scholarship at the Service of a Living Liturgy," in Joanne M. Pierce and Michael Downey, eds., *Summit and Source: Commemorating Josef A. Jungmann, s.j.* (Collegeville, MN: Liturgical Press, 1999), 31.

[25] See Maura K. Lafferty, "Translating Faith from Greek to Latin: *Romanitas* and *Christianitas* in late Fourth-Century Rome and Milan," *Journal of Early Christian Studies* 11 (2003): 21–62.

[26] Thomas Talley, *The Origins of the Liturgical Year* (2nd, emended ed. Collegeville, MN: Liturgical Press, 1991).

historical scholarship is such that researchers will continue to analyze and nuance Talley's review of the evidence and his conclusions for years to come.[27] One historical issue in particular stands out: his use of the so-called Secret Gospel of Mark. In his attempt to understand the origins of the forty-day Lent, Talley argued that those origins were to be found not in a pre-paschal period (i.e., a forty-day Lent leading up to Easter and the celebration of Christian initiation) but rather in a post-Epiphany fast in Alexandria that ended with initiation and was distinct from the celebration of Easter. A major building block of that argument was his claim that the so-called Secret Gospel of Mark, "discovered" by Morton Smith in the late 1950s and published in 1973, provided a missing link in the lectionary system of Constantinople and that Constantinople's system in turn was dependent on Alexandria. Talley noticed that the lectionary tenth-century *Typikon* of the Great Church at Constantinople had the following sequence of Lenten gospels: Mark 10:32-45 on Sunday of the fifth week of Lent followed by John 11:1-45, the raising of Lazarus on the sixth Saturday, the day before Palm Sunday. Why the switch from Mark's gospel to John's? asks Talley. He hypothesizes that the Secret Gospel was inserted between vv. 34 and 35 of Mark 10 in early Alexandrian practice and so would have logically been read at the Saturday liturgy. But since it was non-canonical (to put it mildly!) the Lazarus account from John's gospel was substituted in Constantinopolitan practice. Now this is brilliant conjecture on Talley's part and it is based on years of meticulous scholarship, but it is almost certainly wrong. It shows how fragile a basis even the best of us can use to build our theories. Talley's theory about Alexandrian Lent is gravely put in doubt if Morton Smith's "Secret Gospel" never existed. Two recent books have argued fairly persuasively that Smith's Secret Gospel and the so-called Letter of Clement to Theodore in which it was contained were an elaborate hoax.[28]

---

[27] See, e.g., Martin Connell's new two-volume work on the liturgical year: vol. 1: *Eternity Today: On the Liturgical Year: On God and Time, Advent, Christmas, Epiphany, Candlemas* and vol. 2: *Eternity Today: On the Liturgical Year: Sunday, Lent, the Three Days, the Easter Season, Ordinary Time* (New York: Continuum, 2006).

[28] Peter Jeffery, *The Secret Gospel of Mark Unveiled*, and Stephen C. Carlson, *The Gospel Hoax: Morton Smith's Invention of Secret Mark* (Waco, TX: Baylor University Press, 2005). Three articles in the *Journal of Early Christian Studies* 11:2 (2003) were devoted to the debate over the Secret Gospel.

Sometimes theories like Talley's become the basis for suggested reforms of the liturgy. Needless to say, we must be careful about assessing their status—and even their weight when the evidence is well founded. Paul Bradshaw once said that he reckoned that the contemporary Roman Catholic Rite of Christian Initiation of Adults (and its cousins in other churches) could not have taken the shape it had without the nineteenth-century discovery of the *Apostolic Tradition*, whose questionable dating and authority I have alluded to above. Much the same can be said of the effect of the discovery of the pilgrimage diary of Egeria (an *unicum* in 1884 by J. F. Gamurrini) on proposals for what is called "the cathedral office." To give him his due, Talley himself realized the inadvisability of taking the work of other scholars at face value when he took the trouble to question the dating for the Egyptian solstice that everyone had simply accepted. He did his own investigation of ancient Egyptian calendars and found that the calendar on which many based their theory had never existed.

So one can safely claim that liturgical history is a demanding and delicate, but necessary, enterprise for making theological and reformatory claims. I want to illustrate that contention with a final example, one that I think has profound consequences for Christian theology and practice: the notion of consecration in the eucharistic prayer.

What is an institution narrative for?

On 20 July 2001 the Vatican's Pontifical Council for the Promotion of Christian Unity issued a declaration titled "Guidelines for Admission to the Eucharist between the Chaldean Church and the Assyrian Church of the East."[29] This declaration has profound (if perhaps unintended) consequences for the theology of the Eucharist and (relevant to my theme) it rests on historical scholarship. I am not so much interested here in the argumentation for eucharistic sharing provided by these guidelines (important as that issue is) as I am in what it says about the place of the institution narrative in the eucharistic prayer. Here is the document's summary of the decision on this point:

> As the Catholic Church considers the words of the Eucharistic Institution a constitutive and therefore indispensable part of the Anaphora or Eucharistic Prayer, a long and careful study was undertaken of the Anaphora of Addai and Mari, from a historical, liturgical and

[29] Online at http://www.vatican.va/roman_curia/pontifical_councils/chrstuni/documents/rc_pc_chrstuni_doc_20011025_chiesa-caldea-assira_en.html.

theological perspective, at the end of which the Congregation for the Doctrine of Faith on January 17th, 2001 concluded that this Anaphora can be considered valid. H. H. Pope John Paul II has approved this decision. In the first place, the Anaphora of Addai and Mari is one of the most ancient Anaphoras, dating back to the time of the very early Church; it was composed and used with the clear intention of celebrating the Eucharist in full continuity with the Last Supper and according to the intention of the Church; its validity was never officially contested, neither in the Christian East nor in the Christian West. Secondly, the Catholic Church recognises the Assyrian Church of the East as a true particular Church, built upon orthodox faith and apostolic succession. The Assyrian Church of the East has also preserved full Eucharistic faith in the presence of our Lord under the species of bread and wine and in the sacrificial character of the Eucharist. In the Assyrian Church of the East, though not in full communion with the Catholic Church, are thus to be found "true sacraments, and above all, by apostolic succession, the priesthood and the Eucharist" (U.R., n. 15). Finally, the words of Eucharistic Institution are indeed present in the Anaphora of Addai and Mari, not in a coherent narrative way and *ad litteram*, but rather in a dispersed euchological way, that is, integrated in successive prayers of thanksgiving, praise and intercession.

This statement is astounding in its implications for eucharistic theology as well as for ecumenical rapprochement. In the words of Robert Taft, it is "the most remarkable Catholic magisterial document since Vatican II."[30] His colleague, Cesare Giraudo, calls "this recognition . . . an authentic miracle, a true work of the Holy Spirit."[31]

In its elaboration of the earlier paragraphs I have cited above, the Council for Christian Unity says the following specifically with regard to the use of liturgical history:

[30] Robert Taft, "Mass Without the Consecration? The Historic Agreement on the Eucharist between the Catholic Church and the Assyrian Church of the East Promulgated on 26 October 2001," *Worship* 77 (2003): 482–509, here at 484.

[31] Cesare Giraudo, "L'Anafora degli Apostoli Addai e Mari: La 'Gemma Orientale' della Lex Orandi," *Divinitas* n.s. 47 (2004): 107–24, here at 122. *Divinitas* is the Vatican's semiofficial journal of theology. It devoted the entire issue of twelve articles (including an Italian translation of Taft's "Mass Without a Consecration," to the "Guidelines." Several of the authors are quite critical of the guidelines and very aware of the implications with regard to the notion of eucharistic consecration. See, for example, Brunero Gherardini, "Le parole della Consecrazione eucaristica" (141–70), and David Berger, "'Forma huius sacramenti sunt verba Salvatoris'—Die Form des Sakramentes der Eucharistie" (171–200).

For many years, scholars discussed which version of the Anaphora of Addai and Mari might have been the original one. Some scholars argued that the original formula of the Anaphora of Addai and Mari was longer and did contain an Institution Narrative. Other scholars are convinced that the Anaphora of Addai and Mari did not contain a coherent Institution Narrative and that the short version is consequently the original one. Nowadays, most scholars argue that it is highly probable that the second hypothesis is the right one. Anyhow, this historical question cannot be resolved with absolute certainty, due to the scarcity or absence of contemporary sources. The validity of the Eucharist celebrated with the Anaphora of Addai and Mari, therefore, should not be based on historical but on doctrinal arguments.[32]

One might perhaps be forgiven some skepticism with regard to the last sentence. I would not quarrel with the Roman Church's (or for that matter any church's) obligation to teach on doctrinal grounds, but it is precisely because the weight of historical scholarship has shown the shorter form of Addai and Mari (namely the one without an institution narrative) as likely to be original that one needs to raise the doctrinal question in the first place. What makes it more probable is also the historical scholarship over the past fifty years or so that has been willing to question whether the eucharistic prayers of the first three centuries had an institution narrative as we know it. (We will return in a moment to the phrase "as we know it.") The dossier on the introduction of the institution narrative to the early eucharistic prayers is a familiar one. It includes the studies of excellent scholars like Louis Ligier, Cesare Giraudo, Enrico Mazza, Herman Wegman, Thomas Talley, and Edward Kilmartin.[33] It refers to prayers (which Mazza calls paleo-anaphoras) in *Didache* 9–10, *Apostolic Constitutions* 7, Papyrus Strasbourg Greek 254, and perhaps even those alluded to in Cyril of Jerusalem's *Mystagogical Catechesis* 5 and the *Baptismal Homilies* of Theodore of Mopsuestia.[34] So the issue becomes not: how did a

[32] See n. 29 above.

[33] See the excellent summary of the scholarship in Taft's "Mass Without the Consecration?"

[34] These texts can be found in Anton Hänggi and Irmgard Pahl, eds., *Prex Eucharistica: Textus e Variis Liturgiis Antiquirioribus Selecti*. Spicilegium Fribourgense 12 (Fribourg: Universitätsverlag, 1968) and in English translation in R. C. D. Jasper and G. J. Cuming, eds., *Prayers of the Eucharist: Early and Reformed* (3rd ed. Collegeville, MN: Liturgical Press, 1990). For Mazza's treatment see his *The Origins of the Eucharist Prayer*, trans. Ronald Lane (Collegeville, MN: Liturgical Press, 1995).

eucharistic prayer grow out of Christ's words of institution? But rather: how did Christ's words of institution (a narrative, after all) end up in a eucharistic prayer?[35]

The "Guidelines" do recognize the historical roots of this important theological question. As a matter of fact, the longer argument in a later part of the document explicitly recognizes that the question at hand is related to the ancient nature of Addai and Mari and the fact that its validity was never questioned. But the crux of the question comes with the following statement: "The words of Eucharistic Institution are indeed present in the Anaphora of Addai and Mari, not in a coherent narrative way and *ad litteram*, but rather in a dispersed euchological way, that is, integrated in successive prayers of thanksgiving, praise and intercession." The document is clearly trying to reconcile this ancient anaphora (and by implication what seems to be the tradition of the first three centuries) with the very explicit statement of the fifteenth-century Council of Florence that "the form of this sacrament are the words of the Saviour" (DS 1321).

This is what the Pontifical Council seems to be saying: the narrative of institution is certainly necessary for eucharistic consecration, but that narrative can be present in an anaphora in diverse ways—by reference to the Lord's institution rather than by quoting his words directly. This is the solution adopted by both Robert Taft and Enrico Mazza, and I think it is correct.[36]

I have dwelt on this example of the relation between historical scholarship and contemporary theology at some length because I think it demonstrates how very important attentiveness to historical scholarship can be for the churches today. To my mind the Gordian knot of how the ordained minister represents Christ can be rather easily cut if we are willing to reconsider the historical formulation of eucharistic praying. We will be free to consider other ways of talking about

[35] In addition to Taft's article cited in n. 30 and Enrico Mazza, "La Récent Accord Entre L'Église Chaldéene et L'Église Assyrienne d'Orient sur l'Eucharistie," *Divinitas* 47 (2004): 125–37; see Andrew McGowan, "'Is There a Liturgical Text in This Gospel?': The Institution Narratives and Their Early Interpretive Communities," *Journal of Biblical Literature* 118 (1999): 73–87.

[36] Taft, "Mass Without the Consecration?," 502–06 and Mazza, "La Récent Accord," 136–37. At this point I prefer Mazza's more modest approach, that the way the institution narrative is formulated can differ, to Taft's argument that there is in reality only one eucharistic consecration: the historical words of Jesus spoken (once) at the Last Supper.

eucharistic consecration: for example, by the articulation of the whole prayer. Of course, I hope it is clear that I am not arguing in any way against the traditional institution narrative, but I am trying to understand its role in eucharistic praying in a way that would be somewhat novel for Roman Catholic theology.

A student in my medieval liturgy seminar recently asked what difference it made if Taft was correct in his contention that the Lauds psalms (Pss 148–150) were original to so-called Cathedral Morning Prayer (as opposed to Bradshaw's opinion that they were original to monastic vigils).[37] It was a fair question. I suppose that behind it was his desire to know whether there was any relevance at all to liturgical history. I tried to explain as best I could that Taft's argument could better support present-day practice of communal prayer as a truly popular activity rather than one that is more proper to clergy and religious. I am not certain that the student was convinced, but I do think studies on the origin and development of liturgical prayer or the eucharistic prayer or the feasts and seasons of the liturgical year and other examples I have adduced or left out of this presentation do show that the work of liturgical history is no mere antiquarian exercise, much less irrelevant to contemporary liturgical theory and practice. Liturgical history is certainly not about finding some pristine form of worship and then forcing people to return to it. It is about understanding how we got to where we are and (just as important in many ways) the different cultural and social contexts in which our liturgical forms developed. Liturgical historians will not have the last word in assessing these developments. That is for the academy in general and for various religious authorities. But liturgical historians will always have something important to add to the mix, and that makes the work that we liturgical historians do very worthwhile indeed.

---

[37] Bradshaw came to accept Taft's opinion: see Paul Bradshaw, "Cathedral vs. Monastery: The Only Alternatives for the Liturgy of the Hours?" in Neil Alexander, ed., *Time and Community: In Honor of Thomas Julian Talley* (Washington, DC: Pastoral Press, 1990): 123–36.

Bibliography

Alberigo, Giuseppe. *A Short History of Vatican II*. Maryknoll, NY: Orbis Books, 2006.

———, and Joseph Komonchak, eds. *History of Vatican II*. 5 vols. Maryknoll, NY: Orbis Books, 1995–2006.

Alison, James. "Worship in a Violent World." *Studia Liturgica* 34 (2004): 133–46.

Allen, John. *Cardinal Ratzinger: The Vatican's Enforcer of the Faith*. New York: Continuum, 2000.

Archer, Anthony. *The Two Catholic Churches: A Study in Oppression*. London: SCM Press, 1986.

Baldovin, John F. "Concelebration: A Problem of Symbolic Roles in the Church." *Worship* 59 (1985): 32–47.

———. "Kyrie Eleison and the Entrance Rite of the Roman Eucharists." *Worship* 60 (1986): 334–47.

———. *The Stational Character of Christian Worship: The Origin, Meaning and Development of Stational Liturgy in Jerusalem, Rome and Constantinople*. Orientalia Christiana Analecta 228. Rome: Pontifical Institute for Oriental Studies, 1987.

———. "Liturgical Presidency: The Sacramental Question." In *Disciples at the Crossroads: Perspectives on Worship and Church Leadership*, edited by Eleanor Bernstein, 27–44. Collegeville, MN: Liturgical Press, 1993.

———. "The Eucharist and Ministerial Leaderships." In Judith Dwyer, ed., *Proceedings of the Catholic Theological Society of America* 52 (1997): 63–82.

———. "The Changing World of Liturgy: The Future of Anglican Worship." *Anglican Theological Review* 82 (2000): 65–81.

———. "Lo, the Full Final Sacrifice: On the Seriousness of Christian Liturgy." *Antiphon* 7 (2002): 10–17.

———. *Bread of Life, Cup of Salvation: Understanding the Mass*. Lanham, MD: Rowman and Littlefield, 2003.

———. "Developing a Solid Eucharistic Theology of the Anaphora." *Liturgical Ministry* 14 (2005): 113–19.

———. "The Priest as Sacramental Minister." In *Priests for the 21st Century*, edited by Donald Dietrich, 19–32. New York: Crossroad, 2006.

———. "The Usefulness of Liturgical History." *Proceedings of the North American Academy of Liturgy* (2007): 8–32; also published as "The Uses of Liturgical History." *Worship* 82 (2008): 2–18, and as "The Uses of Liturgical History," the appendix to this book.

Becker, Ernest. *Escape from Evil*. New York: Free Press, 1974.

Bell, Catherine. "Ritual Tensions: Tribal and Catholic." *Studia Liturgica* 32 (2002): 15–28.

Benedict XVI, Pope. Post-Synodal Apostolic Exhortation *Sacramentum Caritatis* (On the Eucharist as the Source and Summit of the Church's Life and Mission).

———. "Christmas Address to the Roman Curia for 2005." http://www .vatican.va/holy_father/benedict_xvi/speeches/2005/december/ documents/hf_ben_xvi_spe_20051222_roman-curia_en.html.

Bonneterre, Didier. *The Liturgical Movement from Dom Gueranger to Annibale Bugnini: or The Trojan Horse in the City of God*. Kansas City, MO: Angelus Press, 2002 (orig. 1980).

Borgmann, Paul. *Crossing the Postmodern Divide*. Chicago: University of Chicago Press, 1993.

Botte, Bernard. *From Silence to Participation: An Insider's View of Liturgical Renewal*. Washington, DC: Pastoral Press, 1988.

Bouyer, Louis. *Liturgy and Architecture*. Notre Dame, IN: University of Notre Dame Press, 1967.

Bradshaw, Paul. "*Diem baptismo sollemniorem*: Initiation and Easter in Christian Antiquity." In *Living Water, Sealing Spirit: Essays on Christian Initiation*, edited by Maxwell Johnson, 137–47. Collegeville, MN: Liturgical Press, 1995.

———. *The Search for the Origins of Christian Worship*. 2nd ed. Oxford: Oxford University Press, 2002.

Braga, Carlo. "Per la Storia della Riforma Liturgica: La Commissione di Pio XII e di Giovanni XXIII," *Ephemerides Liturgicae* 117 (2003): 401–4.

Bugnini, Annibale. *The Reform of the Liturgy 1948–1975*. Collegeville, MN: Liturgical Press, 1990.

Cabié, Robert. "La Place de l'Histoire dans les Etudes Liturgiques." *Ecclesia Orans* 23 (2006): 321–35.

Caldecott, Stratford. "Radical Orthodoxy." http://www.catholicculture.org/ library/view.cfm?recnum=4174.

———, ed. *Beyond the Prosaic: Renewing the Liturgical Movement*. Edinburgh: T&T Clark, 1998.

Cameron-Mowat, Andrew. "Sacramentum Caritatis." *Pastoral Review* 3 (2006): 45–49. http://acameronmowatsj.com/Articles/Sacramentum%20 Caritatis.pdf.

———. "*Summorum Pontificum*: A Response." *Pastoral Review* 4 (2007): 4–11.

Caputo, John. *God, the Gift and Postmodernism*. Bloomington: Indiana University Press, 1999.

Catholic News Agency, "Cardinal Ruini proposes "re-reading" of Vatican II," Rome, June 22, 2005. http://www.catholicnewsagency.com/new .php?n=4201.

Cattaneo, Enrico. *Il Culto Cristiano in Occidente: note storiche*. Rome: Centro Liturgico Vincenziano, Edizioni Liturgiche, 1978, 643–707.

Cecada, Anthony. *The Problem with the Prayers of the Modern Mass*. Rockford, IL: Tan Books, 1991.

Chauvet, Louis-Marie. *Symbol and Sacrament: A Sacramental Rereading of Christian Existence*. Collegeville, MN: Liturgical Press, 1995.

Chavasse, Antoine. "La structure du carême et les lectures des messes quadragésimales dans la liturgie romaine." *La Maison-Dieu* 31 (1952): 76–120.

Chupungco, Anscar. *Liturgies of the Future: The Process and Methods of Inculturation*. New York: Paulist Press, 1989.

Collins, Mary. "Ritual Symbols and the Ritual Process: The Work of Victor W. Turner." *Worship* 50 (1976): 336–46.

Congregation for Divine Worship and the Discipline of the Sacraments. "Response to Questions on the new General Instruction of the Roman Missal" (2000), quoted in Lang, *Turning Towards the Lord* (2004), 26–27.

———. *Liturgiam Authenticam: On the Use of Vernacular Language in the Publication of the Books of the Roman Liturgy, Fifth Instruction on the Implementation of the Constitution on the Sacred Liturgy*. Washington, DC: United States Conference of Catholic Bishops, 2002.

Consilium ad exsequendam Constitutionem de sacra liturgia. Instruction *Comme le prévoit, on the translation of liturgical texts for celebrations with a congregation, 25 January 1969* (= *Documents on the Liturgy 1963–1979: Conciliar, Papal, and Curial Texts*, 123). Collegeville, MN: Liturgical Press, 1982.

Crouan, Denis. *The History and the Future of the Roman Liturgy*. San Francisco: Ignatius Press, 2005.

———. *The Liturgy Betrayed*. San Francisco: Ignatius Press, 2000.

———. *The Liturgy after Vatican II: Collapsing or Resurgent?* San Francisco: Ignatius Press, 2001.

Cullen, Christopher, and Joseph Koterski. "The New IGMR and Mass *versus populum*." *Homiletic and Pastoral Review* 102 (2001): 51–54.

Cziksentmihalyi, Mihalyi. *Beyond Boredom and Anxiety*. San Francisco: Jossey-Bass, 1975.

———. *Flow: The Psychology of Optimal Experience*. San Francisco: HarperSan Francisco, 1993.

Daly, Robert. "Images of God and the Imitation of God: Problems with Atonement." *Theological Studies* 68 (2007): 36–51.

———. "Robert Bellarmine and Post-Tridentine Eucharistic Theology." *Theological Studies* 61 (2000): 239–60.

———. "Sacrifice Unveiled or Sacrifice Revisited: Trinitarian and Liturgical Perspectives." *Theological Studies* 64 (2003): 24–42.

Day, Thomas. *Where Have You Gone, Michelangelo? The Loss of Soul in Catholic Culture*. New York: Crossroad, 1993.

———. *Why Catholics Can't Sing: The Culture of Catholicism and the Triumph of Bad Taste*. New York: Crossroad, 1991.

Derrida, Jacques. *The Gift of Death*. Chicago: University of Chicago Press, 1995.

—. "Writing and Difference," and especially the preface "Plato's Pharmacy." In idem, *Dissemination*, trans. Barbara Johnson. Chicago: University of Chicago Press, 1981.

Dobszay, Laszlo. *The Bugnini-Liturgy and the Reform of the Reform*. Front Royal, VA: Catholic Church Music Associates, 2003.

Douglas, Mary. *Natural Symbols*. New York: Random House, 1970.

Duffy, Eamon. "Pope Benedict XVI and the Liturgy." *Inside the Vatican* (November 2006): 38.

—. "Rewriting the Liturgy: The Theological Implications of Translation." In *Beyond the Prosaic*, edited by Stratford Caldecott, 97–126. Edinburgh: T&T Clark, 1998.

Dulles, Avery. *The Catholicity of the Church*. Oxford: Clarendon Press, 1985.

Dumas, André. "Les oraisons du nouveau missel romain." *Questions Liturgiques* 25 (1971): 263–70.

Finlan, Stephen. *Problems with Atonement*. Collegeville, MN: Liturgical Press, 2005.

Fisichella, Rino, ed. *Il Concilio Vaticano II: Recezione e attualità alla luce del Giubileo*. Milan: San Paolo, 2000.

Flanagan, Kieran. *Sociology and Liturgy: Re-presentations of the Holy*. New York: St. Martin's Press, 1991.

Gamber, Klaus. *Ordo Antiquus Gallicanus: Der gallikanische Meßritus des 6. Jh.* Textus Patristici et Liturgici 3. Regensburg: Pustet, 1965.

—. *Codices Liturgici Latini Antiquiores*. Spicilegii Fribourgensis Subsidia 1. 2nd ed. Fribourg: Universitätsverlag, 1968 (supplement 1988).

—. *Domus Ecclesiae: Die ältesten Kirchenbauten Aquilejas sowie in Alpen- et Donaugebiet bis zum Beginn des 5. Jh. liturgiegeschichtlich untersucht*. Studia Patristica et Liturgica 2. Regensburg: Pustet, 1968.

—. *Ritus Modernus: Gesammelte Aufsätze zur Liturgiereform*. Studia Patristica et Liturgica 4. Regensburg: Pustet, 1972. (Henry Taylor, trans. *The Modern Rite: Collected Essays on the Reform of the Liturgy*. Farnborough: St. Michael's Abbey Press, 2002.)

—. *Liturgie und Kirchenbau: Studien zur Geschichte der Meßfeier und des Gotteshauses in der Frühzeit*. Studia Patristica et Liturgica 6. Regensburg: Pustet, 1976.

—. *Der altgallikanische Meßritus als Abbild himmlischer Liturgie*. Beiheft zu den Studia Patristica et Liturgica. Regensburg: Pustet, 1984.

—. *Die Meßfeier nach altgallikanischem Ritus anhand der erhaltenen Dokumente dargestellt*. Studia Patristica et Liturgica 14. Regensburg: Pustet, 1984.

—. *Sacramentorum: Weitere Aufsätze zur Geschichte der Meßritus und der frühen Liturgie*. Studia Patristica et Liturgica 13. Regensburg: Pustet, 1984.

—. *Fragen in der Zeit: Kirche und Liturgie nach dem Vatikanum II*. Regensburg: Pustet, 1989.

—. *The Reform of the Roman Liturgy: Its Problems and Background*. Translated by Klaus D. Grimm. Harrison, NY: Foundation for Catholic Reform, 1993.

Ganss, George E. *The Spiritual Exercises of Saint Ignatius: A Translation and Commentary*. St. Louis: Institute of Jesuit Sources, 1992, 32.

Garriga, Tena. "La sacra liturgia fonte e culmine della vita ecclesiale." In Fisichella, ed., *Il concilio Vaticano II* (2000), 46–65.

General Instruction of the Roman Missal (Washington, DC: USCCB, 2003).

Gese, Hartmut. "The Origin of the Last Supper." In idem, *Essays on Biblical Theology*. Translated by Keith Crim. Minneapolis: Augsburg, 1981.

Gy, Pierre-Marie. "Is Cardinal Ratzinger's *L'Esprit de la Liturgie* Faithful to the Council?" (translation of an article originally published in *La Maison-Dieu* 229 [2002]). *Doctrine and Life* 52 (2002): 426–32.

Harrison, Brian. "Postconciliar Eucharistic Liturgy: Planning a "Reform of the Reform." In *The Reform of the Reform?* edited by Thomas Kocik, 170–93. San Francisco: Ignatius Press, 2003.

Heim, S. Mark. *Saved from Sacrifice: A Theology of the Cross*. Grand Rapids: Eerdmans, 2006.

Hen, Yitzhak. *The Royal Patronage of Liturgy in Frankish Gaul to the Death of Charles the Bald (877)*. London: Boydell Press (Henry Bradshaw Society), 2001.

Hitchcock, James. *The Recovery of the Sacred*. New York: Seabury, 1974.

———. "Saint Nowhere's." *Adoremus Bulletin* 3:6 (September 1997), at http://www.adoremus.org/9-97St.%20Nowhere.html.

Holeton, David. "Presidential Address for the International Ecumenical Societas Liturgica." *Studia Liturgica* 38 (2008, forthcoming).

Hovda, Robert. "The Vesting of Liturgical Ministers." In *The Amen Corner*, edited by John Baldovin. Collegeville, MN: Liturgical Press, 1994.

International Commission on English in the Liturgy. *Documents on the Liturgy 1963–1979: Conciliar, Papal, and Curial Texts*. Collegeville, MN: Liturgical Press, 1982.

Irwin, Kevin. *Context and Text: Method in Liturgical Theology*. Collegeville, MN: Liturgical Press, 1993.

Jeffery, Peter. *Translating Tradition: A Chant Historian Reads* Liturgiam Authenticam. Collegeville, MN: Liturgical Press, 2005.

John Paul II, Pope. Apostolic Letter *Vicesimus Quintus Annus* (On the 25th Anniversary of the promulgation of the conciliar constitution *Sacrosanctum Concilium*, on the Sacred Liturgy), 1988. http://www.vatican.va/holy_father/john_paul_ii/apost_letters/documents/hf_jp-ii_apl_04121988_vicesimus-quintus-annus_en.html.

Jungmann, Josef. *Missarum Sollemnia: The Mass of the Roman Rite*. Translated by Francis Brunner. 2 vols. New York: Benziger, 1950.

Kavanagh, Aidan. *On Liturgical Theology*. Collegeville, MN: Liturgical Press, 1992.

———. "Liturgical Business Unfinished and Unbegun." *Worship* 50 (1976): 354–64.

———. *The Elements of Rite: A Handbook of Liturgical Style*. New York: Pueblo, 1982.

Kelleher, Serge. "Whatever Happened to the Liturgical Movement? A View from the East." In *Beyond the Prosaic*, edited by Stratford Caldecott, 74. Edinburgh: T&T Clark, 1998.

Kiefer, Ralph. *To Give Thanks and Praise*. Washington, DC: Pastoral Press, 1980.

Klauser, Theodor. *A Short History of the Western Liturgy*. Translated by John Halliburton. 2nd ed. New York: Oxford University Press, 1979.

Klöckener, Martin, and Benedikt Kränemann, eds. *Liturgiereformen: Historische Studien zu einem bleibenden Grundzug des christlichen Gottesdienstes*. 2 vols. Liturgiewissenschaftliche Quellen und Forschungen 88–89. Münster: Aschendorff, 2002.

Kocik, Thomas, ed. *The Reform of the Reform? A Liturgical Debate: Reform or Return?* San Francisco: Ignatius Press, 2003.

Lakeland, Paul. *Postmodernity: Christian Identity in a Fragmented Age*. Minneapolis: Fortress Press, 1997.

Lang, Uwe Michael. *Turning Towards the Lord: Orientation in Liturgical Prayer*. San Francisco: Ignatius Press, 2004.

———. "The Direction of Liturgical Prayer." In *Ever Directed Towards the Lord: The Love of God in the Liturgy of the Eucharist Past, Present, and Hoped For*, edited by idem. Edinburgh: T&T Clark, 2007.

Lara, Jaime. "*Versus Populum* Revisited." *Worship* 68 (1994): 210–21.

Lathrop, Gordon. *Holy Things: A Liturgical Theology*. Minneapolis: Fortress Press, 1993.

Lewis, C. S. *Letters to Malcolm, Chiefly on Prayer*. London: G. Bles, 1964.

Lonergan, Bernard. *Method in Theology*. New York: Herder & Herder, 1972.

Lysik, David. *The Liturgy Documents: Volume Two*. Chicago: Liturgy Training Publications, 2000.

Mannion, M. Francis. "Catholic Worship and the Dynamics of Congregationalism." *Chicago Studies* 33 (1994): 57–66.

———. "The Catholicity of the Liturgy: Shaping a New Agenda." In *Beyond the Prosaic*, edited by Stratford Caldecott, 11–48. Edinburgh: T&T Clark, 1998.

———. "The Church and the City." *First Things* 100 (2000): 31–36.

Marini, Piero. *A Challenging Reform: Realizing the Vision of the Liturgical Renewal*, edited by Mark Francis, John Page, and Keith Pecklers. Collegeville, MN: Liturgical Press, 2007.

Marion, Jean-Luc. *Being Given: Toward a Phenomenology of Givenness*. Stanford: Stanford University Press, 2002.

Mateos, Juan. *La célébration de la parole dans la liturgie byzantine*. Rome: Pontifical Oriental Institute Press, 1971.

McNamara, Denis. "Can We Keep Our Churches Catholic?" *Adoremus Bulletin* 4:1 (February/March 1998). http://www.adoremus.org/98-03_mcnamara .htm.

Metzger, Marcel. "La Place des Liturges a l'Autel." *Revue des Sciences Religieuses* 45 (1971): 113–45.

Milbank, John. *On Being Reconciled: Ontology and Pardon.* London: Routledge, 2003.

———. *Theology and Social Theory: Beyond Secular Reason.* Oxford: Blackwell, 1991.

———, Catherine Pickstock, and Graham Ward, eds. *Radical Orthodoxy: A New Theology.* London: Routledge, 1999.

Miller, Vincent. *Consuming Religion: Christian Faith and Practice in a Consumer Culture.* New York: Continuum, 2005.

Mitchell, Nathan. *Meeting Mystery: Liturgy, Worship, Sacraments.* Maryknoll, NY: Orbis Books, 2007.

———. "The Amen Corner: Back to the Future?" *Worship* 73 (1999): 60–69.

———. "The Amen Corner: Life Begins at Forty?" *Worship* 77 (2003): 56–69.

———. "The Amen Corner: Rereading Reform." *Worship* 80 (2006): 453–66.

———. "The Amen Corner: Worship as Music." *Worship* 73 (1999): 249–55.

Mohrmann, Christine. *Liturgical Latin: Its Origins and Character.* London: Burns & Oates, 1957.

Moore, Gerard. *Vatican II and the Collects for Ordinary Time: A Study in the Roman Missal (1975).* San Francisco: Scholars Press, 1998.

Nichols, Aidan. *Looking at Liturgy: A Critical View of Its Contemporary Form.* San Francisco: Ignatius Press, 1996.

O'Malley, John. "Vatican II: Did Anything Happen?" *Theological Studies* 67 (2006): 3–33.

Parsons, John. "A Reform of the Reform?" In *The Reform of the Reform?* edited by Thomas Kocik. San Francisco: Ignatius Press, 2003.

Paul VI, Pope. Apostolic Constitution *Divinae consortium naturae*, 15 August 1971 (*DOL* 303).

———. Apostolic Exhortation *Evangelii Nuntiandi*, December 8, 1975. http://www.vatican.va/holy_father/paul_vi/apost_exhortations/documents/hf_p-vi_exh_19751208_evangelii-nuntiandi_en.html.

Pecklers, Keith. *Dynamic Equivalence: The Living Language of Christian Worship.* Collegeville, MN: Liturgical Press, 2003.

Pelikan, Jaroslav. *The Christian Tradition: A History of the Development of Doctrine.* Vol. 1: *The Emergence of the Catholic Tradition* (100–600). Chicago: University of Chicago Press, 1971.

Pickstock, Catherine. "A Short Essay on the Reform of the Liturgy." In *Liturgy in Dialogue*, edited by Paul Bradshaw and Bryan Spinks. London: SPCK, 1993.

———"Asyndeton: Syntax and Insanity. A Study in the Revision of the Nicene Creed." *Modern Theology* 10 (1994): 321–40.

———. "A Sermon for St. Cecilia." *Theology* 100 (1997): 411–18.

———. "Liturgy and Modernity." *Telos* 113 (1998): 19–40.

———. *After Writing: On the Liturgical Consummation of Philosophy.* Oxford: Blackwell, 1998.

———. "Thomas Aquinas and the Quest for the Eucharist." *Modern Theology* 15 (1999): 159–80.

———. "Liturgy, Art and Politics." *Modern Theology* 16 (2000): 159–80.

———. "Medieval Liturgy and Modern Reform." *Antiphon* 6 (2001): 19–25.

Pristas, Lauren. "*Missale Romanum* 1962 and 1970: A Comparative Study of Two Collects." *Antiphon* 7 (2002): 29–33.

———. "Theological Principles that Guided the Redaction of the Roman Missal (1970)." *The Thomist* 67 (2003): 157–95.

———."The Orations of the Vatican II Missal: Policies for Revision." *Communio* 30 (2003): 621–53.

Rahner, Karl. "The Concept of Mystery in Catholic Theology." *Theological Investigations* IV. London: Darton, Longman & Todd, 1966, 36–73.

Rappaport, Roy. *Ecology, Meaning, and Religion*. California: North Atlantic Books, 1979.

Ratzinger Joseph. "The Spirit of the Liturgy or Fidelity to the Council: A Reply to Pierre-Marie Gy, O.P." *Doctrine and Life* 52 (2002): 494–500.

———. Preface to Klaus Gamber, *La réforme liturgique en question*. French translation of his *Reform der römischen Liturgie*. Caromb: Editions Sainte-Madeleine, 1992.

———, with Vittorio Messori. *The Ratzinger Report: An Exclusive Interview on the State of the Church*. San Francisco: Ignatius Press, 1985.

———. "The Theology of the Liturgy." In *Looking Again at the Question of the Liturgy with Cardinal Ratzinger*, edited by Alcuin Reid, 18–31. Farnborough: St. Michael's Abbey Press, 2003.

———. *A New Song for the Lord: Faith in Christ and Liturgy Today*. Translated by Martha M. Matesich. New York: Crossroad, 1996.

———. *God Is Near Us: The Eucharist at the Heart of Life*. San Francisco: Ignatius Press, 2003.

———. *Milestones: Memoirs 1927–1997*. San Francisco: Ignatius Press, 1987.

———. *The Feast of Faith: Approaches to a Theology of the Liturgy*. Translated by Graham Harrison. San Francisco: Ignatius Press, 1986.

———. *The Spirit of the Liturgy*. Translated by John Saward. San Francisco: Ignatius Press, 2000.

Reid, Alcuin. *The Organic Development of the Liturgy: The Principles of Liturgical Reform and Their Relation to the Twentieth-century Liturgical Movement Prior to the Second Vatican Council*. Farnborough: St. Michael's Abbey Press, 2004.

———. "*Sacrosanctum Concilium* and the Reform of the *Ordo Missae*." *Antiphon* 10 (2006): 277–95.

———. "The Fathers of Vatican II and the Revised Mass: The Results of a Survey." *Antiphon* 10 (2006): 170–90.

———, ed. *Looking Again at the Question of the Liturgy with Cardinal Ratzinger: Proceedings of the July 2001 Fontgombault Liturgical Conference*. Farnborough: St. Michael's Abbey Press, 2003.

Reno, Russell R. "The Radical Orthodoxy Project." *First Things* 100 (2000): 37–44.

Ricoeur, Paul. *The Symbolism of Evil*. Boston: Beacon Press, 1967, 352–54.

Robinson, Jonathan. *The Mass and Modernity: Walking to Heaven Backwards*. San Francisco: Ignatius Press, 2005.

Romano, John. *Ritual and Society in Early Medieval Rome*. Dissertation, Harvard University, 2007.

Rose, Michael. *Ugly as Sin: Why They Changed Our Churches and How We Can Change Them Back Again*. Manchester, NH: Sophia Institute Press, 2001.

Russell, James C. *The Germanization of Early Medieval Christianity: A Sociohistorical Approach to Religious Transformation*. New York: Oxford University Press, 1994.

Sacrosanctum Concilium, Constitution on the Sacred Liturgy (4 December 1963). In Austin Flannery, OP, ed., *Vatican Council II*. Vol. 1: *The Conciliar and Postconciliar Documents*. Northport, NY: Costello, 1975, 1–36.

Schloeder, Steven J. *Architecture in Communion*. San Francisco: Ignatius Press, 1998.

Schloesser, Stephen. "Against Forgetting: Memory, History, Vatican II." *Theological Studies* 67 (2006): 275–319.

Scott, R. Taylor. "The Likelihood of Liturgy: Reflections upon Prayer Book Revision and its Liturgical Implications." *Anglican Theological Review* 62 (1980): 103–20.

Seasoltz, R. Kevin. *God's Gift Giving: In Christ and Through the Spirit*. New York: Continuum, 2007.

Smolarksi, Dennis. *Sacred Mysteries: Sacramental Principles and Liturgical Practice*. New York: Paulist Press, 1995.

Society of St. Pius X. *The Problem of the Liturgy Reform*. Kansas City, MO: Angelus Press, 2001.

Spinks, Bryan. "Review of *After Writing*." *Scottish Journal of Theology* 51 (1998), 508–11.

Stevenson, Kenneth. "After Writing: On the Liturgical Consummation of Theology" (review). *Journal of Theological Studies* n.s. 50 (1999), 452–54.

Taft, Robert F. *A History of the Liturgy of St. John Chrysostom*. 6 vols. Rome: Pontifical Oriental Institute Press, 1975.

———. "Anton Baumstark's Comparative Liturgy Revisited." In *Comparative Liturgy*, edited by idem and Gabriele Winkler, 191–232. Rome: Pontifical Oriental Institute, 2001.

———. "The Structural Analysis of Liturgical Units: An Essay in Methodology." In *Beyond East and West: Problems in Liturgical Understanding*, edited by idem, 187–202. 2nd rev. ed. Rome: Pontifical Oriental Institute Press, 2001.

———. "Sunday in the Byzantine Tradition." In idem, *Beyond East and West*, 51–72.

———. "Mass Without the Consecration? The Historic Agreement on the Eucharist Between the Catholic Church and the Assyrian Church of the East, Promulgated 26 October 2001." *Worship* 77 (2003): 482–509.

———. "A Poetics of the Eucharist." *Telos* 131 (2005): 83–91.

———, and Gabriele Winkler, eds. *Comparative Liturgy Fifty Years after Anton Baumstark (1872–1948): Acts of the International Congress, Rome, 25–29 September 1998*. Orientalia Christiana Analecta 265. Rome: Pontifical Oriental Institute, 2001.

Taylor, Charles. *Hegel*. Cambridge: Cambridge University Press, 1975.

Torevell, David. *Losing the Sacred: Ritual, Modernity and Liturgical Reform*. Edinburgh: T&T Clark, 2000.

Trautman, Donald. "The Relationship of the Active Participation of the Assembly to Liturgical Translations." *Worship* 80 (2006): 290–309.

Turner, Victor. "Ritual, Tribal and Catholic." *Worship* 50 (1976): 504–26.

United States Conference of Catholic Bishops. *Built of Living Stones: Art, Architecture and Worship* (2000), §§73–80.

———. "Fifth Instruction" on translation (*Liturgiam Authenticam*). English translation. Washington, DC: USCCB, 2001. http://www.usccb.org/liturgy/livingstones.shtml#chaptertwo.

———. *Sing to the Lord: Music in Divine Worship* (Nov. 14, 2007). http://www.usccb.org/liturgy/SingtoTheLord.pdf.

United States Conference of Catholic Bishops Committee on the Liturgy. *Environment and Art in Catholic Worship (EACW)*. In *The Liturgy Documents*. Vol. 1, 313–40. 3rd ed. Chicago: Liturgy Training Publications, 1991.

Van Gennep, Arnold. *The Ritual Process: Structure and Anti-structure*. Chicago: Aldine, 1969.

———. *Dramas, Fields and Metaphors: Symbolic Action in Human Life*. Ithaca: Cornell University Press, 1975.

Vogel, Cyril. *Medieval Liturgy: An Introduction to the Sources*. Washington, DC: Pastoral Press, 1986.

Wainwright, Geoffrey. *Eucharist and Eschatology*. New York: Oxford University Press, 1981.

Ward, Anthony. "The Discipline of the Eucharist: The Instruction 'Redemptionis Sacramentum.'" *Ephemerides Liturgicae* 118 (2004): 209–43.

———. "The Instruction 'Liturgiam Authenticam': Some Particulars." *Ephemerides Liturgicae* 116 (2002): 197–221.

West, Fritz. *Scripture and Memory: The Ecumenical Hermeneutic of the Three-Year Lectionary*. Collegeville, MN: Liturgical Press, 2002.

Wilkins, John. "Lost in Translation: The Bishops, the Vatican, and English Liturgy." *Commonweal* 132:21 (December 2, 2005): 12–20.

Wright, Craig. *Music and Ceremony at Notre Dame of Paris 500–1500*. Cambridge: Cambridge University Press, 1989.

Index

Talley, Thomas, 167–69
Taft, Robert, 20, 49–50, 141, 162, 165, 170
Torevell, David, 92–95
Tracy, David, 163–64
translation, standards of, 27–28, 116–26
  and inclusive language, 123–24
transubstantiation, 29–30
Trautman, Donald, 120, 123
Turner, Victor, 90–92

Urban Character of Christian Worship, The (Baldovin), 164–65

Vatican Council II
  historiography of, 11–12
  Sacrosanctum Concilium, 1–6, 20–21, 40–41, 56–57, 61–62, 68, 96–97, 114–15, 136–37, 143, 161
Varietates Legitimae (CDWDS), 3, 7
vernacular, and reform, 46, 58, 78, 113–16, 144–45
  in *Sacrosanctum Concilium*, 114–15
versus populum. See orientation, liturgical
von Balthasar, Hans Urs, 83

Ward, Graham, 14
Why Catholics Can't Sing (Day), 154–55
Winkler, Gabriele, 166